Breaking into Windows

PLEASE NOTE—USE OF THE DISK(S) AND THE PROGRAMS INCLUDED ON THE DISK(S) PACKAGED WITH THIS BOOK AND THE PROGRAM LISTINGS INCLUDED IN THIS BOOK IS SUBJECT TO AN END-USER LICENSE AGREEMENT (THE "AGREEMENT") FOUND AT THE BACK OF THE BOOK. PLEASE READ THE AGREEMENT CAREFULLY BEFORE MAKING YOUR PURCHASE DECISION. PURCHASE OF THE BOOK AND USE OF THE DISKS, PROGRAMS, AND PROGRAM LISTINGS WILL CONSTITUTE ACCEPTANCE OF THE AGREEMENT.

Breaking into Windows

Matthew Lake

Ziff-Davis Press
Emeryville, California

Development Editor	Jeff Green
Copy Editor	Kate Hoffman
Technical Reviewer	Dale Lewallen
Project Coordinator	Kim Haglund
Proofreader	Cort Day
Cover Illustration	Carrie English
Cover Design	Carrie English
Book Design	Paper Crane Graphics, Berkeley
Screen Graphics Editor	Dan Brodnitz
Word Processing	Howard Blechman, Cat Haglund, and Allison Levin
Page Layout	Anna L. Marks, Bruce Lundquist, and Tony Jonick
Indexer	Mark Kmetzko

Ziff-Davis Press books are produced on a Macintosh computer system with the following applications: FrameMaker®, Microsoft® Word, QuarkXPress®, Adobe Illustrator®, Adobe Photoshop®, Adobe Streamline™, MacLink®*Plus*, Aldus® FreeHand™, Collage Plus™.

Ziff-Davis Press
5903 Christie Avenue
Emeryville, CA 94608

Copyright © 1993 by Ziff-Davis Press. All rights reserved.

Ziff-Davis Press and ZD Press are trademarks of Ziff Communications Company.

All other product names and services identified throughout this book are trademarks or registered trademarks of their respective companies. They are used throughout this book in editorial fashion only and for the benefit of such companies. No such uses, or the use of any trade name, is intended to convey endorsement or other affiliation with the book.

No part of this publication may be reproduced in any form, or stored in a database or retrieval system, or transmitted or distributed in any form by any means, electronic, mechanical photocopying, recording, or otherwise, without the prior written permission of Ziff-Davis Press, except as permitted by the Copyright Act of 1976 and the End-User License Agreement at the back of this book and except that program listings may be entered, stored, and executed in a computer system.

EXCEPT FOR THE LIMITED WARRANTY COVERING THE PHYSICAL DISK(S) PACKAGED WITH THIS BOOK AS PROVIDED IN THE END-USER LICENSE AGREEMENT AT THE BACK OF THIS BOOK, THE INFORMATION AND MATERIAL CONTAINED IN THIS BOOK ARE PROVIDED "AS IS," WITHOUT WARRANTY OF ANY KIND, EXPRESS OR IMPLIED, INCLUDING WITHOUT LIMITATION ANY WARRANTY CONCERNING THE ACCURACY, ADEQUACY, OR COMPLETENESS OF SUCH INFORMATION OR MATERIAL OR THE RESULTS TO BE OBTAINED FROM USING SUCH INFORMATION OR MATERIAL. NEITHER ZIFF-DAVIS PRESS NOR THE AUTHOR SHALL BE RESPONSIBLE FOR ANY CLAIMS ATTRIBUTABLE TO ERRORS, OMISSIONS, OR OTHER INACCURACIES IN THE INFORMATION OR MATERIAL CONTAINED IN THIS BOOK, AND IN NO EVENT SHALL ZIFF-DAVIS PRESS OR THE AUTHOR BE LIABLE FOR DIRECT, INDIRECT, SPECIAL, INCIDENTAL, OR CONSEQUENTIAL DAMAGES ARISING OUT OF THE USE OF SUCH INFORMATION OR MATERIAL.

ISBN 1-56276-144-7

Manufactured in the United States of America
10 9 8 7 6 5 4 3 2 1

To Caroline and Chris—of course

■ Contents at a Glance

Introduction		xvii

PART 1	**Window Dressing**		1
Chapter 1:	Start Wasting Time		3
Chapter 2:	This Old Windows		21
Chapter 3:	Passing the Screen Test		41
Chapter 4:	Cursors! Foiled Again!		59
Chapter 5:	I Think Icon, I Think Icon		71
Chapter 6:	Disturbing the Neighbors		89
Chapter 7:	Font Mania		107

PART 2	**Mismanaging Your Time**		124
Chapter 8:	Program Mismanagement		127
Chapter 9:	File Mismanagement		147
Chapter 10:	Recorder Macrocosm		165

PART 3	**Start Wasting Time**		184
Chapter 11:	Playing to Win		187
Chapter 12:	Hunting for Easter Eggs		203

Appendix: Programs on the Disk	221
Index	237

Table of Contents

Introduction   xvii

PART 1   Window Dressing   1
How to Make Redecorating Your Desktop into a Full-time Job

Chapter 1:   Start Wasting Time   3

WIN a Few   4
    WIN Slash What?   4

The Business of Bootup   6

That Start-up Logo Has Gotta Go!   6
    Ditching the Windows Start-up Logo   7
    Replacing the Windows Start-up Logo   8

Building Your Own Windows Start-up Logo   10

INI Beginning…   14
    Now You See It…   16
    Run versus Load   17

What Was the Point of This Chapter?   19

Chapter 2:   This Old Windows   21

Wallpaper Hanging Made Complex   22
    Hang That Wallpaper Left of Center…Or Right…Or Up a Bit…   23
    Wallpaper Lite: Looks Great, Less Filling   25
    A Regular Change of Wallpaper   27

New Sources of Wallpaper—Print Screen and Paintbrush   27
    .BMP and .PCX: Formats and Substance   29
    Exploring the Graffiti Artist Within   30
    "Danger, Will Robinson!"—A Meaningful Error Message   31

Decorating without Wallpaper   35
    Rose-Tint Your World, Paint It Black, or Sing the Blues   35
    Advancing with the General Pattern   36

What Was the Point of This Chapter?   38

Chapter 3: Passing the Screen Test   41

Primal Screens   42

Screened for Security   46

Oh, for a Speedily Saved Screen   46
    Hit the Hot Spot   49

More and Better Animations   50
    A Different Saver Every Time   52

What Has Gills and Looks Great on Screen?   54
    A Piscine Premium   56

What Was the Point of This Chapter?   56

Chapter 4: Cursors! Foiled Again!   59

Hit the Mouse Trail   60

The Cursor as a Beacon   61

Change That Cursor's Behavior   62
    Quick! Stop That Cursor!   62
    Click! Click! On the Double!   63

Something in Another Color, Perhaps?   64
    Blinking in Disbelief   65
    Mouse Cursor Metamorphosis   66

Plug in a Few More Cursors   67
    What's a .CUR In?   69

What Was the Point(er) of This Chapter?	69

Chapter 5: I Think Icon, I Think Icon   71

New Icons for Old	72
Give Your Icons Their Space	73
Put the Squeeze on Your Upstairs Neighbor 75	
Plug In a New Group Icon	76
Build Your Own Icons	78
The Right Tool for the Job: AZ Icon Edit 78	
The Right Job for the Tool 81	
Hang Them in a Gallery	84
Retouch the Rough Edges 86	
Install an Icon in a Permanent Collection 86	
What Was the Point of This Chapter?	87

Chapter 6: Disturbing the Neighbors   89

Give Your PC Its Voice	90
Installing the PC-Speaker Driver 90	
Catch a WAV	92
The Big Event (and What It Actually Means) 93	
When an Unstoppable Sound Meets an Immovable Event 93	
Replay with the Sound Recorder	95
The Wall of Sound 96	
More Sound Ideas	99
A Better-Packaged Sound Scrapbook 101	
What Was the Point of This Chapter?	104

Chapter 7: Font Mania — 107

In Your (Type)Face Font Trivia — 109

Windows Typecasting — 110
    Lose a Font   111
    Gain Seven Fonts   111

The Uses and Overuses of Fonts — 113

Fonts 101 and More — 113
    Strength of Character (Map)   115
    Fonts in Folders Make Windows Faster   116

Putting a New Face on Windows — 119
    More Fonts for Menus and Title Bars   119
    Even More System Fonts   121
    A Change of Icon Label   122

What Was the Point of This Chapter? — 123

PART 2   Mismanaging Your Time — 125
    Keep Busy without Actually Getting Anything Done

Chapter 8: Program Mismanagement — 127

Trash the Program Manager's Settings — 128

Five Steps to a Better Program Manager — 130
    Toolkit Groups—A Place for Everything and Everything in Its Place   132

Two-fisted Program Management — 132

Shuffling the Program Deck — 133

Five Ways Plug-In Improves Program Management — 137

Cram the Most Icons in the Smallest Space—
　　　A Button Bar　　　　　　　　　　　　　　　　140

Manage Program Installations with (gasp!) Batch Files　　142

What Was the Point of This Chapter?　　　　　　　　144

Chapter 9:　File Mismanagement　　　　　　　147

Bend the File Manager to Your Will　　　　　　　　148
　　Face-lift Your File Manager　149
　　Files from Another Point of View　149

An Aside: File Management Made Incredibly Difficult　　154

A Sensible Arrangement　　　　　　　　　　　　　156

Dragon Dropping Your Way to Cleaner Windows
　　　Directories　　　　　　　　　　　　　　　　157

An Association of Files, Desktop, and Printer　　　　158

Space Case: Too Many Files Spoil the Disk　　　　　160
　　Zip 'em Up　160
　　Flushing out Superfluous Files　162

What Was the Point of This Chapter?　　　　　　　　163

Chapter 10: Recorder Macrocosm　　　　　　　165

Aliens Ate My PC! The Daily Macro Tells All　　　　166

The File Manager's Friends　　　　　　　　　　　　170

Beating a Hasty Retreat Using Macros　　　　　　　174
　　Quit the Recorder Using a Macro　174
　　Quit Everything at Once　176

Cut! Print! Taking Pictures from the Silver Screen 178

You Are Now a Professional. Attempt This at Home! 180

What Was the Point of This Chapter? 182

PART 3 Start Wasting Time 185
Windows Activities You Can't Pass Off As Work

Chapter 11: Playing to Win 187

Solitaire 188

    The Object of the Game 189
    Playing the Game 189
    Scoring 191
    Dealer! Fresh Deck, Please! 192
    Gain a Tactical Advantage 192

Minesweeper 194

    The Object of the Game 195
    Playing the Game 196
    Clear around a Square 197
    Scoring 198
    The Minefield You Always Wanted 199
    Gain a Tactical Advantage 200

What Was the Point of This Chapter? 201

Chapter 12: Hunting for Easter Eggs 203

Windows Wasters 204

    The Wallpaper That Built Windows 3.0 204
    The Windows 3.1 Cartoon Carnival 205
    Norton Desktop for Windows Photographs and Philosophy 206

Wasting Words — 207
    The Day the Word Stood Still   207
    Word for Windows 1's Fire in the Sky   208
    Ami Pro 2.0's Video Tribute to Elvis   209

The Chronicles of Wasted Spreadsheets — 210
    Excel 4.0's Bug Buster   211
    So Much for Pathos   213
    Terminator 1-2-3 1.1: Judgment Day   214
    Quattro Pro for Windows and the Elegant Meal   215

A la recherche des screens perdus — 215
    CorelDRAW and the Hot Air Mouse   216
    Paradox for Windows Plays Pdox and the Wolf   217

A Final Challenge — 218

What Was the Point of This Chapter? — 218

Appendix: **Programs on the Disk**   221

Index   237

■ Acknowledgments

This book would be decidedly slimmer but for the diligent programming and commitment of software developers. The software bound into this book was culled from dozens of programs that I trawled from online services, and these are the cream of the crop. For their hard and often thankless work, my hat is off to these developers.

The authors and editors I work with daily have, by attrition, raised my Windows IQ and sense of fun, for which I'm also grateful. Particular thanks go to Dylan Tweney for his humor, creativity, and a relentless stream of good ideas, to say nothing of the way he developed some of my stray ideas for this book and came up with his own. Good on you. Thanks too to John Taschek for invaluable (if frivolous) research.

For his work in developing this book, editor Jeff "Control Panel" Green should have his name somewhere on the cover. Copy editor Kate "WordPerfect" Hoffman and project coordinator Kim "File Manager" Haglund also have my lasting gratitude. For handling the screen shots and overcoming some major technical difficulties, Dan Brodnitz earns a gold medal for patience in the face of adversity. Nice job. For knocking the technical content into shape and a keen eye with a keen sense of humor, thanks also to technical reviewer Dale "SysEdit" Lewallen. And, for having the faith and good taste to accept my book proposal, thanks to Cindy "Program Manager" Hudson.

For general inspiration, thanks go to two *PC/Computing* editors, Ron White and Craig Stinson, whose excellent work in the Help section has taught me much. Craig filled his monthly Windows column with a depth, character, and awareness of deadlines that made editing his work a pleasure. I'd know a lot less about Windows if it weren't for him. And Ron's professionalism and guidance helped me through some of the tricky times as I was holding down several projects at once.

Major thanks go to my wife Caroline, who cast a trained eye over early drafts and vastly improved them with her critiques. She deserves even more thanks for putting up with an obsessive author during the entire conception, writing, editing, and production of this book without complaint. And Chris did his part too, with frequent reminders for me to go work on the 'puter. Without you two it would not have been possible.

I'd also like to thank the Academy for this award, and for all the little people behind the scenes.

■ Introduction

Microsoft and MIS departments around the globe rightly point out that Windows combines an iconic graphical user interface with cooperative multitasking. The rest of us take advantage of this fact—we admire the pictures onscreen and run Solitaire and Minesweeper at the same time. Of course, we also keep Excel running in the background to switch to whenever somebody we want to impress wanders by.

Industry analysts assert that the Clipboard, dynamic data exchange, and object linking and embedding can enhance our productivity by enabling us to share data between applications. While this is true, it doesn't quite offset the fact that most people can spend half a day just deciding which screen saver they prefer. *Breaking into Windows* celebrates the fact that even in a multitasking environment with the power to run a dozen programs at once and to share megabytes of data, productivity easily can take a back seat.

■ What This Book Is—and Isn't

There are plenty of more instructive, more tip-filled books about Windows. Three of my favorites are Gus Venditto's *Guide to Using Windows 3.1,* Mike Edelhart's *2001 Windows Tips,* and Microsoft's own Windows manuals—including the excellent *Windows Resource Kit*. If you can spare a few more bucks, buy the ones you don't already have. You won't regret it.

This book won't replace any standard Windows desk references. Instead, Breaking into Windows combines a guided tour of Windows's back roads with a grab bag (grab disk?) of graphics, sound, and software files—and I've even thrown in a collection of time-consuming and ultimately futile projects for stamping your own personality on your Windows desktop.

This guide is designed for people who get in and out of Windows to do work, but who feel like hanging around after work to relax in Windows. While it's written for people who are already familiar with the way Windows looks and operates, it doesn't assume too much of the new user. If you don't know the Windows terrain when you pick up this book, you'll know it like a native by the time you put it down. All you need is enough time.

An Apology:

Occasionally, I have to concede, you'll find a procedure or tip that will come in handy when you have to do work in Windows. I offer no excuse for the useful tips that slip in, except to say that sometimes you have to save a little time at work to waste it later in frivolity.

■ About the Disk That Accompanies This Book

The stiff back cover of this book conceals a disk stuffed with 1.44MB of Windows-based entertainment. Some of the programs on this disk are just for fun. Some of them are both useful and fun. And some of the files there aren't programs at all—they are icons, wallpaper bitmaps, and strange sounds.

You'll be using the programs in a few of the exercises in wasted time you'll be going through in the book—but once you've been through the rigorous training this book provides, each of the programs and files will offer hours of free-form fun to the dedicated timewaster.

PART 1

Window Dressing

How to Make Redecorating Your Desktop into a Full-time Job

- *Start Wasting Time ... 2*

- *This Old Windows ... 20*

- *Passing the Screen Test ... 40*

- *Cursors! Foiled Again ... 58*

- *I Think Icon, I Think Icon ... 70*

- *Disturbing the Neighbors ... 88*

- *Font Mania ... 106*

- *WIN a Few*
- *The Business of Bootup*
- *That Start-up Logo Has Gotta Go!*
- *Building Your Own Windows Start-up Logo*
- *INI Beginning…*
- *What Was the Point of This Chapter?*

CHAPTER 1

Start Wasting Time

How to move from the DOS prompt to Windows with the maximum effort

Conventional wisdom has it that all you need do to start Windows is type **WIN** at the DOS prompt and press the Enter key. If you think that's all there is to it, you need a few lessons in creative time-wasting. The first rule is to remember the New Age maxim "Success is in the quality of the journey," and the old age maxim about stopping to smell the roses. Thereafter, observe no rules. To really *know* Windows, you have to explore every way to get from point A (the DOS command line) to point B (Icon City).

■ WIN a Few

So you are missing the point of Windows altogether. You want to save time by avoiding direct contact with Windows itself and diving directly into your applications. In theory, you can do that by running Windows and a program in one command. In theory, you can begin crunching away at your spreadsheet in seconds by entering

```
WIN EXCEL BUDGET.XLS
```

at the DOS prompt.

Luckily, DOS's PATH usually gets in the way of the theory. For this command to work, the directory that contains Excel must be in the DOS PATH—and even if it is, your data files must be in the same directory. So you'll get at least one error message and lose time. And of course, entering the command

```
WIN C:\EXCEL\EXCEL D:\FINANCE\BUDGET.XLS
```

is likely to consume more of your time than it's actually worth—unless you're a fair typist who can manage a long string of characters with nary an error and who can remember where you saved your budget file in the first place. Most of us find it much quicker to wield the mouse once we get into Windows, click on an icon, and select a few menu options to reach the same end.

The moral of this tip? Whenever you're feeling cocky, try loading your favorite Windows application and a file you want to work on using the command line only. Each time you get it right, reward yourself with a couple of opportunities to cheat at Solitaire the next time you play (more on how to do this later in the book).

WIN Slash What?

In the interest of wasting more time outside of Windows, let's look at the DOS program that starts it all, WIN.COM. You can modify WIN.COM with a number of parameters and switches, most of which are documented. If you don't have the Windows manual handy, use the help switch to see a list of the switches. Most Microsoft products in recent years use the slash-query key combination (/?) to reveal the program's legitimate switches. Try this with the Windows program file (type **WIN /?**), and you'll get an imposing series of options, including the redoubtable /3, /S, /B, and /D (see Table 1.1). It's unlikely that you'll use any of these, but you might want to try the one Microsoft doesn't show you, which is simply a colon (:). More about this later.

The first two options that WIN /? reveals set the mode that Windows will run in: /3 runs Windows in 386 enhanced mode, which is the default if you've installed Windows on a 386- or 486-based PC; and /S (or /2) runs Windows in standard mode, the standard for Windows on 286 machines. Since you can't

WIN a Few 5

Table 1.1

How to Complicate Starting Up Windows

Switch	Function
/3	Starts Windows in 386 enhanced mode
/S	Starts Windows in standard mode
/B	Creates BOOTLOG.TXT, a log of system messages generated as Windows starts up
/D	Used for troubleshooting problems when Windows doesn't start correctly
	:F Turns off 32-bit disk access (also called FastDisk)
	:S Specifies that Windows should not use the ROM address space between F000:0000 and 1MB for a break point
	:V Specifies that the ROM routine will handle interrupts from the hard disk controller
	:X Prohibits Windows from using the adapter area of memory
:	Suppresses the Windows start-up logo; not recommended by Microsoft

Detour: If you look over all the start-up switch options, you'll see there's an obvious reason for each letter or number used *except* /D. What can the D stand for? These are all troubleshooting options, so T would make more sense. Any insights into this would be most welcome.

run Windows in 386 enhanced mode on a 286, the only time you would use either switch is to step down an enhanced-mode Windows installation to standard mode. The only reasons you'd do that is if you were encountering serious problems with virtual memory or you wanted Windows to run slower. You'd use /3 to switch a 386 into enhanced mode when you'd already set it to run in standard mode.

You would only run the /D switch options when you're having problems with Windows. If you are, these switches save a lot of time when you're editing Windows's system initialization file, SYSTEM.INI.

The one command line parameter not recommended by Microsoft is the colon (though why they don't is a mystery, since they put it there in the first place). All it appears to do is suppress the Windows start-up graphic, so that you cut straight from the DOS prompt to your Program Manager. But every time this tip appears in print, droves of technoids write vaguely troubling letters about how the colon "makes some systems unstable" and how there must be *some* reason it's not documented by Microsoft.

It's true that Microsoft doesn't mention it in any of their documentation, but they never mentioned the /AUTOTEST switch for DOS's FORMAT command either, and that's a godsend for anyone wanting to initialize a new floppy disk (try it sometime). Whether typing WIN : will make your system unstable or not is a risk you'll have to take on your own. It's a real waste of time.

■ The Business of Bootup

Ever wonder why Windows takes so long to get started? It's not loading the start-up graphic that takes time—try a stopwatch test, starting Windows first with a plain WIN command and then with a WIN : command. If there's more than a second's difference, either your machine or your stopwatch thumb is too slow. No, while you're staring at Microsoft's ad for the program you've already bought, Windows is chugging away at initializing a stack of files for you to have at your beck and call during your Windows session.

To have a gander at what Windows loads while it starts, type **WIN /B** at the DOS prompt. This creates a text file called BOOTLOG.TXT, which you'll find in your Windows subdirectory. To read it, double-click on the Notepad icon, select the File menu's Open option, and click on BOOTLOG.TXT. Exactly what you'll see depends on your system setup, but it will include many lines beginning with *LoadStart=,* followed by a file name and many corresponding lines beginning with *LoadSuccess=*. There will also be several lines beginning with *INIT* and corresponding *INITDONE* and *STATUS* lines.

Most of the files named in BOOTLOG.TXT are the drivers and fonts that Windows needs to run its most basic functions. You'll also find the files listed (if you look for them in File Manager) in your SYSTEM subdirectory, and you'll find mention of them in the two Windows initialization files, WIN-.INI and SYSTEM.INI. If there's something wrong with Windows's startup, you'll find a *LoadFail=* line and a cryptic failure code.

The most common cause for LoadFail lines (at least, the most common cause that doesn't halt Windows startup and signal that there's a problem somewhere) is an unavailable font file. If a font file is either deleted or corrupted, and not removed from your system properly (don't worry, I'll show you the right way later in the book), Windows looks for it, can't find it, and, if Windows doesn't crash, it leaves no trace of the problem—except in BOOTLOG.TXT.

Because of this, it's a good idea to run Windows periodically from a /B switch. In fact, if Windows crashes during startup, it's the first thing you should do. By the way, don't be surprised to see the BOOTLOG file size swelling over time. The /B switch doesn't overwrite start-up information from an existing BOOTLOG.TXT, but instead fills in the new information at the end of the original file.

■ That Start-up Logo Has Gotta Go!

Pop Quiz: What's the similarity between the commands WIN *filename,* WIN /B, and WIN :? *Answer*: All of them suppress the Windows start-up logo. WIN.COM calls up this little graphic during startup to distract you while

Gratuitous Tip: Fast Fix for BOOTLOG Failures

If you find an unexpected LoadFailure report in a BOOTLOG.TXT file, you can replace the corrupted file that caused it directly from your Windows installation disks without having to reinstall the whole shebang. From the DOS prompt (and you thought Windows would make everything graphical!), use the EXPAND program that's in your Windows subdirectory. For example, if there's a LoadFailure on the file VGASYS.FON, check the Windows floppies with the DIR command until you find the one containing the same file name, but ending in an underscore—VGASYS.FO_—and then enter this command from the Windows directory:

```
EXPAND A:\VGASYS.FO_ VGASYS.FON
```

EXPAND does the rest.

Windows is going through its paces, and it takes the graphic away shortly before it hangs the wallpaper file. This little graphic is actually embedded in WIN.COM, but it started life as a separate file called VGALOGO.RLE (or, for EGA monitors, EGALOGO.RLE), hidden away in Windows's SYSTEM subdirectory. (RLE stands for Run Length Encoded, which is a subset of the .BMP graphics format—but at around two-fifths the size, it's far more economical for your hard disk.)

Some people assume that displaying this graphic makes startup slower (which it may do, but usually by no more than a second). Some people assume it's subliminal advertising of the most insidious kind. Some people brood over the logo. Some people want to blast it away—without being told that doing so makes their system unstable. The next section is for those people.

Ditching the Windows Start-up Logo

Whenever you change part of Windows setup—such as the video driver, keyboard, or mouse—the setup procedure creates a new WIN.COM file using several files from the SYSTEM subdirectory. One is the start-up graphic file VGALOGO.RLE (or its equivalent for other display standards, such as EGA), another is WIN.CNF, and a third called VGALOGO.LGO helps integrate the graphic. If you want to wave goodbye to the start-up graphic, you need to create your own WIN.COM file without using the RLE file.

Hacking a program file like this presents two hazards: First, it might not work, and if it doesn't, you can't run your program; second, it might well invalidate your software license with Microsoft. If you want to waste a lot of time, read the fine print on the envelope that contained the Windows installation disks. You'll find that by breaking the seal, you agreed to abide by all the fine print, and hacking WIN.COM is not in the spirit of the agreement and is probably outside the letter of it, too. So bearing this in mind, here's how to do it:

1. If you're in Windows, get back to DOS. Don't click on the MS-DOS icon to shell out, but instead exit Windows entirely by selecting File, Exit from Program Manager. You'll be plopped into your Windows subdirectory.

2. Back up your original WIN.COM in case anything goes wrong. Don't be overconfident. Just do it by entering this line:

   ```
   REN WIN.COM WINBAK.COM
   ```

   With this backup file in place, if anything goes wrong, you can restore your old file.

3. Next, create a new Windows program file—totally logo-free—from the WIN.CNF file:

   ```
   COPY /B SYSTEM\WIN.CNF WIN.COM
   ```

   This command makes a binary copy (copy /B) of WIN.CNF and calls it WIN.COM. That's all there is to it. Now run Windows by entering WIN at the DOS prompt. Nothing will happen for a few seconds, and then you'll cut abruptly to Windows. Pretty dull, wasn't it? If you're getting bored with the start-up logo, simply getting rid of it may not be the best answer. Why not change it instead?

Replacing the Windows Start-up Logo

We established earlier that WIN.COM contains a graphics file called VGA-LOGO.RLE and that a short DOS command can create a new WIN.COM. Here's where the fun starts. You can use another DOS command to insert a different RLE file into the program to replace the Windows start-up logo (see Figure 1.1). This process isn't for the timid, but if you maintain the necessary backups, you won't risk corrupting your Windows program file. On the disk in the back of this book, there's a collection of RLE files suitable to the task. For grins and gratuitous self-promotion, let's insert a spoof start-up logo from the file WASTING.RLE.

That Start-up Logo Has Gotta Go!   9

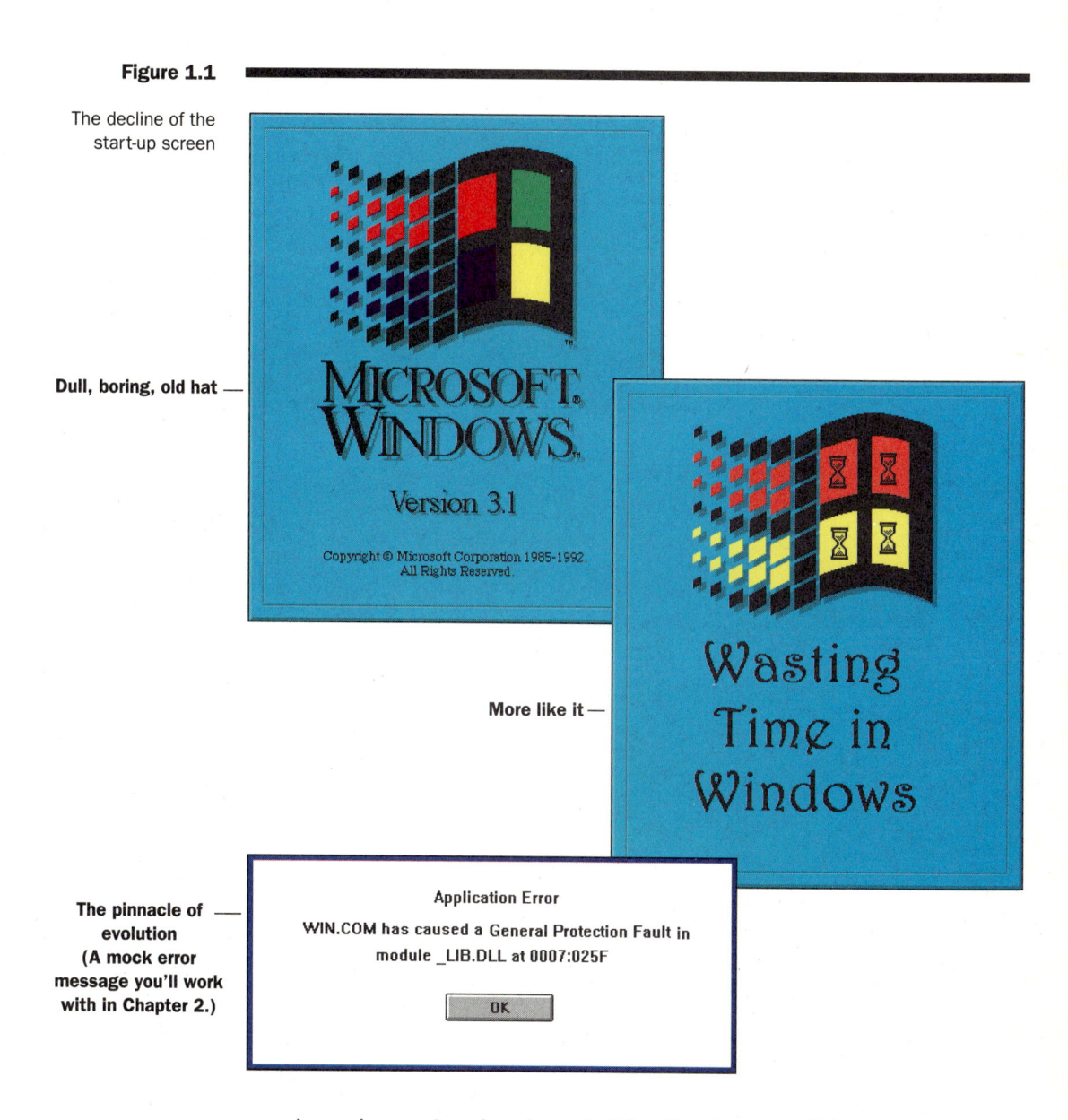

Figure 1.1

The decline of the start-up screen

Dull, boring, old hat —

More like it —

The pinnacle of evolution (A mock error message you'll work with in Chapter 2.)

> **Application Error**
>
> WIN.COM has caused a General Protection Fault in module _LIB.DLL at 0007:025F
>
> [OK]

Assuming you've already copied the files from our disk onto your hard drive (see the Appendix if you haven't yet), the first step now is for you to copy the WASTING.RLE file from your WASTING subdirectory into your Windows SYSTEM subdirectory. With the file safely copied into your Windows SYSTEM subdirectory, it's time to hack into WIN.COM again. As before, this involves quitting Windows.

Use DOS's CD command to change to the Windows directory (if necessary). Now get ready to enter a fiendishly long DOS command that you'll need to double-check several times before committing yourself to the Enter key. This line takes WIN.CNF, a logo introductory file called VGALOGO-.LGO, and the new logo file WASTING.RLE from the SYSTEM subdirectory, and copies them all into a new WIN.COM file in the Windows directory. Here goes:

```
COPY /B SYSTEM\WIN.CNF + SYSTEM\VGALOGO.LGO + SYSTEM\WASTING.RLE WIN.COM
```

Once you're sure you've got it right, press Enter. The DOS COPY command will show the names of each file as it copies it. Enter a quick DIR WIN.COM and check the time and date stamp—it should be current. Now fire up the new Windows.

Isn't that a little better?

■ Building Your Own Windows Start-up Logo

Like any graphic that stares at you while you're waiting to do something important, even WASTING.RLE will get stale. That's why there are several RLE files for you to choose from on the disk accompanying this book. Before you do so, you'll want to check what the graphic looks like. Of course, that's not as straightforward as it should be. Windows's own and only graphics program, Paintbrush, can't read RLE files. To preview these files, you need to seek outside resources, such as the shareware graphics program PaintShop Pro from JASC Inc., which you'll also find (by a remarkable coincidence) on the floppy disk bound into the back of this book.

To check out an RLE graphic (in this case, Windows's own VGALOGO-.RLE) in PaintShop Pro, double-click on the PaintShop Pro icon to start it running. Until you register the shareware, you'll see a reminder that this is an evaluation unit. Click on OK to get to the program's opening screen, and then follow these instructions:

1. Select File, Open.

2. Scroll down the Format box, and highlight RLE.

3. Under Directories, click on the drive and directory that contain Windows, and then select the SYSTEM subdirectory.

4. Under Files, click on VGALOGO.RLE.

You can see where this is leading. PaintShop Pro gives you access to files in quite a few formats—.TIF, .GIF, .TGA, .WPG, .BMP, .PCX, .MAC, .MSP, .IMG, .PIC, .DIB, and .JAS—and can save them as RLE files. You can convert a lot of files you might have lying around into files you can use as

Building Your Own Windows Start-up Logo   **11**

start-up logos. But you must observe one limitation: Before you try, make sure that the RLE file is smaller than 64K. Any larger than that and it will cause problems.

But even a stack of prefabricated graphics files won't make your Windows system unique—and certainly won't waste enough time. To do that, you need to create your own graphics—or, for more fun, butcher somebody else's. In art, this is called parody. On your desktop, it's called messing with VGALOGO.RLE some more.

Since PaintShop Pro's myriad virtues don't include a robust library of bitmap editing tools, this exercise requires another paint program. In this case, I'll describe how to do it in Paintbrush. These instructions start off where those for examining RLE files left off:

1. From within Paintshop Pro, select File, Save As, BMP - Windows - RGB Encoded, and click on OK. Then select File, Close, and either File, Quit or change to Program Manager.

2. Start Paintbrush, and open the file VGALOGO.BMP.

3. To make a suitably anarchic parody, click on the irregular selection tool (the icon at the top left of the toolbar), and make a jagged selection of the Windows flag logo—one that looks like a broken piece of glass (see Figure 1.2).

Figure 1.2

The beginning of the end: Shattering an image starts with Paintbrush's irregular selection tool

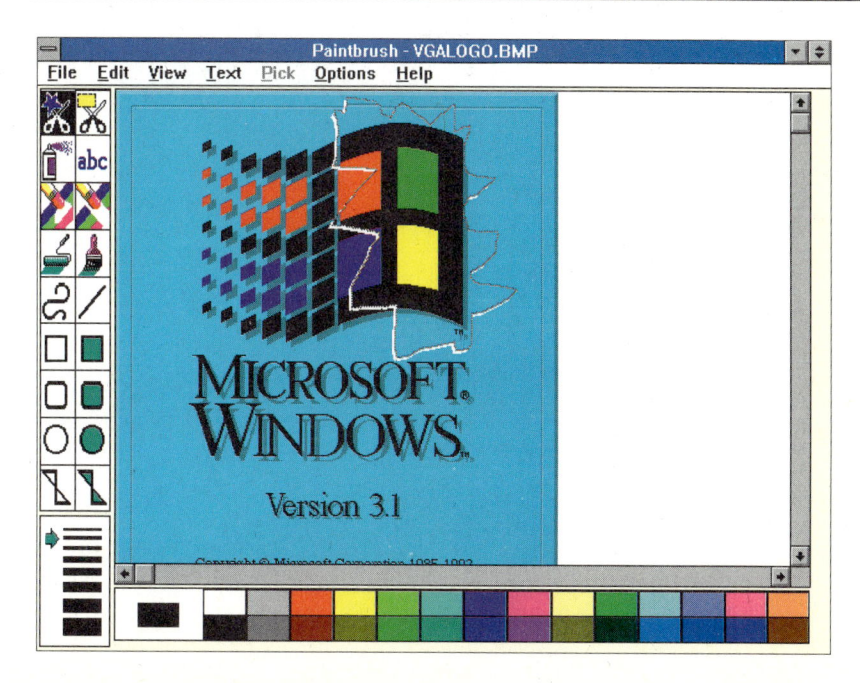

4. Once you've connected the lines, release the mouse button, move the pointer to the center of the selection, hold down the mouse button, and drag the selection over a little.

5. Continue to work on the flag, selecting portions and dragging them away until the graphic is a real mess.

6. To make way for your own caption, draw a loop around the word Microsoft, and then press Shift+Del to delete it (see Figure 1.3).

Figure 1.3

The decomposition continues: Once the logo is in tatters, prepare the ground for wordplay

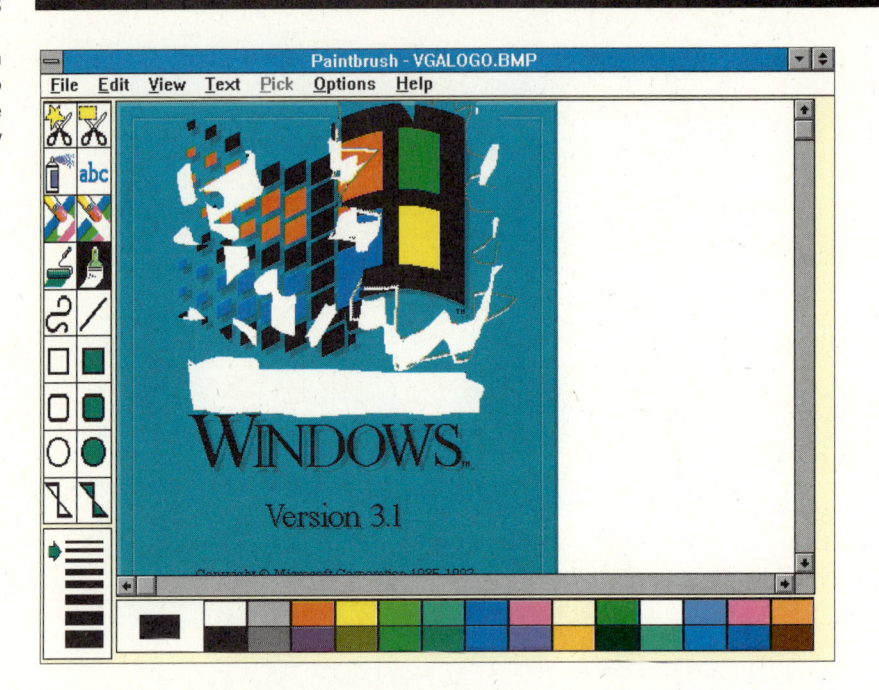

7. To fill in the white space, click on cyan in the color palette, and select the roller tool. Click on the white space, and the roller fills the whole range with cyan (see Figure 1.4). If you screw up (which is easy to do with the roller), just select Edit, Undo.

8. Select the Text, Fonts menu option, and pick a font that either matches or contrasts with the word Windows (whatever you prefer). Increase the point size to 26. Then click on OK. On the color palette, click on black, and then select the text tool. Click on an insertion point above the word Windows, enter the word **Shattering**, and choose File, Save to save the results (if you think they're good enough). Compare your screen with ours in Figure 1.5.

Building Your Own Windows Start-up Logo   **13**

Figure 1.4

Getting there: Fill the gap using the roller (or fill) tool

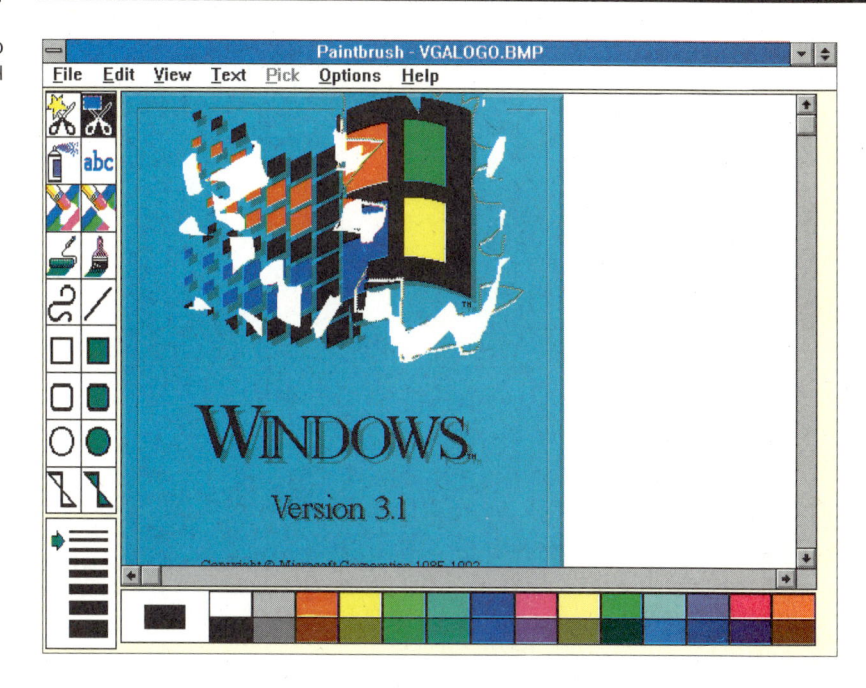

Figure 1.5

The crowning glory: When in doubt, use a well-worn pun

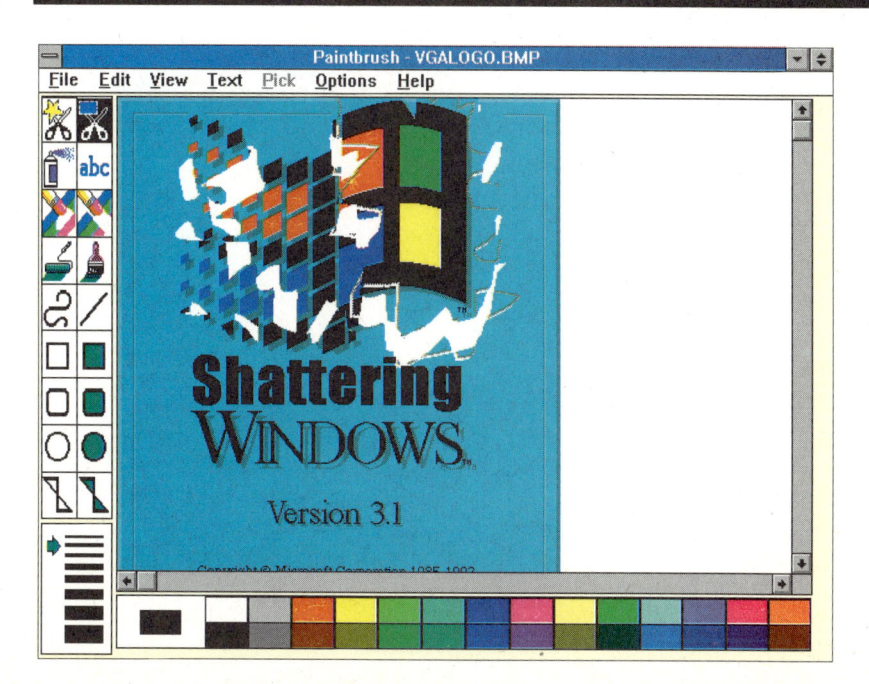

The file is, of course, in RGB-encoded .BMP format—and needs to be opened in PaintShop Pro and saved as an RLE-encoded .BMP file. That done, you're ready to go through the COPY /B rigmarole to incorporate the file into a new WIN.COM. And good luck to you.

Now go back and think up your own joke screens.

■ INI Beginning…

Every significant Windows application you can think of has an initialization or .INI file. These are text files (and as such, are easy to edit) with long lists of program parameters, drivers, and functions, written in a software engineer's shorthand (and as such, are tough to edit). Windows itself has more than its share of initialization to do.

The listing you saw in the BOOTLOG trick earlier in the chapter isn't the only hoop Windows jumps through to throw itself on your screen. As soon as WIN.COM gets started, three .INI files come into play.

The first, SYSTEM.INI, is a listing that's mainly concerned with the contents of your system—the hardware drivers, network, and device drivers that Windows needs to know about to make your system cooperate. The next, WIN.INI, tells Windows details about the desktop and programs you have set up, and encroaches on SYSTEM.INI's turf by listing the printer and communications ports your system has. As if in retribution, SYSTEM.INI holds the key to one crucial Windows program—it defines the shell that will be your main contact with Windows. This is usually Program Manager, though other apps can do an equally good or better job (depending on your tastes). Some folks go for Norton Desktop, others prefer the Windows File Manager. Whichever program you use as your shell, its .INI file is the third one processed during Windows startup. I'm assuming that most people are using the default shell, Program Manager, whose .INI file is PROGMAN.INI.

These and other .INI files have certain things in common. They are divided into paragraphs with headings in square brackets, such as [Desktop] and [Windows]. If one of their lines is preceded by a semicolon, it's a comment that the program won't act upon. And .INI files can be edited using a text editor—after all, they're nothing but unformatted text files.

Although Notepad is the primary Windows text processor, it isn't the best choice for editing WIN.INI and SYSTEM.INI. Sure, it has a search function and is a functional (if basic) text-editing program, but it doesn't create backups automatically. Instead, use the System Configuration Editor—or Sysedit to its friends. From the Program Manager or File Manager, select File, Run, and type **SYSEDIT**. A four-window subset of Notepad will appear with the SYSTEM.INI and WIN.INI files, along with DOS's CONFIG.SYS

The Five Laws of .INI File Editing

There are many good reasons for editing WIN.INI and SYSTEM.INI (most of which we'll look at later), but only if you do it right. If you're going to tinker with files that affect the way programs work—especially files like WIN.INI that will take hours to recreate—you need to observe a few guidelines very closely:

- Make a backup file before you change a single word—you'd be nuts not to. Try the same file name with a different extension, such as .BAK, .OLD, or a number (if you make several changes in a day).

- Make only one change at a time. If you screw up an .INI file, it's easier to figure out what you did wrong if you only did one thing.

- Don't use a word processor. It's only a matter of time before you accidentally save the file formatted—and the next time you fire up Windows, it'll throw up its hands and surrender.

- Add comments to your changes. Add a new line before the line you've changed, type a semicolon (;) as the first character on that line, and make a note of what you did, why you did it, and who told you to do it (so you can blame them later).

- Instead of deleting or replacing a line, comment it out by placing a semicolon before the line to make it a comment line. It's easier to restore a line like ; LOAD=SOL.EXE by deleting the semicolon than by typing LOAD=SOL.EXE. Make life easy for yourself.

and AUTOEXEC.BAT. Change any of these files, and Sysedit will make a backup when you leave the program, and the backup will have the same file name but with the extension .SYD. You may want to make the System Configuration Editor a part of your Program Manager—you'll be using it often enough as you read through this book to make it worthwhile. Pick a suitable program group, select File, New, click on Program Item, and press Enter. In the Command Line box, type **SYSEDIT**.

Armed with this information, you're ready to render Windows completely unrecognizable. Read on.

Harmless Trick: Edit an Edited Files List

Any program that has a list of the most recently used files under its File menu (for you to reopen quickly) stores that information in its .INI file. Use Notepad to open up Excel's or Ami Pro's .INI file, for example (but not WinWord's, which uses an encryption technique that makes it uneditable), and look for the lines that read *LastOpen=* or *[Recently Edited Files]*. Then perk up a boring morning by replacing the file names with some cheery message, like the one shown to the right.

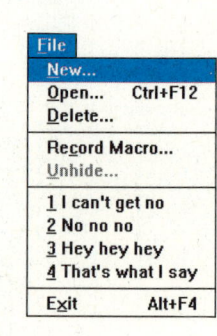

    First, make a backup, and then edit away at the words after the equals sign. Save your changes and quit Notepad. Then fire up the program. If you click on any of the "files" under the program's File menu, all you'll get is an error message dialog box and no harm done.

File	
New...	
Open...	Ctrl+F12
Delete...	
Record Macro...	
Unhide...	
1 I can't get no	
2 No no no	
3 Hey hey hey	
4 That's what I say	
Exit	Alt+F4

Now You See It...

Three things will determine what you'll see once Windows is loaded: SYSTEM.INI's *shell=PROGMAN.EXE* line, WIN.INI's *Run=* and *Load=* lines, and the contents of your Startup group. Unsurprisingly, since I brought it up, none of these is cast in stone. Here's what you can do to change each of them.

Switch the Shells

First, fire up Sysedit. Select SYSTEM.INI and search for the word *shell*. The *shell=* statement can be followed with pretty much any executable file name. If you're an obsessive card player, you could make Windows a bloated, multi-megabyte version of Klondike by using Solitaire as your shell.

    If you're a DOS shell buff, try making File Manager the shell with the line

```
shell=WINFILE.EXE
```

File Manager has all the requisites of a good shell: It enables you to launch programs at a double-click, manage files, and waste hours reconfiguring.

    If you hanker for the good old days of the '80s, resurrect the MS-DOS Executive—the bare-bones file manager that greeted users of Windows 286 and 386 before the Windows 3.*x* series came along. Before committing yourself to it as your shell, road-test it first. Select File, Run in File Manager or

Program Manager, and type **MSDOS**. When you press Enter, a black-and-white screen full of file names appears in a yummy system font. Crude graphics of disk drives with letters beside them line up across the top of the screen. The three menu options (Help is considered unnecessary) provide the basics for file management, and the listings provide file names ripe for the double-clicking (anything to get away from the Executive itself). Ponder for a moment that for five years before 1990, this was what people thought Windows was all about. Then put it out of your mind for good.

Run versus Load

Note. Running a program brings it up in a window when Windows first starts up. Loading a program brings up a minimized icon at the bottom of your desktop.

Early in WIN.INI's [Windows] paragraph are the lines *Run=* and *Load=*, each of which can be followed by a program's file name. (If you don't see these lines, you can add them yourself.) The Run and Load lines are throwbacks to versions of Windows where Program Manager didn't use a Startup group. They're useful if you're running another shell, but the Startup group does everything these lines can do (except for one thing—these lines can't be bypassed by pressing the Shift key, and the Startup group can). Use these lines to run programs you always want running—like Solitaire. Enter a program name preceded by the directory path Windows will need to follow to find it (followed by a file name and its path, if you like).

Start-up Strategies

Switch to Program Manager, and find the Startup group (if you have one)—or use File, New, Program Group to create a group called Startup (if you don't). Now decide which programs you want to run every time you start Windows—let's say, File Manager, the Clock, and Calendar. Copy them from their groups into the Startup group by holding down the Ctrl key and dragging each program's icon over the Startup group or its icon. When you're done, open the Startup group (if it's minimized) and decide which programs you'll run and which you'll load minimized. If you want the clock to run minimized, for example, press Alt and double-click on the Clock icon. In the Program Item Properties dialog box that appears, click on the Run Minimized box so that an X appears in it, and then click on OK.

Make Any Group a Startup Group   Met all your deadlines and want to slack off? It's possible, nay, easy, to make a Startup group of the Games group (or any other group that takes your fancy). Here's how:

1. Open PROGMAN.INI in Notepad.

2. Make a backup file by saving the file as PROGMAN1.INI.

3. At the end of the [settings] paragraph, enter the line

   ```
   STARTUP="Games"
   ```

   Alternatively, use any other program group name, copying it exactly as it appears in the group's title bar.

4. Save your changes to PROGMAN.INI, quit Notepad, and restart Windows to see the changes take effect.

Rename Program Manager   The very name Program Manager is enough to strike up a chorus of yawns. When—not if—you get tired of seeing it blazoned across the top of your screen, use the Startup group to change it. First, open your Startup group, and then select File, New, Program Item. In the Description box, think of any word, phrase, aphorism, insult, name, or line of poetry you'd like to see in the title bar of Program Manager. Then in the Command Line box, type the word **PROGMAN**. Click on OK, and an icon will appear in the Startup group with your banner witticism under it. Double-click on the icon and look at the Program Manager title bar (see Figure 1.6). That's the way it'll appear every time you start Windows until you change the Program Item Properties box again.

Figure 1.6

A ProgMan by any other name... To change what you see on Program Manager's title bar, run Program Manager from your startup group and change its label.

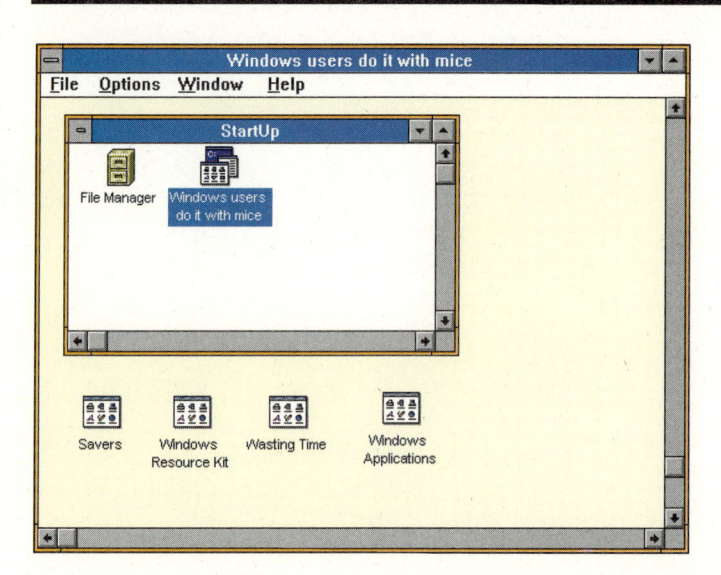

Gratuitous Tip: Bypass the Start-up Items

Need to run a resource-hog of a Windows app that crowds out the contents of your Startup group? Then don't load your Startup group. When you first run Windows, press the Shift key and hold it down while the start-up logo is on screen. Windows will cut to the shell, but won't load any other programs. Note that you can't bypass programs this way if they are run or loaded by a line in WIN.INI.

■ What Was the Point of This Chapter?

"Start Wasting Time" described:

- How to start Windows and a Windows application in one command—and advised against it
- Which of WIN.COM's switches and parameters you should care about
- How to remove, replace, and otherwise mutilate the Windows start-up graphic
- Ways to edit .INI files that will change what you first see when you load Windows
- How to set up and change your Startup group

- *Wallpaper Hanging Made Complex*
- *New Sources of Wallpaper—Print Screen and Paintbrush*
- *Decorating without Wallpaper*
- *What Was the Point of This Chapter?*

CHAPTER 2

This Old Windows

Turn redecorating your screen into a full-time job

THE FIRST PROJECT YOU TAKE ON WHEN YOU MOVE INTO A NEW house is redecorating. Nothing makes a place feel more like your own than slapping on some wallpaper and painting the woodwork in colors you like. And if you've been living in the same place for years, a lick of paint and some new drapes make it feel like new again.

The same is true of Windows. You can't really be comfortable in Windows unless you've tried out a few "looks." And interior design for your graphical user interface offers advantages over mere house overhauls: Experimentation is easy and free, you don't have to spend a fortune hiring a designer, and you won't get paint on your carpets.

But like domestic decoration, customizing the look of Windows involves time, a few extra tools, and a handful of professional tips. If you're in search of better looking Windows, here's what you need to get the job done.

■ Wallpaper Hanging Made Complex

One Windows utility can change the appearance of almost the entire Windows environment, and that is the Control Panel. Though you can control many other elements by editing lines in various .INI files (most of which I'll go into later), the Control Panel is the best starting point. When you minimize all your application windows, you're staring at the wallpaper, and to adjust it, you need to use the Control Panel's Desktop option, shown in Figure 2.1.

Figure 2.1

Desktop's Wallpaper option isn't much help—it shows only .BMP files in the Windows subdirectory. But you can enter the path for a wallpaper file located anywhere on your system.

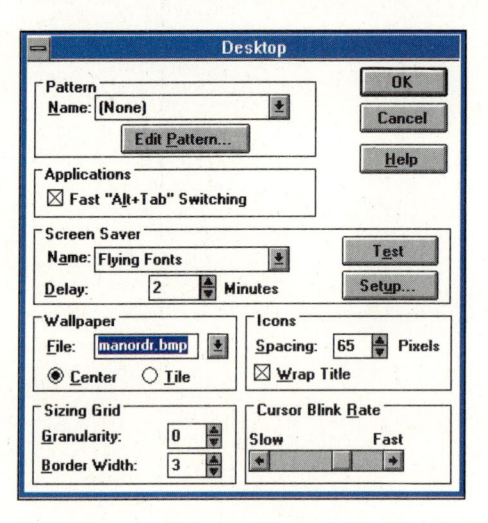

Among the Desktop options is one entitled Wallpaper. In the File combo box, you can choose from various .BMP files. In fact, the list shows only the .BMP files in your Windows subdirectory—if you can remember the names of .BMP files located elsewhere, enter the path and full name of one of them to load it as your wallpaper. Just don't expect any help from Windows in finding such files. The best you can do to find the path to another subdirectory is to use the File Manager.

Wallpaper Hanging Made Complex

This much information about wallpaper is common knowledge. What's not so well known is that Windows can use compact RLE-encoded .BMP files for wallpaper as well as regular, inefficiently coded, Paintbrush-style, RGB-encoded .BMP files. The surest way to prove the truth of this to yourself is to enter **system\vgalogo.rle** in the File combo box in the Control Panel Desktop's Wallpaper section. This line looks in the SYSTEM subdirectory for the start-up logo, and once you press Enter, it loads it on your desktop as wallpaper. You can substitute any of the RLE-encoded bitmaps you created in the first section or retrieved from the accompanying disk to make wallpaper of those, too.

Gratuitous Tip: Direct to the Control Panel's Desktop

To cut straight to one of the options on the Control Panel—quickly and without wielding a mouse—use the Program Manager's or File Manager's File, Run command. To run the Color options, for example, enter **control color** in the Run dialog box's Command Line box, as shown here:

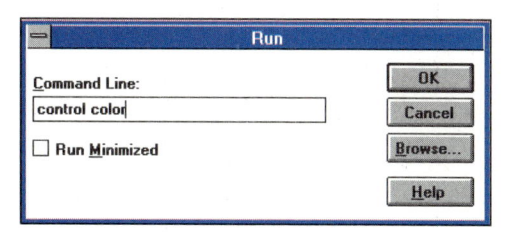

For other options, substitute *desktop*, *fonts*, *ports*, *mouse*, *sound*, and so forth for *color*. (Be sure to include *control* as the first word in each of these command lines.) The Control Panel will load more quickly and take you straight to your choice in one step.

Hang That Wallpaper Left of Center...Or Right... Or Up a Bit...

Once you've selected the bitmap of your choice, you need to make only one other basic decision: Do you want the wallpaper tiled (stacked shoulder-to-shoulder with multiple iterations of itself) or centered (stuck on its own in the middle of the screen)?

This caters to most people's wishes, but Windows provides a little-known option for adjusting the center point of your wallpaper. In general, when you center wallpaper in the Control Panel, it ends up in the dead center of the screen. But let's suppose you want centered wallpaper to appear a little off-center so you can see it peeking around your application windows. There are two undocumented lines you can add to WIN.INI to shift your wallpaper out of line:

```
WallPaperOriginY=n
WallPaperOriginX=n
```

These two lines belong at the end of the [DeskTop] section, and both must be followed with a number (*n*), which represents the offset value of the graphic. The default value for each is zero, meaning that Windows calculates the starting point (0,0) for its wallpapers based on the upper-left corner of the screen. To move an image down, complete the *WallPaperOriginY=* line with a number which represents the number of pixels needed to shift the image down. To shift an image right, adjust the *WallPaperOriginX=* line. Depending on where you want an image and how big the image is, you'll need to experiment with offset numbers to get the best results.

Figure 2.2

Off-center wallpaper can show more of your favorite image, even while you're working in an application. This image has been positioned with a WallpaperOriginX value of 350 (that is, 350 pixels from the left boundary of the screen) and a WallpaperOriginY value of 10 (or 10 pixels down).

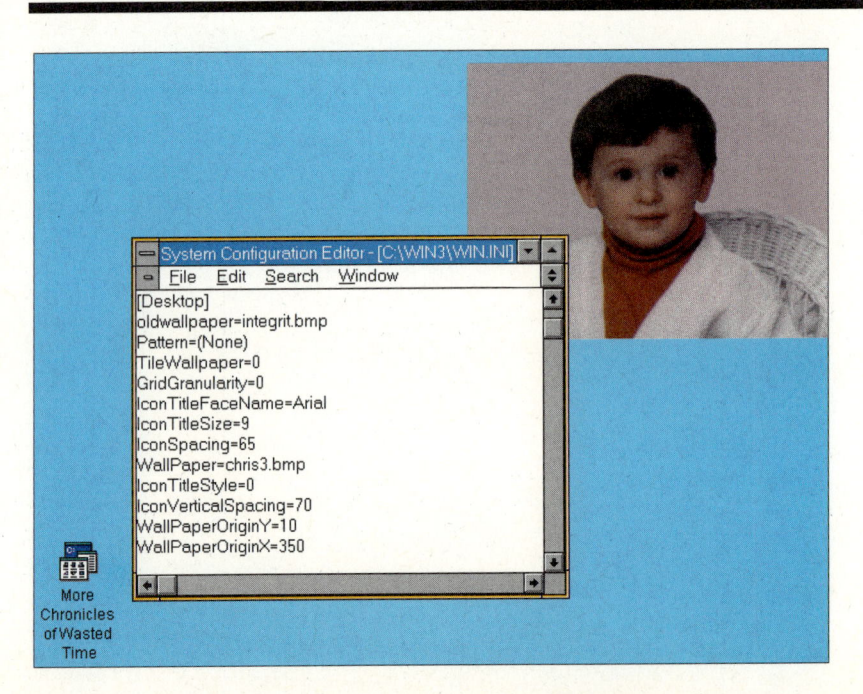

Wallpaper Lite: Looks Great, Less Filling

You've already learned that Windows is happy to use RLE-encoded .BMP files for wallpaper. The .BMP files that Windows provides for use are RGB-encoded. Check them out in the File Manager by changing to your Windows subdirectory, clicking on View, By File Type, and selecting *.BMP in the Name box. Assuming your view includes all file details, you'll see that the .BMP files are extremely varied in size. This is because they contain different color depths—from 2 colors to 256—and different dimensions—from 16 pixels square to 640-by-480 pixels (depending on whether they are intended to be tiled or centered).

In many cases, you can save a chunk of hard disk space by converting the .BMP files to RLE-encoded .BMP files, which is a snap in PaintShop Pro. If you do this, Windows will still recognize the files as a subset of .BMP, and you can still use them for wallpaper. The technique is simple:

1. Open a .BMP file in PaintShop Pro.

2. Check the numbers in parentheses on the title bar. A reading of (640 × 480 × 256) means the image is 640 pixels wide by 480 deep, saved with a 256-color palette.

3. If the number is more than 256, reduce the color palette to enable the conversion to work. Select Colors, Decrease Color Depth, and pick either 256 Colors (8-bit) or 16 Colors (4-bit). Stick with the default settings for Palette, Reduction Method, and Options. Then click on OK.

4. Select File, Save As, and under Format, select BMP-Windows-RLE Encoded.

5. To retain the original file so you can compare the file sizes, enter a new name in the Filename box. (PaintShop Pro retains the .BMP extension, so don't try to use another extension with the same file name).

6. Switch to the File Manager, and compare the before and after file sizes. Delete the larger file.

This technique will stand you in good stead as you start making your own wallpaper files—try it out on any .BMP, .PCX, or .TIF file, or on other graphics files you've finished editing. But you have to be careful—contrary to popular opinion, .RLE bitmaps aren't always smaller than RGB-encoded ones. Before obliterating your original .BMP files, check the comparative file sizes in Table 2.1. And remember that you won't be able to edit any RLE-encoded .BMP files in Paintbrush without opening them first in PaintShop Pro; selecting Edit, Copy; switching to Paintbrush; and selecting Edit, Paste. Selecting File, Open is easier, so unless you see a greatly reduced file size, this conversion process may be more trouble than it's worth.

Chapter 2: This Old Windows

Table 2.1

Use PaintShop Pro to convert Windows .BMP files to RLE-encoded format, which takes up fewer bytes than .BMP—except when it doesn't.

File Name	.BMP File Size	.RLE File Size	Difference in File Size	Percentage Change
256COLOR	5078	5572	+494	10% added
ARCADE	630	672	+42	7% added
ARCHES	10358	6734	–3624	35% off
ARGYLE	630	622	–8	1% off
CARS	630	690	+60	10% added
CASTLE	778	882	+104	13% added
CHESS	153718	31744	–121974	79% off
EGYPT	630	596	–34	5% off
FLOCK	1630	1226	–404	25% off
LEAVES	15118	8352	–6766	45% off
MARBLE	27646	23616	–4030	15% off
PAPER	9662	*	*	*
PARTY	38518	39512	+944	3% added
PYRAMID	630	564	–66	10% off
REDBRICK	630	742	+112	18% added
RIBBONS	38518	31556	–6962	18% off
RIVETS	630	342	–288	46% off
SLASH	2038	2032	–6	Less than 1% off
SPOTS	4558	2968	–1590	35% off
SQUARE	630	432	–198	31% off
STEEL	7174	4564	–2610	36% off
TARTAN	32886	6598	–26288	80% off
THATCH	598	628	+30	5% added
WEAVE	190	*	*	*
WINLOGO	38518	34506	–4012	10% off
ZIGZAG	630	494	136	22% off

* A two-color bitmap, which cannot be RLE-encoded

A Regular Change of Wallpaper

Want to rotate your wallpaper files without going to the fuss and bother of entering the Control Panel every time you run Windows? There's a freeware application on the disk bound into the back of this book that will do it for you. One of the pioneers of shareware, Jim Button, wrote the Newpaper utility that cycles through all the .BMP files in your Windows subdirectory; each time you start Windows, you are greeted with a newly decorated desktop.

The utility runs transparently, but it's not the kind of program that installs itself—some assembly is required (though fortunately, that's not assembly language). To install Newpaper, follow these steps:

1. Copy the file NEWPAPER.EXE into a directory on your hard disk, and make a note of the disk letter and directory name.

2. Open Sysedit, switch to WIN.INI, and add the full path to Newpaper to the *RUN*= line. If the .EXE file is in your D:\UTILITY directory, for example, the line should read

   ```
   RUN=D:\UTILITY\NEWPAPER.EXE
   ```

3. If you're already using *RUN*= to start a program, simply leave a space after the existing program's name, and enter the Newpaper command after it.

That's all there is to installing Newpaper. After finishing this step, you'll never quite know what to expect the next time you start up Windows.

■ New Sources of Wallpaper—Print Screen and Paintbrush

Want to add a little variety to your wallpapers, but your graphic skills are lacking? Use the little-publicized Print Screen key to capture a Program Manager screen (rich in icons for the editing) to the Clipboard. A single press on Print Screen should do the trick on most keyboards, but check the cursor to see whether it disappears momentarily. If it doesn't, press Print Screen again, and if that still doesn't do it, try pressing Shift+Print Screen. To capture just the active window (the one with the colored-in title bar), press Alt+Print Screen.

Once the screen is in the Clipboard, you can paste it into Paintbrush, but not before jumping through a few hoops first. Paintbrush accepts only those bits that fit into its screen, so to paste an entire Program Manager screen into a Paintbrush window, put on your hoop-jumping shoes:

1. Click on Paintbrush's maximize button (the up-arrow in the upper-right corner of the application's window).

Chapter 2: This Old Windows

2. Under Options, Image Attributes, click on the Pels (that is, pixels) radio button, and check that the width and height boxes read 640 and 480 (or, if your screen is Super VGA, either 800-by-600 or 1,024-by-768, depending on which resolution you run).

3. Select View, Zoom Out, and when the window has zoomed out completely, press Shift+Insert to paste the image in.

4. You'll see a gray hatch pattern. Click on some point outside the pattern (not on it, as this will cause the pasted-in image to shift around and take an excruciating length of time to redraw). A wobbly-looking rendition of the screen will appear in the zoomed-out Paintbrush window (see Figure 2.3).

Figure 2.3

Wallpaper madness! Press Print Screen to capture the whole Windows screen to the Clipboard, paste it into Paintbrush, and use it as a source of wallpaper graphics.

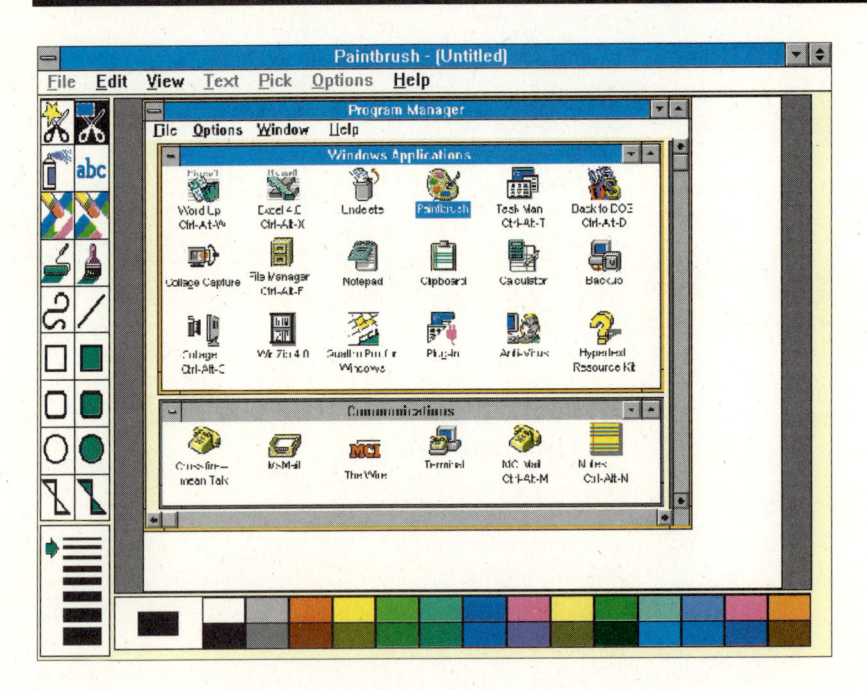

5. Select View, Zoom In, and the details will become sharper.

To make a wallpaper from several icons, lasso them with the selection tool and drag them into a free corner. (If necessary, clear some space by selecting an area and cutting it to the Clipboard using the Shift+Delete key combination.) Once you've arranged three or four icons in a group, select a fill color from the palette, select the Fill roller tool, and click on the white background to the screen. When the background color fills in, select the group of icons and copy them to the Clipboard (using either Ctrl+Ins to copy or Shift+Delete to cut them). Then paste the Clipboard's contents into a new Paintbrush file of the appropriate size (see the gratuitous tip "Size Your Image Exactly" for details), and save the file.

Gratuitous Tip: Size Your Image Exactly

Want to determine the exact size in pixels of a Paintbrush image? Select View, Cursor Position, and a little box with two numbers appears on the title bar. These numbers are the horizontal and vertical location of the cursor, measured in pixels. To obtain the exact size of an image, move the cursor to the lower-right corner, and read off the numbers in the cursor position box. To gauge the size of a portion of a screen, draw a box around it with the selection tool, and press Ctrl+Ins to copy it to the Clipboard. If necessary, scroll to the upper-left corner of the screen, and press Shift+Ins to paste the portion of the image back into the Paintbrush file. The insertion point of a pasted image is always at the upper-left corner of the visible screen, so you can judge the size of the portion by bringing the cursor to its lower-right corner. To remove the pasted portion from the image, just press Shift+Delete to cut it to the Clipboard.

.BMP and .PCX: Formats and Substance

If the size difference between RLE- and RGB-encoded bitmaps is sometimes unclear, the same is seldom true of any .BMP file and its .PCX equivalent. .BMP files are the most inefficient of all bitmapped graphics file formats, except encapsulated PostScript–EPS files—and those don't bear consideration. .BMP files are routinely 30 to 50 percent larger than their .PCX equivalents. Although .PCX files cannot be used as wallpaper, they can and should be used to store works-in-progress.

There is, of course, a drawback. Like many Windows programs, Paintbrush makes assumptions about which file extensions you want to load. While Paintbrush happily deals with the .PCX file format, it chooses to look first and foremost for .BMP files. In fact, if you look closely at Paintbrush's File Open dialog box, you'll see that it actually looks for two extensions—.BMP and the all-but-extinct .DIB (device independent bitmap) files. Assuming that you can part with the .DIB option, it's a relatively easy step to hack PBRUSH.EXE to look for both .BMP and .PCX files each time you choose File, Open.

Cracking Microsoft's Code, Again

Willing to ignore Microsoft's vehement recommendation that you don't hack into their code? Then use a little-known programming tool that ships with Windows to change the way Paintbrush works—namely, the word processor Write. This humble word processor does a fine job of changing the requisite settings. First, use the File Manager to make a backup copy of PBRUSH.EXE, and then follow these steps:

1. Fire up Write, and choose File, Open to open PBRUSH.EXE from the Windows directory.

2. Click on the No Conversion button.

3. When the file has opened, select Find, Replace. In the Find What box, enter *.**DIB**, and in the Replace With box, enter *.**PCX**.

4. Click on the Match Case check box to enter an *X* into it, and click on the Replace All button.

5. Press the Close button to return to the editing windows, and save the changes to PBRUSH.EXE.

Next time you start Paintbrush, the File, Open command will list both .BMP and .PCX files.

Exploring the Graffiti Artist Within

The graffiti wall is one wallpaper-hanging project for the juvenile delinquent languishing inside many otherwise upstanding citizens born in the 1950s or later. Channel those nascent antisocial tendencies into acts of virtual vandalism using Windows's brick wallpapers, screen capture, and Paintbrush. As you can see in Figure 2.4, the possibilities are endless. Although anarchy will undoubtedly reign before long, begin your wall with these steps:

1. In the Control Panel's Desktop, choose either CASTLE.BMP or REDBRICK.BMP as the tiled wallpaper.

2. Once the wallpaper is up, minimize all your windows, and use Print Screen to capture the entire screen—which will mostly be bricks.

3. Then open Paintbrush, zoom out the view, and press Shift+Insert to paste the contents of the Clipboard into Paintbrush.

4. Click away from the gray hatch pattern to bring up the image of the bricks, and select View, Zoom In.

5. Use the scrollbars to move down to the lower-left corner of the image, and look for minimized programs icons. To conceal these icons on your graffiti wall, use the selection tool to lasso an area of brick big enough to cover them.

New Sources of Wallpaper—Print Screen and Paintbrush   31

Figure 2.4

You too could have a desktop like this.

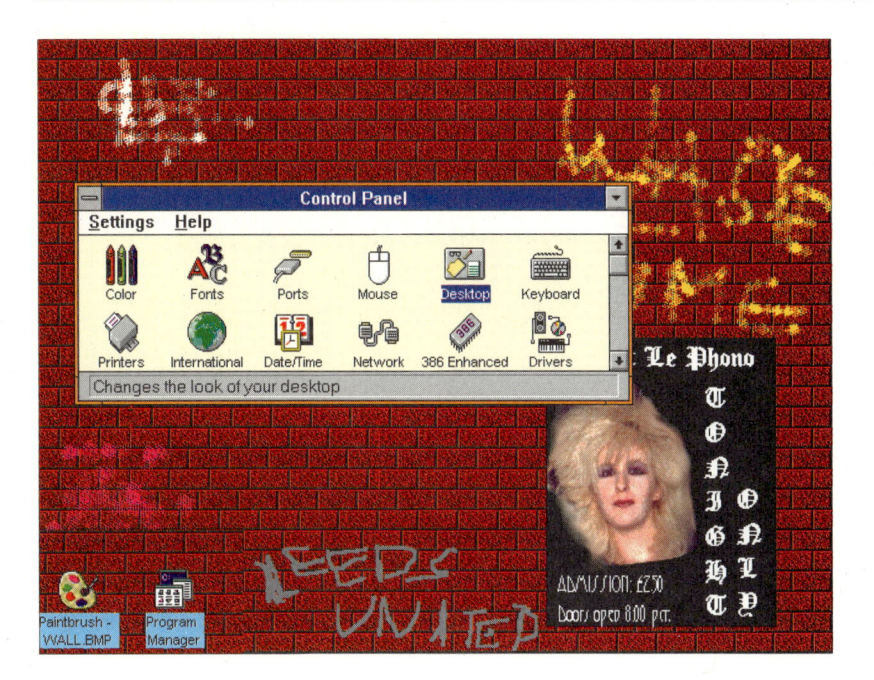

6. Press Ctrl+Insert to copy the portion of brick to the Clipboard, and Shift+Insert to paste it into the upper-left corner of the screen.

7. Use the mouse cursor to drag the pasted portion of brick over the icons, and make the necessary fine adjustments to line up the bricks.

8. When you're done aligning the bricks, select the spray paint tool, pick a color from the palette that will clash violently with the color of the brick, and spray away.

9. When you're satisfied with your graffiti, switch to the Program Manager, and run PaintShop Pro or another iteration of Paintbrush.

10. Open other graphics files, cut them to the Clipboard, and paste them onto your graffiti wall.

11. When you're done, save the file and make it your wallpaper (as described earlier in this chapter).

"Danger, Will Robinson!"—A Meaningful Error Message

Check out the file BOX_MINE.PCX on the disk accompanying this book (see Figure 2.5). It contains all the elements necessary to build your own error message wallpaper—just insert the appropriate error message and button, and you're cooking.

Figure 2.5

Delve into BOX_MINE.PCX for the raw materials you can use in making a start-up .RLE file or wallpaper.

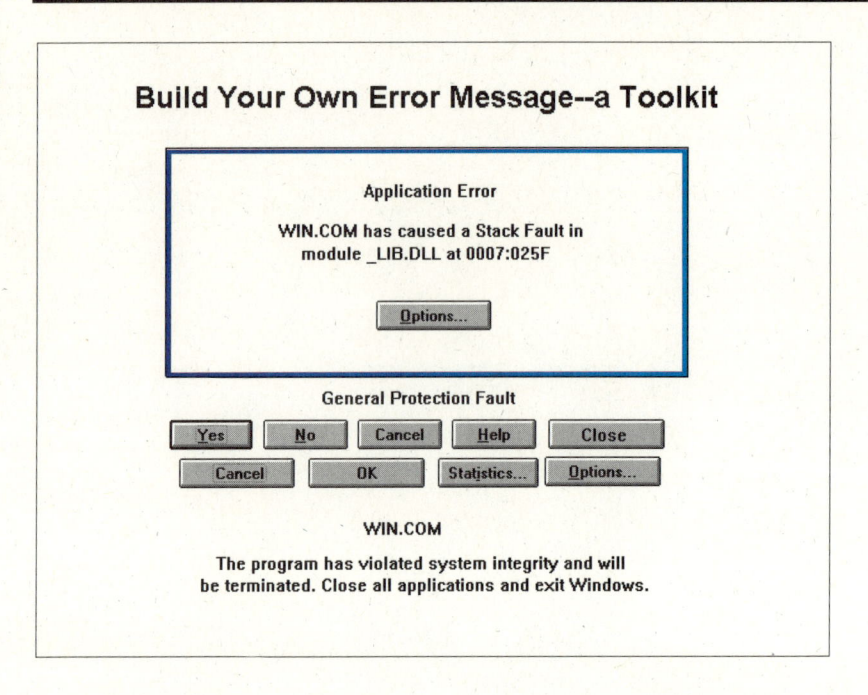

Build Your Own Error Message--a Toolkit

Application Error
WIN.COM has caused a Stack Fault in
module _LIB.DLL at 0007:025F

[Options...]

General Protection Fault

[Yes] [No] [Cancel] [Help] [Close]
[Cancel] [OK] [Statistics...] [Options...]

WIN.COM
The program has violated system integrity and will
be terminated. Close all applications and exit Windows.

The format for most Windows error messages is standard:

```
Application Error
SOMEFILE has caused SOME KIND OF ERROR in
module ANOTHER.COM at A BINARY MEMORY ADDRESS
```

To personalize an error message, open BOX_MINE.PCX in Paintbrush, click on the text tool (which by default uses the system font you'll see in all error message boxes), and type a message off to the side of the box, which you will drag in and align later. The error could be anything from a Stack Overflow to a General Protection Fault (in Windows 3.0, it was Unrecoverable Application Error—referred to by the cynical as Unavoidable Application Errors).

Remember to use initial capital letters for each word in the error's name—this is a throwback to German or Old English in which Anything Important (especially Nouns) must start with a big letter. Binary memory addresses contain two sets of four numbers and letters separated by a colon, such as 000C:0B47.

When your mock error message is complete, use the selection tool to lasso the message currently in the dialog box, and press Shift+Delete to remove it. Then select each line of the error message separately, and drag it into place between the heading and the button. Center each line by eye, and if necessary, adjust them when both lines are in place.

When the box looks good, grab it with the selection tool, and press Ctrl+Ins to copy it to the Clipboard. Select File, New, and don't save the changes to the original BOX_MINE.PCX. Under the new file's Options, Image Attributes, select Pels, and enter 485-by-180 as the dimensions for the new image. Click on OK, and then, in the new window, press Shift+Insert to paste the error message box. Save this file under a suitable name, and run it as a centered wallpaper.

When you start Windows with this screen as your wallpaper, the first thing you will see is a distressing error message that doesn't respond to mouse clicks. The pranksters in the audience will probably cotton to the practical joke possibilities. The author of this book feels the same way about this behavior as he does about hacking into code—I'm merely saying it can be done, I'm not *forcing* you to do it. If you use such a technique on your own system, you can justify it with this rationale: If snoops try to break into my system, an error message may put them off, and they deserve no better.

A favorite error message for this kind of activity is the extremely worrisome one shown in Figure 2.6. Like most error messages, it appears with the Close button on the assumption that you're not going to argue about closing down the application.

More Dirty Desktop Deeds

Another way of tricking potential snoops is to capture an entire Windows screen—exactly as you see it when you start Windows—and use this as your wallpaper. There are a few tricks to make this technique watertight, but the basics are very straightforward.

First, press Print Screen from a regular Program Manager screen to capture it to the Clipboard, run Paintbrush with the View in Zoom Out mode, and press Shift+Insert to paste the screen in. Click away from the hatch pattern, select View, Zoom In to change back to a regular view, and save the screen under the Windows directory as something like SCREEN.BMP. Under Control Panel's Desktop, make this the centered wallpaper.

To deter snoops with this for more than two seconds, you need to prevent Windows from responding to mouse clicks. This takes two steps: Minimize every application at startup, especially the Program Manager, and disable the Task List that pops up whenever you double-click on the desktop or wallpaper. These are both easy steps to manage.

To ensure that all your start-up applications run minimized, open your Startup group. Press Alt and double-click on each icon in turn to bring up its Program Item Properties box. Click on the Run Minimized box in each instance to put an *X* in it.

Figure 2.6

Imagine this wallpaper greeting you every time you load Windows.

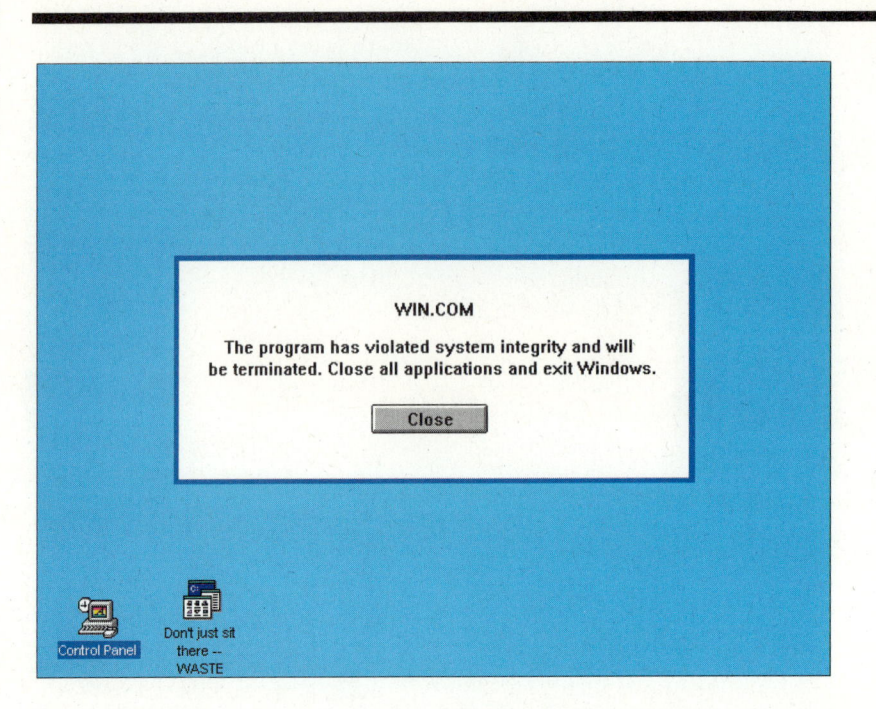

If the Program Manager isn't in your Startup group, select File, New Program Item to put it there. In the Properties box, give it a different name, check off the Run Minimized box, and for good measure, change the icon so that it won't be the first icon a snoop will click on.

To disable the Task List, first start Sysedit, and then switch to SYSTEM.INI. Search for the line

```
TASKMAN.EXE=TASKMAN.EXE
```

To disable the Task List temporarily, place the cursor between the equals sign and the T of the second TASKMAN.EXE, press Enter, and insert a semicolon (;). This does three things: First, it disables the Task Manager; second, it makes a comment line of the second TASKMAN.EXE; and third, it makes reversing the move as simple as deleting a hard return and a semicolon. Save the changes and leave Sysedit.

When you're finished, restart Windows. You'll see the desktop appear as wallpaper, and it won't respond to mouse clicks. It's by no means a foolproof method—click on the right minimized icon, and you'll bring up a window (and Alt+Tab will do the same). However, it'll put off the casual intruder, and give you a chuckle in the meantime.

■ Decorating without Wallpaper

If you run your small wallpaper bitmaps centered, the gray wall that usually surrounds the image is a rather dull backdrop. For that reason, Windows contains two other decorating tools—colors and Desktop patterns. Both come with a passel of predetermined looks, which you can accept, keep on hand, or remove from your system at will. If none of them accelerates your bit-blits (so to speak), both colors and patterns can be edited, saved, recycled, and implemented. Clearly, budding interior decorators can use them to waste a lot of time, too.

Rose-Tint Your World, Paint It Black, or Sing the Blues

There are several reasons for not discussing the adoption of color schemes in depth. One man's Plasma Power Saver is another man's Hot Dog Stand. One monitor may show color differently from another. Forty percent of all males have some color perception disability. And you may actually like Windows's Valentine color scheme. It's all a matter of taste (poor taste, actually).

But taste isn't the only issue. Templates of any kind, even Windows color schemes, discourage experimentation. But just try running the Color option on the Control Panel once (see Figure 2.7). Look at the preset color schemes (except for Valentine). It doesn't take much to realize that there's more to life than the Windows Default. Try out one or two preset color schemes—even Hot Dog Stand is tolerable for a while (though Valentine is not, unless Pepto-Bismol tops your aesthetic polls). It's much better to develop your own schemes.

Start by clicking on the Color Palette button beneath the mock-up Windows screen. A series of boxes will appear to the right. Click on one of the elements on the mock-up screen in the left panel. To liven up some of the gray in Windows's default scheme, for example, click on the backdrop. The Screen Element box at the upper-right will change to Desktop. Click on any of the Basic Colors in the palette, and you will see it previewed in the mock-up screen. Once you have the perfect color, take a deep breath—you now have 20 more elements to assign.

From the look of the schematic desktop in the Color box, it's hard to make out all 21 separate screen elements. To get more of an idea of what's going on, cycle through the options in the Screen Elements box. Starting with the one we've already worked on—namely, Desktop—the Screen Elements box lists Application Workspace, Window Background, Window Text, Menu Bar, Menu Text, Active Title Bar, Inactive Title Bar, Active Title Bar Text, Inactive Title Bar Text, Active Border, Inactive Border, Window Frame, Scroll Bars, Button Face, Button Shadow, Button Text, Button Highlight, Disabled Text, Highlight, and Highlighted Text.

Figure 2.7

Don't rely on Windows's color schemes—in fact, remove Valentine sight unseen. Concoct your own color scheme by clicking on screen elements on the left and colors from the right.

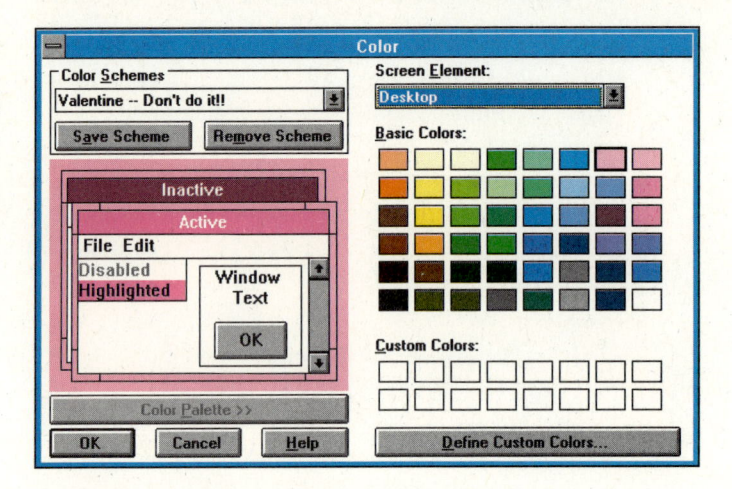

Most of elements are easy to figure out from their titles, but if you can't fathom them right away, use the color palette to make one stand out: Pick the mystery element and assign it a contrasting color such as bright yellow. If that doesn't make it obvious, nothing will.

If you find that none of the colors in the palette quite matches the color you have in mind, click on the Define Custom Colors button. A Custom Color Selector window (shown in Figure 2.8) will appear over the left side of the screen, showing a rainbow gradation of color that looks really impressive if you have a 24-bit color video system (instead of the $50 VGA board most of us put up with). The rest of us will see a dithered rainbow that shows some marginal differences between colors. Click on one of the blank Custom Color boxes, and drag the mouse around the rainbow until the sample Color Solid box shows the color you're after. Then click on the Add Color button, and then on Close.

Once you have the perfect series of colors for each of the 21 elements in a Windows screen, click on the Save Screen button, and assign a name to the masterpiece you've created. In a week, you'll hate it, and you'll be able to start all over again.

Advancing with the General Pattern

Once you've taken care of your colors (for the next few days, at least), try turning your attention to the pattern that appears on your desktop. By default, there isn't one. But go into the Control Panel's Desktop, and a pattern option will be waiting for you. But don't just assign patterns at random. Before plugging one into the desktop, click on the Edit Pattern button for a preview and zoom view of the small pattern that's repeated in the desktop pattern.

Figure 2.8

Move the target sights around the custom color selector, and check out the color you're making in the Color|Solid box.

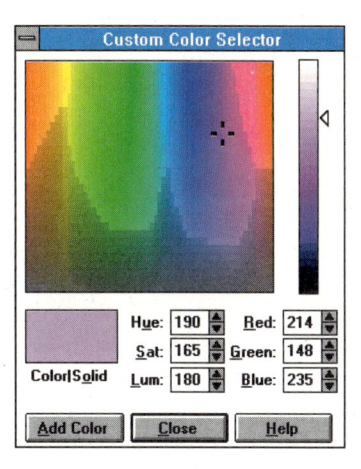

The zoomed-in view is also a primitive bitmap editor that you can use to make your own background patterns, as shown in Figure 2.9. All you do is press the left mouse button to change the color of the bit on which the cursor is resting. The effects are immediately reflected in the window on the left. When you've designed a pattern you like, name it, click on Add, and then on OK. When you click on OK again to leave Desktop, the new pattern will appear on the desktop.

Figure 2.9

Desktop's bit editor helps you make tiny repeat patterns to surround your centered wallpapers.

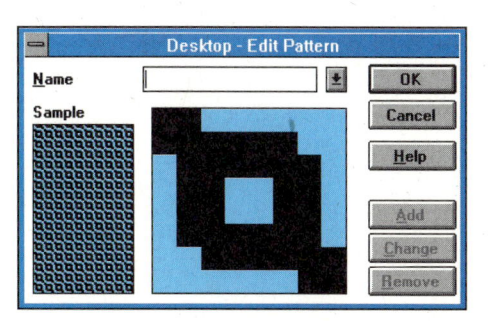

Because there are only 64 pixels to edit in the repeat pattern, this is a good exercise in bit editing and on the effects of repeat patterns. The instant feedback provided by the Pattern Editor can prove useful in designing repeat patterns for tiled wallpaper. But editing the background patterns is rather labor-intensive, considering that each takes up less than $1/18$ of an inch when you see it on screen. Most people barely register that there is a pattern involved at all. So pattern editing really is a waste of time.

■ What Was the Point of This Chapter?

In "This Old Windows," you learned:

- How to hang Windows wallpaper
- How to hang Windows wallpaper off-center
- How run-length encoded .BMP files can save you disk space and still be used as wallpaper
- How to use Buttonware's Newpaper to hang a new wallpaper every time you run Windows
- How to use Print Screen to generate wallpaper
- How to make Paintbrush look for .BMP and .PCX files together
- How to vandalize your Windows walls
- How to use wallpaper to fluster interlopers
- How to use color schemes and patterns to decorate a desktop without wallpapers

- *Primal Screens*
- *Screened for Security*
- *Oh, for a Speedily Saved Screen*
- *More and Better Animations*
- *What Has Gills and Looks Great On Screen?*
- *What Was the Point of This Chapter?*

CHAPTER

3

Passing the Screen Test

Make your PC do tricks when you take a break

Anyone who's used a bank's automated teller machine and seen the ghost image of the opening menu etched permanently into the screen's phosphors knows that fixed images can damage screens. But it's rare these days to see phosphor burn-in, especially on a uniformly-lit Windows screen. If truth be told, screen savers for Windows aren't really useful at all. The ones that blank out the screen altogether don't even save a cent in power consumption. Screen savers are there for only two reasons: They hide what you've been doing from prying eyes, and they give you something to look at while you're goofing off.

Of course, they do serve another purpose to the dedicated time-waster—they can be configured minutely in those moments when you feel like being busy, but don't want to do any real work. And you can always claim with authority that having a moving image on screen isn't just for fun—it's illuminating the phosphors cyclically to prevent burn-in. It sounds good, even if it is baloney.

■ Primal Screens

The basics of screen saving go a little deeper than "don't touch the mouse or keyboard for a certain length of time, and your screen goes blank." To decide which Windows screen-saving option you want to see each time you're not working, open the Control Panel's Desktop option. In the middle of the dialog box, you'll see the four Screen Saver controls—Name, Delay, Test, and Setup—all visible in Figure 3.1. First, set the delay in whole minutes; this can range from 1 to 99 minutes. Set it to less than two minutes, and you'll find the screen saver an unwelcome distraction from your work. Set it to more, and you'll rarely see it at all. Start out at two minutes, and if necessary adjust the time later to suit your tastes.

Figure 3.1

Setting up a screen saver starts here in Control Panel's Desktop: Once you've selected a saver and its delay, click on Setup for more options

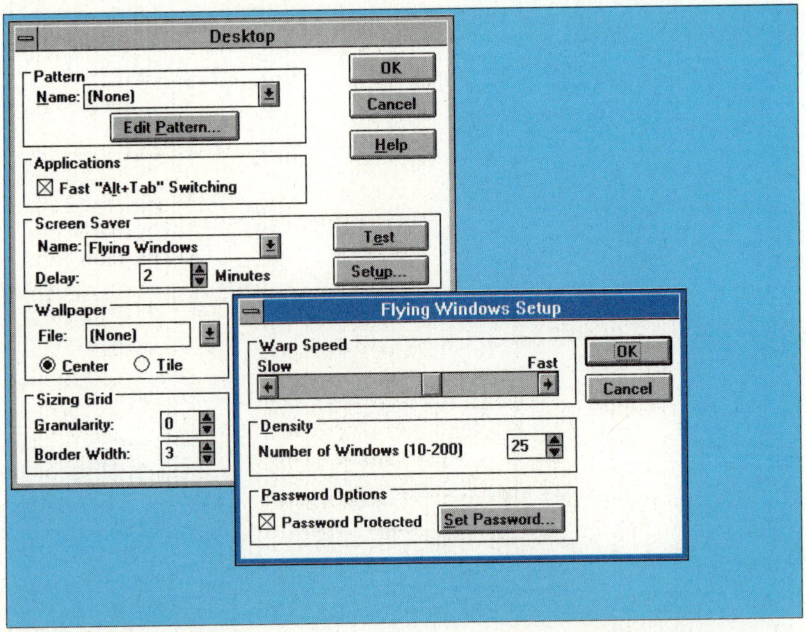

Next, click on the arrow next to the Screen Saver section's Name box, and Windows drops down a list of six options: None, Blank Screen, Flying Windows, Marquee, Mystify, and Starfield Simulation. None and Blank Screen are discreet but patently dull. All the others can be set according to your preferences—assuming you know how you want them set up. To select one, highlight its name. To see how it looks, click on the Test button. To configure it, click on Setup, and read on.

Screen Stars

Starfield Simulation and Flying Windows are variations on the same theme. Starfield Simulation mimics the view from the bridge of the Starship Enterprise—stars fly past but mysteriously never crash into you. Flying Windows cutely substitutes the Windows 3.1 logo for the stars. You can vary the number of stars or Windows logos visible at any given time between 10 and 200, and you can adjust the speed from slow to fast by clicking on the Setup button and changing the relevant settings in the pop-up dialog box.

Behind the Mystery Screen

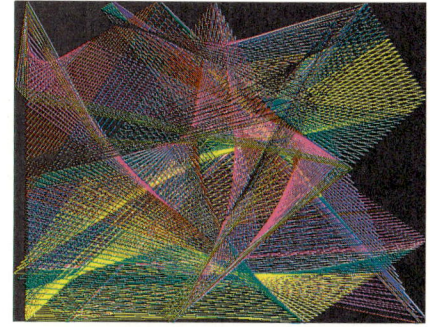

Mystify is a combination of geometry, color, and animation. Large shapes made up of many thin lines twist and contort across your screen, changing color as they go. There are more controls over the appearance of this screen than the previous two. Here's the Mystify Setup dialog box:

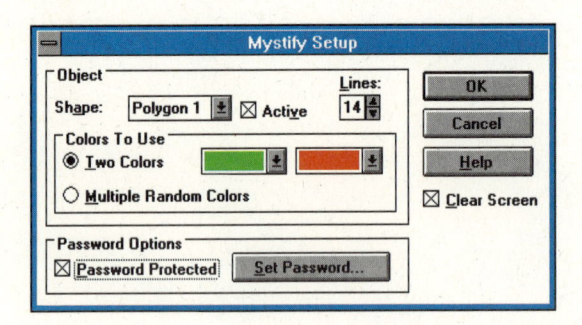

You can choose between two shapes—Polygon 1 or Polygon 2—under the setup box's Shape drop-down list. To select one, click on the Active check box to put an *X* in it while the appropriate name appears in the Name box. You can set the number of lines of the active selection to between one and fifteen by choosing a setting from the Lines drop-down list. (For details about the password options in Mystify's Setup box, see the section, "Screened for Security.")

Want to set the colors? Click on the Two Colors radio button, and pick the colors from the drop-down palettes. Or just leave the choice to Windows with the Multiple Random Colors option.

Finally, you can choose whether the screen's background turns immediately black when the screen saver comes up (the default setting) or whether the moving lines gradually erase the contents of your screen. For a quick blackout, make sure the Clear Screen check box is marked. For a gradual fade-out, click on the square to remove the *X*.

Marquee—My Words

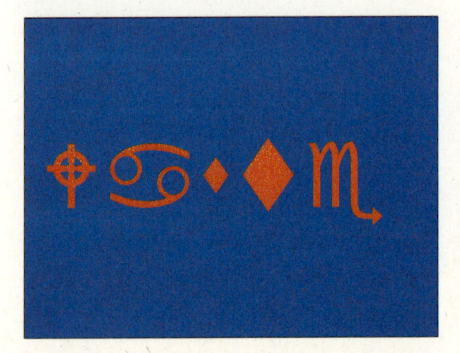

At first sight, the Marquee screen saver is the least appealing. All you see are the words "Windows 3.1" scudding across the middle of your screen, which hardly makes for compelling viewing. But the Setup button for this screen saver provides the best options of all, enabling you to change the contents, color, speed, and position of the screen-saver elements.

Want to leave an informative message (such as "Out to lunch") when you leave your desk? Prefer something more inspirational (such as "Wasting time again")? Just enter them in the Marquee Setup screen's Text box. Feel free to be wordy—you can enter up to 254 characters. As long as the Centered Position button is selected, you'll be able to preview your message. When Position is set to Random, you won't see the scrolling preview. Save yourself some tedious steps back and forth between the Desktop and Marquee Setup boxes—keep the position centered while you set up the message.

Want to change the font to Symbol or WingDings so that nobody can understand it? Click on Format Text, and in the window that appears (see Figure 3.2), take your pick of fonts, type style (bold is always good), and point size (unless you're using a slow laptop plasma screen, 76 points is a good starting size). Experiment with text and background colors (options found in the Format Text and basic Marquee Setup dialog boxes, respectively). Windows gives you instant feedback in the Marquee Setup's Text Example box.

Figure 3.2

When you set up Marquee's text, always have the text centered so you can see it; then change to Random before you exit.

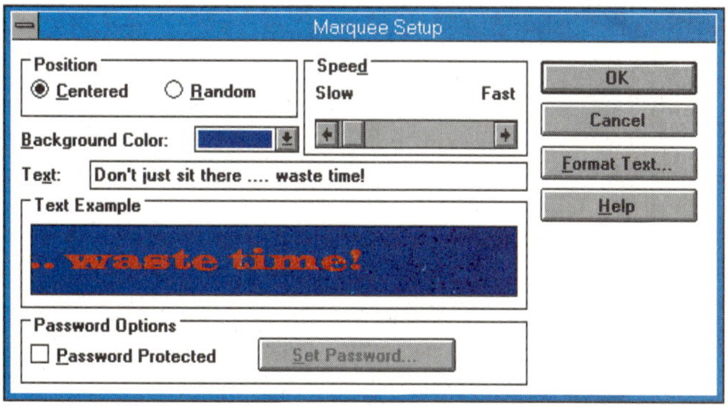

Apart from the regular Speed scroll bar, which is best set on the slow side, there's only one other choice to make—whether to have the text scroll across the center of the screen or to have it start at random points. There's no competition, of course: Random is the only way to go.

■ Screened for Security

All the screen-saver options except Blank Screen have a check box for Password Options. This isn't a foolproof security method, but it does prevent people from gaining easy access to your desktop. And if you don't want to lose the screen saver when you accidentally jog your mouse or hit your keyboard, password protection helps. Press a key or move the mouse, and you'll get a dialog box asking for the password, but you won't lose the screen. Just press the Esc key to can the dialog box. This option is also handy for those with cats or small children who routinely add 450 unwanted characters to Windows documents by leaning or sitting on the keyboard.

Selecting passwords is easy enough. From the screen saver's Setup box, click on the Password Protected radio button so that it's filled, and the grayed letters on the Set Password button become active. Click on the button, and enter the password in the first box; then click in or tab to the second box, and enter it again. Click on OK, and when you quit the Setup dialog box by selecting another OK, your screen saver will be password-protected. To change the password later, click on the Set Password button again, enter the old password in the top box, and then enter the new password twice in the lower two boxes. Click on OK twice to quit the password and screen-saver dialog boxes for the change to take effect.

■ Oh, for a Speedily Saved Screen

Ever wish you could start a screen saver with a quick mouse action or prevent it from appearing until you want it there? Well, Windows doesn't make either customization easy, but there are two workarounds: One involves making the screen savers part of a desktop Program Group; the other requires a shareware program we'll look at a little later.

Putting screen savers on the desktop isn't as easy as it sounds, because the screen-saver modules—intuitively named SCRNSAVE, SSFLYWIN, SSMARQUE, SSMYST, and SSSTARS—are appended with an .SCR extension, which Windows does not recognize as executable. So first, you have to make Windows recognize .SCR files as programs. Here's how:

1. Open SYSEDIT and select WIN.INI.

2. Scroll to the line reading *Programs=PIF EXE BAT COM*. After COM, enter a space, followed by **SCR** (with no punctuation).

3. Save the change, exit SYSEDIT, quit, and restart Windows.

4. In Program Manager, select File, New, Program Group, and name the group Screens. Minimize the group, and move it to the extreme right of the screen.

Oh, for a Speedily Saved Screen **47**

Gratuitous Tip: No-Password Protection

The simplest password of all has no characters to it. Select Password Protected, and don't click on the Set Password button to enter a password. When you try to get back into Windows after the screen saver has kicked in, and the module prompts you for a password, just press the Enter key. If you already have a password and you want to use no-password protection, click on the Set Password button, enter the old password in the top box, and click on OK without entering anything in the other two boxes.

The password you choose for one screen saver works for every password-protected screen saver, so you'll only have to remember one. If it slips your mind, you can remove the password altogether. However, you can't do it through the menu system—try to change a password without entering the old one, and you won't get far, because Windows demands the old password first.

To delete a password that you've forgotten, open CONTROL.INI in Notepad. Scroll down until you find the [ScreenSaver] paragraph. You'll see a line like this, in which the password is encrypted:

```
Password=G/.DhuR3
```

The encryption prevents snoops from learning your password from CONTROL.INI, but you (and they) can remove it by simply deleting everything after the equals sign, saving the changes, and restarting Windows.

5. Run File Manager, and adjust the window size so the Screens group icon is visible. Change to the Windows subdirectory, and under View, By File Type, select *.SCR as the Name.

6. Select all five .SCR files, drag them over to the Screens group, and release the mouse button. Repeat this step so that the programs are copied twice.

You now have two iterations of each screen saver in a Program Manager group. Open the group and arrange the icons so that the five screen savers are in a line with their duplicates next to them. Click on any of these icons, and you'll get a setup screen for it—except, of course, for the Blank Screen option, which has no setup options.

You duplicated the files because it's convenient to have mouse-click access to a screen saver's setup screen. (For the same reason, you can now delete one of the SCRNSAVE icons, since it's the Blank Screen module, which you can't configure. Highlight the icon and press Del to remove it.) To make an icon start its respective screen saver, you need to add an /S switch to the command line that runs them. Here's how:

1. Highlight a screen saver's icon and press Alt+Enter, or press Alt and double-click with the mouse.

2. In the Program Item Properties box, change the Description from an obscure file name to the name of the screen saver.

3. In the Command Line box, move to the end of the line, and add **/S**. Then click on OK.

4. Repeat these steps for each of the five icons you'll be using to activate screen savers.

5. For the setup icons, open the Program Item Properties box, and change the Description to Setup. Then click on OK.

Now you have double-click access to any screen saver and its configuration screen from a Program Manager group like that shown in Figure 3.3. The biggest bonus of this system is being able to access your screen saver's setup box by clicking an icon, which is much quicker and easier than going through multiple levels of Control Panel choices.

Figure 3.3

You too can have access to screen savers and their setup screens at the double-click of a mouse.

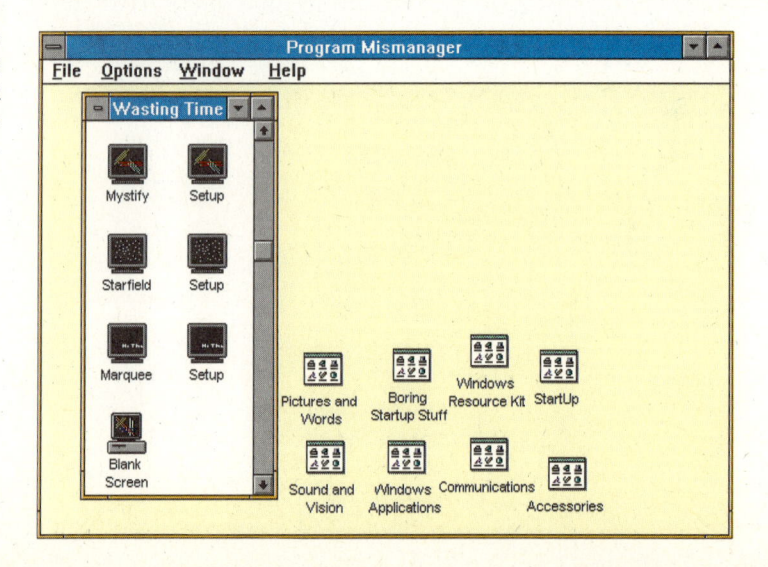

Hit the Hot Spot

While having icons helps you get quick access to your screen savers, it's not as convenient as having a "hot-spot" feature. Most commercial and shareware screen-saving programs start up instantly when you flick the mouse cursor into a predefined corner. Another option prevents the screen from being blanked out; simply sweep the mouse into a different corner. Windows, however, does not offer either option. Fortunately, Washington-based Windows wiz Dave Veith thought this was a shame, so he wrote a Windows app called Hot Spot that performs both tricks. More fortunately, he chose to distribute it as shareware, and it's included on the disk in the back of this book.

Best run as part of the Startup group (so you don't have to think about it), Hot Spot by default tells the screen saver "Now!" when you move the mouse cursor to the lower-left corner of the screen and "Never!" when it's at the lower-right corner. It also beeps to let you know when you've swept the cursor into the "Never" zone.

Configuring the program is easy. It runs as an icon, like the one in Figure 3.4. Click on it once to bring up its control menu (not twice, as this is an alternative way to set off the screen saver), and select the Hot Spot Setup option. In the box that pops up, simply click on the radio buttons in the Activate Saver and Prevent Saver boxes to select the corners you want as the Now and Never zones, and click on OK. That's all there is to it.

Figure 3.4

Hot Spot gives you a choice of corners—drag your mouse to one to turn out the lights, and to the other to keep your screen on permanently.

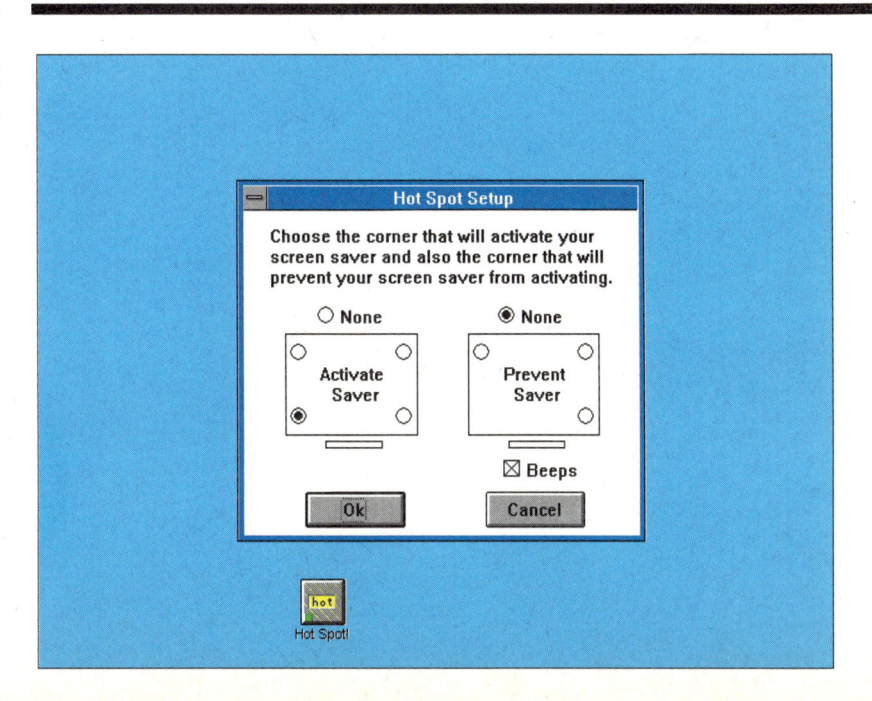

■ More and Better Animations

This is all well and good, but Windows provides only four screen-saving options (or five, if you count a black screen as worthy of wasted time). That's a paltry number—and that's where software developers see an opportunity to make a difference. Commercial ventures have produced the massively popular After Dark and Intermission programs, but undeservedly less well-known is an excellent set of shareware screen savers from Gordon Harris of Data Arts in Minneapolis. His collection is a welcome addition to the Windows offerings (it's called SAVERS.EXE and is easily located on the disk bound into the back of this book). Here's a quick rundown of what to expect:

Clock Saver (CLOCKSVR.SCR) is a large analog clock with an optional second hand, colored face, and hourly chime. The size is also adjustable.

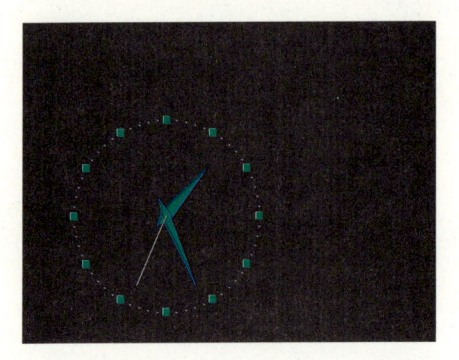

Fishes (FISHES.SCR) is a rudimentary aquarium of snapping tropical fish—with optional bubbles.

Quilt Saver (QUILT.SCR) slaps on screen one of three quilt patterns, which I'll name for the textile buffs in the audience: Double X, Dutchman's Puzzle, and Storm at Sea. The colors rotate at timed increments that you set.

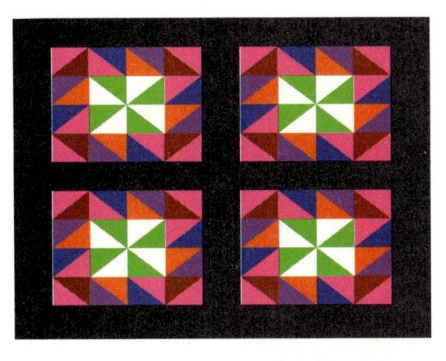

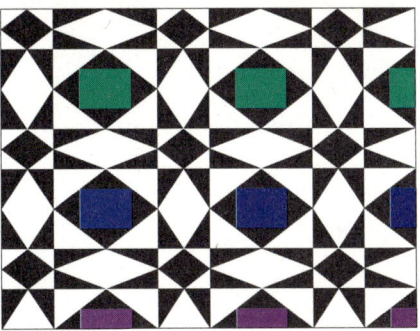

Various Stuff (VARIOUS.SCR) is a succession of geometric shapes with various fill patterns that pile up on the screen. Under Setup, you can pick Miscellaneous (the aforementioned patterns), but there's also Swerve, a filament pattern that zooms around the screen changing color as it goes. Or there's Spheres, a succession of multicolored globes; or Lines, a pile of multicolored sticks; or Random, bits of each of the above. Or there's all of them—five screen savers in one.

Each of the Data Arts modules is an .SCR file like Windows's own; each offers a password-protection box and other setup options. All of them work like native Windows screen savers right down to the smallest detail: Place them in the Windows subdirectory, and they can be selected from the Control Panel's Desktop option; drag them from a window in File Manager into the Screens group, and they'll form icons (assuming you've changed WIN.INI's *Programs=* line as described in the section "Oh, for a Speedily Saved Screen," earlier in the chapter); and edit the icon's properties so the command line ends with /S—the show will begin when you click on the icon.

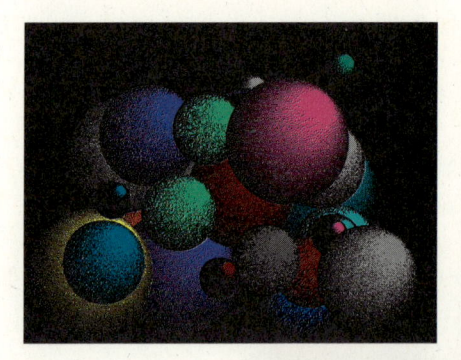

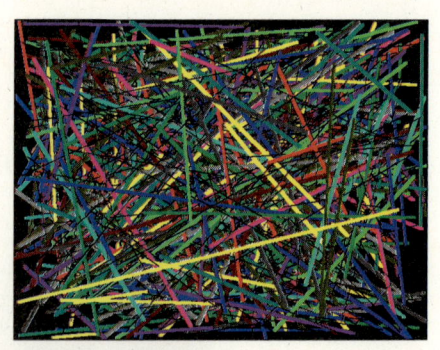

The Data Arts screen savers also go a couple of steps beyond Windows's offerings. Each has a check box in the Setup dialog box entitled "Change wallpaper on exit." When checked, this option rotates cyclically through every .BMP file in your Windows directory, much like Newpaper. Every time you come back to Windows proper from one of these screen savers, you'll have a new wallpaper to greet you.

A Different Saver Every Time

OK—so far, we've examined nine screen savers and how to call up them up from Program Manager or from the corner of the screen. But something's missing. The whole deal is too structured. You always know what to expect next. That's where CYCLE.SCR—the mysterious fifth saver in the Savers collection—comes in. Its sole purpose in life is to launch other screen savers.

To try it out, load Control Panel's Desktop again. Under Screen Saver, select Cycle through All Savers; then click on Setup. You'll see a screen like the one in Figure 3.5. Unlike the Windows screen savers, this one doesn't provide a password-protection box, because it runs other screen savers that do. The options it does offer are intriguing, however. The first option allows you to choose whether the saver cycles through the other savers in a preset order or picks one at random every time. Either way, you win.

Figure 3.5

Feel like a change of screen? Use Data Arts's Cycle Screen Saver to work your way through all your screen savers in rotation.

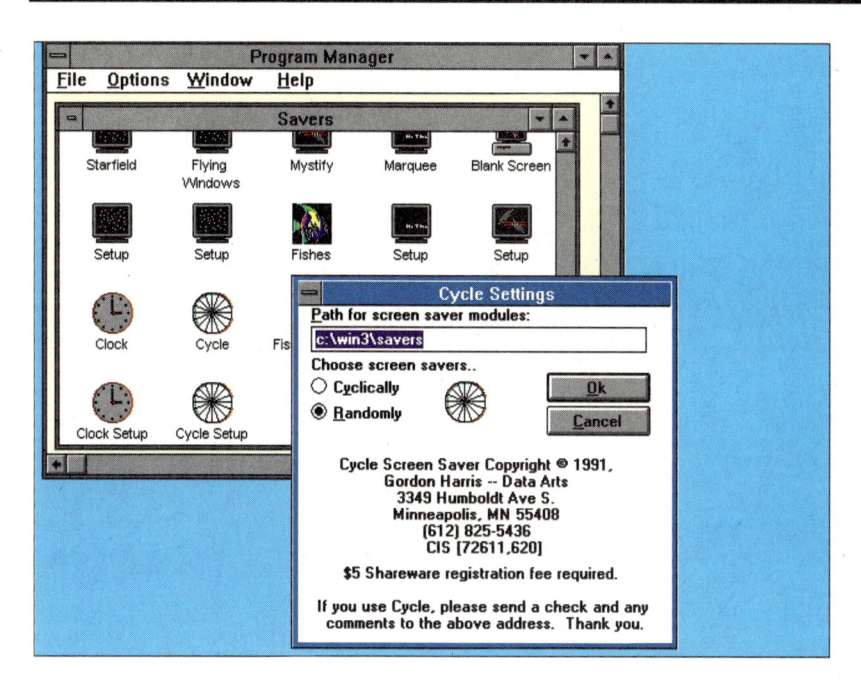

Alternatively, choose a path for screen saver modules, specifying the directory in which the savers you want to cycle through reside. By default, it's the Windows directory. However, if you find some screen savers more appealing than others, but you don't want to remove the less appealing ones from your system, you can restrict the selection of screen savers:

1. In File Manager, click on your Windows directory, and then select File, Create Directory. Create a subdirectory named **SAVERS** under your Windows directory.

2. From within your Windows directory, select View, By File Type, and in the Name box, specify *.**SCR**.

3. Press Ctrl and click on each of the screen savers you like (except Cycle).

4. Click once on one of your selections, and drag them all into the SAVERS subdirectory.

5. Change to Control Panel's Desktop, select Cycle as your screen saver, and click on Setup.

6. Add **\SAVERS** to the end of the line labeled "Path for screen saver modules" (so that it appears as a subdirectory under your Windows directory) and click on OK.

Chapter 3: Passing the Screen Test

■ What Has Gills and Looks Great On Screen?

Back in the dark days of Windows 3.0, screen savers were a different breed altogether. There were no native Windows screen savers, so shareware and commercial models had to be run as separate utilities through WIN.INI's *Load=* command. Those gray, wintry times were brightened up by a screen saver and desktop animator from Bogus Software, ported over from the Macintosh, going under the brief but descriptive name Fish.

As you'd expect, Fish fills your screen with aquatic life. It's the standard against which all marine screens are judged. Data Arts' Fishes is a respectable offering, but it pales by comparison to this. If you want to keep using your current selection of screen savers, Fish can brighten up your desktop just by running as an animated backdrop. Run it, and fish swim around behind your open applications and in front of your wallpaper.

Once you start Fish running, you call up its menu options by clicking anywhere on your wallpaper. Click on the Preferences option to call up a dialog box (like the one in Figure 3.6) that helps control your shoal. By default, a single mouse click on your wallpaper will bring up the Fish menu. If you prefer a double-click, check the Double Click for Menu option in the Preferences dialog box. Then get down to serious trawling.

Figure 3.6

Choose the contents of your digital marine world from the Select a Fish Directory dialog box.

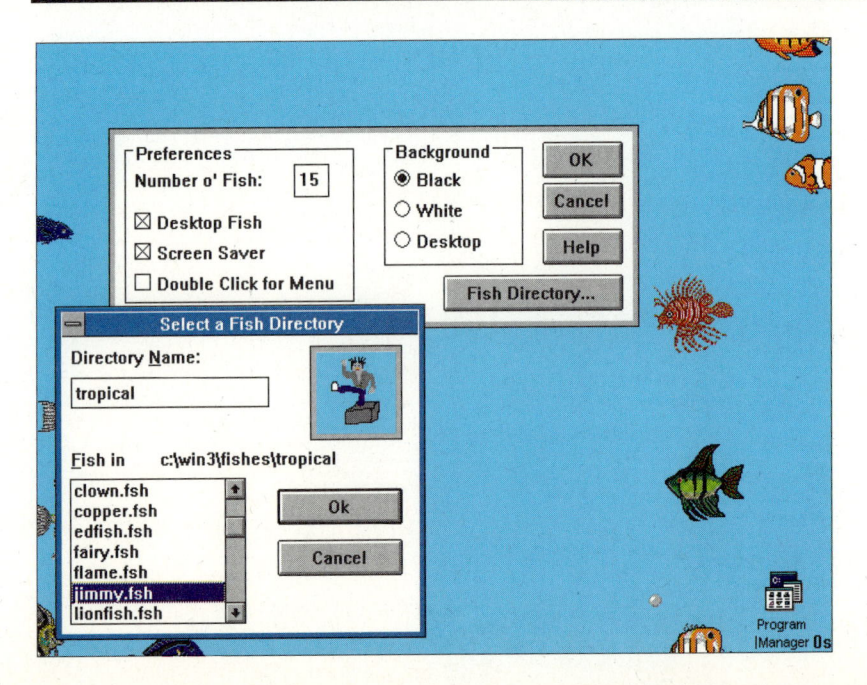

What Has Gills and Looks Great On Screen? 55

You'll undoubtedly want to keep the Desktop Fish option checked—this ensures the fish don't vanish just because you're working in a Windows app. This option will have you running your apps in tiny windows in the middle of the screen, so you can watch your watery menagerie—but hey, that's what wastes the time!

When you select the Number O' Fish, pick a number high enough that you can appreciate the marine life in all its abundance, and small enough that they won't slow down your system too much. Start with 10 to 15 for a medium-fast 386 with a VGA screen, and adjust the figure later if the fish are too few or too slow.

The Fish Directory button helps you select the fish you'll be observing. When Fish stocks your desktop aquarium, it looks for fish species in the directory you specify. This option gives you animated previews of all the fish whose names you highlight. Take the opportunity to refine your taste in fish, and note their names. When you've found the ones you like, press Alt+Tab to cycle to either File Manager (if it's open) or Program Manager to load File Manager. Create a subdirectory under the Fish directory to store your Fish files of choice, and then press Alt+Tab to return to Fish. Change the source directory to the one you just created and filled, and voilà! You have the perfect scaly screen saver. Create different subdirectories for different moods, and periodically change the source directory for a little variety.

The options discussed so far all relate to both the screen saver and the desktop animation portions of Fish. The rest concern screen saving alone. Check the Screen Saver Fish box to enable the screen saver—and when you do, be sure to disable your other screen savers in Control Panel under Desktop. If you don't, you'll waste system resources by having two screen-saving timers running at the same time. Only one of them will bring up a screen saver, and although my tests with Fish and the other screen savers haven't resulted in any system crashes, it could happen. Waste time by all means, but don't waste resources.

The background options determine what your screen-saver fish will swim over. Black and white are as straightforward as they are dull. Desktop uses the wallpaper that you (or Newpaper) have assigned to your desktop. Since the wallpaper changes every time you boot up when you run Newpaper, there's little danger of your getting bored by a wallpaper. This and the fact that wallpaper is intrinsically more interesting than a plain black or white background makes Desktop the option to choose.

Once you've customized the look of the screen saver, quit the dialog box, click on the wallpaper for the Fish menu, and pick the Screen Saver option. Then you can pick which screen corners will be activated by your mouse cursor to call up Fish immediately or disable it indefinitely. You also get the chance to set the delay before your work gets overrun by fins and to demand a password before you banish them behind a windowful of work. *Warning:* Keep that password short—this screen saver doesn't have a password dialog box, so you enter it (amid many beeps) directly into the void and without pressing Enter at the end. Get it wrong and you have to start over—and your ears will suffer the consequences.

A Piscine Premium

There's one more killer element to Fish—but it's not on your hard disk yet. Like all shareware, Fish is distributed for free, but if you use it often, you're expected to pay. Fish gives you an added incentive to pony up. When you do, you receive an upgrade that enables you to edit the fish files and create your own. The first option on the Fish menu, the Fish Editor, is available in the version included on our disk—but you can't save any changes. To get an idea of what goes into a Fish file, run the Fish Editor and open any of the .FSH files you're presented with.

Each fish is made up of two images, shown in the lower-right corner of the Fish Editor, which the program switches between to create the appearance of swimming—a rudimentary but effective animation. Under Options, Motion, check out the paths along which each fish goes. Check the horizontal motion radio button, and you're presented with options like those shown in Figure 3.7 for Top, Middle, or Bottom path, or the random Any option. Unless you deselect either the Left or Right boxes, the fish will travel in either direction. Similar options are available for vertical motion, but for diagonal motion, you only get to choose between up and down.

Even if you don't create any fish (and you should—it's fun), this knowledge will deepen your appreciation of what you're watching as you continue to waste time in Windows.

■ What Was the Point of This Chapter?

"Passing the Screen Test" introduced you to Windows's own screen savers and discussed:

- How to change the way they look
- How to turn idle fun into a security measure using password protection
- How to make your screen savers into icons on the desktop
- Why you need Dave Veith's Hot Spot to call up a screen saver right away (because Windows can't do it alone)
- How to improve your choice of .SCR files (using Data Arts's Savers)
- How to fill your monitor with Fish

What Was the Point of This Chapter? 57

Figure 3.7

Try out the Fish Editor to fathom how your fin-filled screens work.

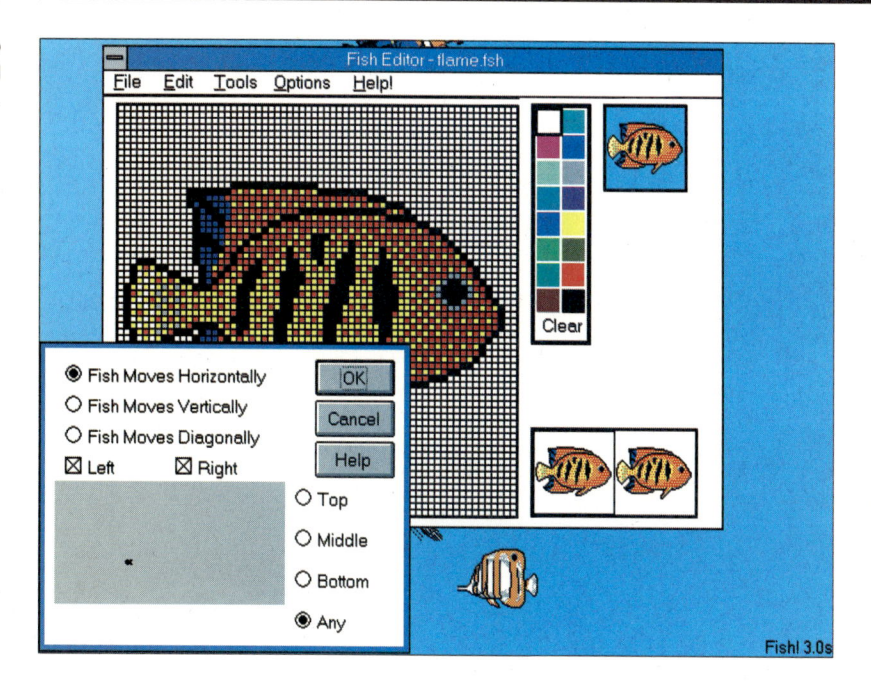

Gratuitous Tip: Task Management, Fish-Style

Fish disables your double-click access to the Task List—mouse clicks on the desktop wallpaper bring up Fish's pop-up menu while Fish is running. But this doesn't prevent you from getting to the Task List altogether. First of all, there's a keyboard shortcut—Ctrl+Esc—that takes you to the Task List from anywhere in Windows (whether you see wallpaper or not). Also, the Fish menu has a Switch To option that calls up the Task List. In fact, since Fish can be brought up with a single click, you still only click twice—but the second one requires a more careful aim.

- *Hit the Mouse Trail*
- *The Cursor as a Beacon*
- *Change That Cursor's Behavior*
- *Something in Another Color, Perhaps?*
- *Plug-In a Few More Cursors*
- *What Was the Point(er) of This Chapter?*

CHAPTER

4

Cursors! Foiled Again!

Screen savers aren't the only sort of moving pictures you get with Windows. The humble cursor—limited as it seems at first sight—is the one you'll see most often. Depending on what program you're running and what else is happening in Windows, cursors come in four basic kinds: the pointer, the I-beam, the hourglass, and the double-headed arrow, shown here:

The basic pointer is what you'll see most of the time, unless you're one of those unlucky souls with a PC without enough memory or processing power, in which case the hourglass may be the most familiar cursor to you. In word processors, Sysedit, Notepad, and other text-related applications, you'll mostly see an I-beam, which is considerably easier to place between two letters than an arrow. When you're resizing windows, you'll see a double-headed arrow cursor.

And that's about it for Windows's own selections—which doesn't provide much variety in the cursor department. Windows imposes the most obvious limitations on the shape and color of cursors. You can't pick a cursor's shape at will—only Windows can. Certain applications provide their own cursors (such as the right-pointing arrow of Word for Windows and the animated hourglass of CorelDRAW), but they still won't yield control to the change-hungry user. And you can change the cursor's color only by changing the Window Background color under the Control Panel's Colors option. This forces the I-beam cursor to become the inverse color from the background. Choose a white background, the cursor's black. A blue background makes for an ochre cursor. Big deal. Lucky for you there's a cursor utility that comes with this book that lets you pick a cursor color (more on this later in the chapter).

But despite Windows's apparent cursor control limitations, you *can* do a few things to spruce up the look and action of your on-screen pointers without running a cursor enhancement utility. In some cases, this involves our old friend the Control Panel. In others, you're back to editing .INI files. Either way, it's a guaranteed time-waster that demonstrates a little more about the way Windows operates.

■ Hit the Mouse Trail

Microsoft provided a minor aid to the owners of laptops with the release of Windows 3.1. Until then, the gray passive matrix display of most laptops earned everyone's vote as the best way to hide a Windows cursor. The theory at Microsoft was that if you simply provided more copies of the pointer, the original would be easier to find. So they added a check box called Mouse Trails under the Control Panel's Mouse option. If you click on this to produce a check mark and then quit the Control Panel, the pointer and hourglass cursors will leave a trail of replicas behind them whenever you move the mouse, like this:

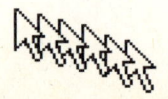

If your only choices for mouse trails were to turn them off or on, they really wouldn't be worth discussing. In fact, you can add a touch of customization to your pointer's speed-blurs by specifying how many shadow cursors trail the "live" cursor. This number is established by a setting in WIN.INI's [windows] section. Once you've checked the Mouse Trails box in the Control Panel's Mouse option (so that there's an *X* in it), open up Sysedit. Use the Search, Find menu to track down Mouse Trails. The search will take you to a line that reads something like

```
MouseTrails=7
```

You can change the number to anything between 1 and 7 (and 0 if you want to turn off the option from Sysedit). Once you've saved the changes you make to WIN.INI, restart Windows to see the change take effect.

■ The Cursor as a Beacon

While mouse trails do make the pointer moderately easier to find on laptop screens, they do nothing for the vertical bar cursor in your word processor that marks your current position in the text. This drawback is a major source of frustration for anyone who spends a lot of time writing and rewriting—in other words, anyone who wants to avoid looking stupid because of spelling or grammar errors. That should cover just about everyone who's reading this book—and a few million others.

To make the vertical bar stand out more on any kind of screen, you must make it blink faster. This technique relies on a basic fact of human perception—if something moves in the periphery of your field of vision, it's easier to detect than something that's stationary. If it moves fast, you see it considerably more easily. (Evolutionists surmise that this vision improvement increases the odds of survival of the species; it allows a species to spot predators moving quickly—especially from out of the corner of the eye.)

Though cursors are unlikely to hunt you for lunch, faster-blinking vertical bar cursors are easier to find, so if you lose yours often, change the blink rate. The setting for the vertical bar's blink rate is in the Desktop section of the Control Panel. Check out the sliding bar in the lower-right corner. It shows a little bar that blinks at the rate you've set so you can get instant feedback about your choice. (The disadvantage of this is that you look directly at it when you're making the settings, and it seems plenty fast enough even at slow settings.) If you're looking for a cursor 2 or 3 pixels wide in an image some 307,200 pixels square (that's a regular VGA screen), you'll detect a faster blinking cursor much more quickly.

■ Change That Cursor's Behavior

There's more to the mouse and cursor relationship than meets the eye. To make the mouse a more comfortable piece of hardware to use, try changing a few settings that affect how the mouse cursor works. As usual, this is a process that starts with the Control Panel, but it becomes infinitely more interesting when you start tinkering with WIN.INI settings.

Quick! Stop That Cursor!

How fast does your cursor move? The chances are it scurries just fast enough across the screen and selects text in your word processor just precisely enough. The default setting is a fair compromise between the ideal for large-scale movements and for detailed work, and like all compromises, it works for most circumstances. However, it can, of course, be improved on.

If you don't currently use the mouse for a great deal of fine-detail work, chances are that you will by the time you've finished reading this book. When it comes down to bit-level editing for creating screen savers or icons or start-up screens, you'll want things pretty finely tuned. The Control Panel's Mouse section has the tool for you.

When you're entering an application session that involves doing detailed work, such as bit editing, start up the Control Panel and keep it running in the background, as follows:

1. In the Control Panel's Mouse section, slide the marker on the Mouse Tracking Speed slide control to its slowest setting.

2. Without clicking on OK, press Alt+Tab (repeatedly, if necessary) until you bring up the graphics application you're using. Continue with your filigree work.

3. If at any stage you find you're having to move the mouse too far to send the cursor where you need it, press Alt+Tab to call the Control Panel back up, and slide the marker a little to the right. Then press Alt+Tab again to get back to your graphics application.

4. When you've finished your graphics work, press Alt+Tab one last time to go back to the Control Panel, and click on Cancel to reinstate the original mouse speed.

Once you've experimented with the mouse tracking speed, you may want to make a more permanent change. Before you do, run the mouse with the new setting for an entire Windows session, and use as many of your regular applications as possible. If you run a whole session comfortably at the new mouse speed, click on OK to save it.

More Experiments with Speed

So you've tried all the mouse tracking speeds that the Control Panel affords, and it's given you a taste for more? Try editing WIN.INI's Mouse settings. Fire up Sysedit, select Search, Find, and search for Mouse. You'll find three lines together that resemble these (the numbers after the equal sign may differ):

```
MouseThreshold1=5
MouseThreshold2=10
MouseSpeed=2
```

MouseSpeed can be set to 0, 1, or 2. If it's at 0, the cursor will track the mouse's movement inch for inch. If it's set at 1, it establishes a mouse tracking speed from the *MouseThreshold1* number.

For a *MouseSpeed=1* setting and a corresponding *MouseThreshold1=5*, if the mouse moves 5 pixels within a given time (namely, a mouse interrupt), the cursor begins traveling twice as fast. If *MouseSpeed* equals 2 and *MouseThreshold2* is 10, the cursor quadruples in speed if you move the mouse 10 pixels per mouse interrupt.

The upshot is this: A *MouseThreshold2* setting of 5 with a *MouseSpeed* of 2 will be hugely fast, suited to those with a really steady hand. Ham-handed oafs like me who wield the mouse like a saber would be better suited to a slower speed—something like *MouseSpeed=0*—which you can set by sliding the Control Panel's Mouse Tracking Speed indicator to Slow.

Editing WIN.INI is by far the most complex way to change the tracking speed. For one thing, every time you change a setting, you have to save your changes and reboot to test them out. But if you've already exhausted the possibilities of the Control Panel, it will give you hours more fine-tuning pleasure.

Click! Click! On the Double!

How quickly do you double-click the mouse once the cursor rests on something you want to select? Way fast? Slow as a snail on Sominex? It doesn't really matter as long as you go straight to the Control Panel's Mouse section and adjust the double-click rate to suit your own mouse-finger's reflexes.

Since I hate triple- and quadruple-clicking, I err in favor of the slower double-click, with the slider at around the midpoint of the sliding control. But this setting carries with it a disadvantage. If you move the mouse even slightly during a double-click, Windows won't accept your action and you'll need to reclick. And it's extremely easy to move a mouse during a double-click. That's why there's a control for it. Of course, Microsoft didn't bother to document this control in the *User's Guide*, but they left it in the WIN.INI file anyway. Here's how to increase the range of your double-click.

By default, you can move the cursor no more than four pixels in any direction between the first and second click of a double-header. That's not at all far, so to increase the range, run Sysedit and bring up the WIN.INI file. Under the [Windows] heading, you may find two lines:

```
DoubleClickHeight=4
DoubleClickWidth=4
```

If the lines aren't there, just enter them yourself. After that, it's a straightforward procedure to make Windows a little more tolerant of your hyperactive mouse-hand. Just increase the figures to 6 or 8, or possibly a little higher. Don't go overboard, however, in increasing these values. If you have a slow double-click setting and a wide double-click width, you might actually set Windows up to refuse your instructions when you're in an application. If, for example, when selecting multiple check boxes, you click in two adjacent check boxes, Windows may interpret it as a double click, instead of two single clicks.

■ Something in Another Color, Perhaps?

So much for the minimal controls Windows affords its faithful users over their cursors. As always, where Microsoft missed an opportunity, shareware authors rush forward with their own offerings. Farpoint Software's Meta-Mouse, among the best of them, brings three things to the show: better-looking cursors, blinking pointers for added visibility, and, best of all, color. The biggest plus: It's on the disk included with this book.

When you double-click on Meta-Mouse's Program Manager icon, it runs minimized, as another icon on your desktop. To configure its settings, click once on the running icon, and select Setup from the pop-up menu. The dialog box in Figure 4.1 will appear.

Your first choice should be Color—this is something you don't find often, and you should jump at the chance while you can. Meta-Mouse's Color settings change the part of the cursor that's usually white into whatever color you really want to see. For the best effect of all, check the setting Oh Wow and never look at the color settings again. Oh Wow changes the cursor's color dynamically whenever you move the mouse. It cycles through Meta-Mouse's color palette as it goes—a real treat for the eyes. Better yet, with this option checked, whenever you move an icon in the Program Manager or on the desktop, the moving icon picks up the cycling colors, too.

Figure 4.1

Meta-Mouse's setup box may not look like much, but you should see what it does to your cursors.

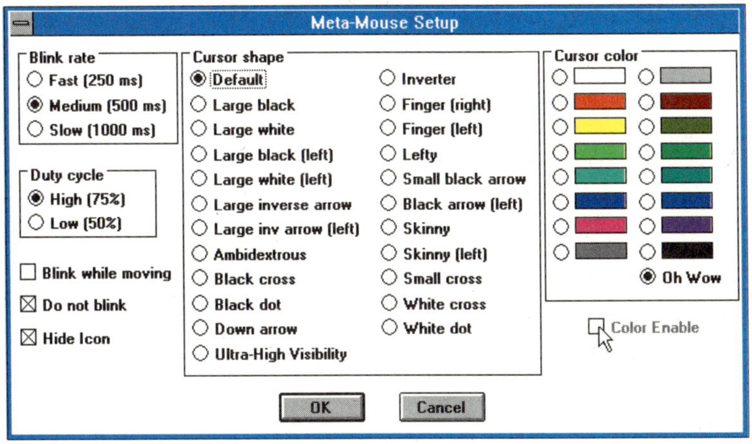

Like all the best things in life, cursor color has a few drawbacks: It may not work with some exotic video drivers (several 1,280-by-1,024 and 24-bit color drivers among them). If the Color Enable check box is grayed out, this means your driver can't handle Meta-Mouse's color enhancement. However, this will not interfere with the program's other settings.

Blinking in Disbelief

Mouse trails don't make your pointer stand out enough? Try making it blink. Meta-Mouse's Setup box provides scads of blinking controls, and implements them immediately for instant feedback on your choices. Given the choice (and of course, you are), pick the slow blink rate first, since higher speeds such as 250 or 500 milliseconds may be too distracting.

The other blinking control—not as obviously named as the first—is duty cycle, which you can set to 50 or 75 percent. Duty cycle sets the ratio of "cursor-on" time to "cursor-off" time. Let's say the blink rate is set to 1000 milliseconds, with a duty cycle of 75 percent. During the 1000 milliseconds, the cursor will show for 750 milliseconds and blink off for 250.

I recommend keeping the *Blink while moving* option unchecked—that way, the cursor will blink only while it's stationary. For my tastes, it's a little too distracting to have your pointer moving and blinking at the same time. Of course, you may find the blink itself distracting—in this case check the *Do not blink* option. After all, there's much more to this program than just blinking.

Gratuitous Tip: That Icon Has Gotta Go!

Meta-Mouse is best run from the Startup group, which means that its icon will be ever-present on your desktop. If you won't put up with the clutter, choose Setup from the program's Control menu, and check Hide Icon. This will run the program but make it invisible too—the Task Manager won't be able to bring it up. When you need to reset a cursor, color, or blink feature, open the Startup group and double-click on the Meta-Mouse icon to run a second iteration of the program. Then single-click on the now-present desktop icon, pick Setup from the System menu, and the icon disappears again.

Mouse Cursor Metamorphosis

Last, but by no means least, Meta-Mouse's setup lets you change the shape of your pointer. To test the appearance of each of these designs on your system, just click on its button. Here's what thay all look like:

The inverse pointer options are translucent and invert the color of the screen beneath them (black becomes white, red becomes green, and so forth), and if you have Oh Wow colors enabled, everything beneath the cursor changes color as the cursor moves, which is quite a treat. Ultra-High Visibility changes the shape of the cursor constantly without actually blinking, so Duty Cycle and the other blink options have no effect on it.

■ Plug in a Few More Cursors

Want a little more variety in your cursors? Install Plug-In for Program Manager from Plannet Crafters, which you'll find on the disk included with this book. The first time you run the program, you will probably notice that your cursor has mutated into a half-black, half-white arrow about three times bigger than the normal pointer. Only after that do you notice some of the other changes to your Program Manager menus and icons (most of which I'll discuss in the chapters on icons and mismanaging your programs).

Predictably, there's more variety in the cursor controls than meets the eye. Since Plug-In doesn't have a desktop icon when it's running, you have to delve into the mutated menu structure it imposes on the Program Manager to examine your options. Select Options, Configure Plug-In, and then click on the Custom Cursors button to reveal some of the exotica that Plug-In lets loose on your screen in lieu of a standard cursor. Check them out in Figure 4.2.

Figure 4.2

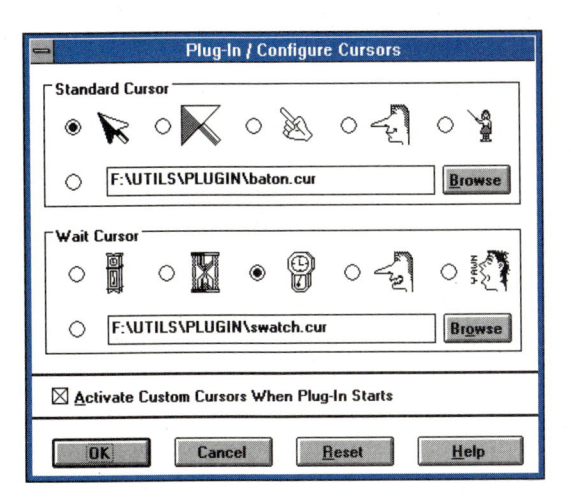

Any of these Plug-In cursors could be floating around your monitor....

A long-nosed man, a pointing finger, and a schoolmarm hoisting a handheld pointer are among the first choices for Standard cursor. To make them all the more interesting, make sure Meta-Mouse is running (without a custom cursor) with Oh Wow color enabled. The sight of a beaky bloke turning from yellow to purple to blue is a sublime experience.

Notice the grandfather-clock that pops up instead of the hourglass when Windows is chugging away at something? That's one of the wait cursors in Plug-In's configuration dialog box. While this and the other well-crafted timepieces are a distinct improvement over Windows's own pale offering, try the empathic yawning man for size. It's guaranteed to perk up the dullest day.

Still not satisfied? Then click on Browse to look at more cursors—this time, ones that aren't actually built into the program. You'll find a conductor's baton, a fat arrow, a pointing finger, two stick figures, and a fob watch, shown here:

Each of these occupies a separate file in a directory created when you install Plug-In.

Gratuitous Tip: Drivers—Round the Bend

The Microsoft mouse driver took a few steps in the direction of cursor changing, which unfortunately causes problems when you run any other custom cursor utility—including Meta-Mouse and Plug-In. If you're using the ballpoint mouse or MS-Mouse 8.10 and 8.20 drivers, take heed: Don't try to use both the built-in Growth option in the MS-Mouse control panel and custom cursors from another program. The best you can hope for from this unlikely union is that you simply don't get a custom cursor. The worst case scenario involves Windows error messages with the dread words "General Protection Fault" in them.

What's a .CUR In?

The cursor file (with its .CUR extension) is the staple of cursor enhancement tools. Every fancy cursor you see—and each of the dull ones too—started life as a .CUR file. Programmers use special graphics editors to create cursors, and once the cursors are completed, they are integrated into the code—not unlike the way VGALOGO.RLE becomes a part of WIN.COM. (In fact, most of the cursors you find in Meta-Mouse started public life as .CUR files that you could integrate into Windows using elaborate batch files.)

While keeping separate cursor files is a bit of a nuisance, it makes upgrading programs like Plug-In very easy. When you register the program with its author (along with the appropriate fee), you get a stack of .CUR files to choose from. (For those with modems and subscriptions to on-line services: You can also download .CUR files by other authors—ready to use in Plug-In—from a variety of sources, including CompuServe, Prodigy, and America Online).

■ What Was the Point(er) of This Chapter?

In "Cursors! Foiled Again!" you learned:

- How to leave a trail behind your cursor
- How to irritate yourself with a blinking I-beam
- How to accelerate a cursor from 0 to 60 pixels per second in no time flat
- Not to take double-clicking for granted
- How to change cursor colors
- How to make a pointer blink
- How to vanquish dull cursors forever

- *New Icons for Old*
- *Give Your Icons Their Space*
- *Plug In a New Group Icon*
- *Build Your Own Icons*
- *Hang Them in a Gallery*
- *What Was the Point of This Chapter?*

CHAPTER 5

I Think Icon, I Think Icon

The little picture that could…

WHAT'S THE FIRST THING YOU THINK OF WHEN YOU HEAR THE word icon? Most of the English (and Latin and Greek) speaking world have a vague image of religious paintings in the churches of Eastern Europe. The linguists in the audience will immediately recognize that the word passed into English and other European languages from the Latin word *icon* (spot the similarity?), which in turn came from the Greek word *eikon*. Both words mean *image*.

The rest of us won't really care about the word's origins, because if you've spent more than a couple of seconds in Windows, OS/2, or the Macintosh, the first thing that springs to mind is any 32-pixel-square graphic that represents an application on your hard disk. Click on the picture, you get the application—that's all you need to know.

Or not. Pick any application at random and ask yourself whether you really *like* its icon. Sure, it's familiar by now, but is it preferable to something—anything—else? Can you think of anything you'd like to see on your desktop *less* than the Calculator icon? Are you always satisfied by everything that's served up for you? Would you rather not ponder these issues, and just go on with your work? If you can answer "yes" to any of the above questions, you're probably leafing through this book in a bookstore and are deciding not to buy it. For the rest of us, the answer is obviously "No, I want more and better icons in Windows, and I want them NOW!" Wait no more. More and better icons will be yours. Read on.

■ New Icons for Old

Windows is pretty good about providing alternatives to the default graphical options. By now you'll probably have tried out some of the options in the Program Item Properties box for many of your Program Manager applications. Pick an application at random (on second thought, make it the Calculator icon—that's dreadful enough to require alteration as soon as possible). Press Alt as you double-click on its icon or highlight the icon's title, and press Alt+Enter.

The default icon will be there in the lower-left corner of the Properties box. Over to the right, you'll find the Change Icon button. Give it a click, and you'll see that CALC.EXE has only one icon incorporated in it. But you'll also see a Browse button. Click on that, and you'll see a list of all the .ICO, .EXE, and .DLL files in the Windows subdirectory. These file types are the ones that contain icons, and there are plenty of them. But save yourself some effort—most of these files provide very little in the way of icon choice. All the Windows mini-apps (Write, Paintbrush, Calendar, and so on) provide one icon only. But PROGMAN.EXE and a special .DLL file called MORICONS are treasure troves for the iconically frustrated. You'll need to scroll through the Current Icon box to see the full selection, because between the two of them, PROGMAN and MORICONS provide around 140 icons, give or take a few dozen duplications (MORICONS.DLL alone provides no fewer than three iterations of a stupefyingly dull MS-DOS blue box icon, for example).

But sure enough, about halfway through PROGMAN.EXE's offerings is an icon to replace the drab greenish rectangle that is the Calculator's burden.

Check it out in Figure 5.1. This icon includes a drab greenish rectangle all its own, but it's made more palatable by being small and outnumbered by a pen and paper.

Figure 5.1

Don't be content with any program's default icon (especially the Calculator's)—check out the PROGMAN.EXE collection. If that doesn't suit your fancy, the icons in MORICONS.DLL or another Windows application may do.

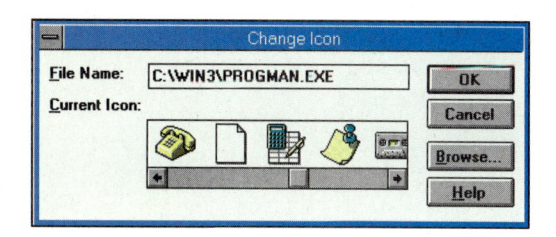

When you've exhausted the possibilities in these two files, trawl around your hard disk for application files. Excel and PowerPoint have five or six offerings of general appeal, Ami Pro has three, and Quattro Pro for Windows has nine. My favorite, however, is Paradox for Windows, which counts among its icons two of the most dreadful visual puns I've seen. The first is an incongruous image of two ducks (what has *that* got to do with database development?), and the second is a couple of wooden platforms jutting out into wave-riddled waters. Yes, that's right, it's a pair o' ducks and a pair o' docks. You've got to hand it to those Borland guys—they know how to waste time in icon-editing software.

■ Give Your Icons Their Space

Like any work of art, an icon is enhanced by its setting. Just as the Mona Lisa would lose a certain something if it were pasted into a scrapbook with Elmer's glue, an icon's impact is lost in a cluttered, uneven screen with overlapping titles.

For art's sake (and, dare I say, enhanced productivity), do your icons a favor. Get them in line. If you have a three-line description under an icon, make it more concise so that it won't invade the space of the icon beneath it. Rename the Microsoft Word for Windows icon "Word," and what do you lose? Two dozen letters, and nothing from the meaning. Think about that sometime.

Next, (unless you have enabled Auto Arrange) select Window, Arrange Icons. Your icons will straighten up in no time. Of course, things may still not appear quite right. For starters, you may now see scrollbars that weren't there before, because when properly spaced, your icons might not fit in the window anymore. If that's the case, call in reinforcements. Go to the Control Panel and get into the Desktop. It will look like Figure 5.2.

74   Chapter 5: I Think Icon, I Think Icon

Gratuitous Tip: Make Windows Arrange Your Icons

If you believe that computers exist to do your work for you, select Program Manager's Options, Auto Arrange menu selection. Now Windows will automatically place every icon in a group at a predetermined distance from its neighbors. When you drag an icon to another area of a Program Manager group, it will automatically be assimilated in its new place, and Windows will shift the other icons to make orderly rows—a much easier technique than using Window, Arrange Icons.

The problem with auto-arrangement, however, is that you lose control over the order in which icons appear. If you're trying to shuffle a few icons around, it becomes annoying when Windows butts in and takes over. My advice? If you don't care much about icon arrangement, enable Auto Arrange, and ignore all my comments about Window, Arrange Icons. If, like me, you want to arrange everything just so and then have Windows tidy up your lines, disable Auto Arrange.

Figure 5.2

The Control Panel's Desktop applet affords only two icon controls—horizontal icon spacing and title word wrap. Anything else requires editing WIN.INI.

The section devoted to icons is in the lower-right corner, just above the cursor blink rate. Two controls, and that's your lot. One generously allows you to mess up your screens altogether by removing word wrap from your icon titles. Do this at your own risk. It turns neat Windows 3.1 screens into unsightly Windows 3.0 screens. In psychological circles it's called regression. Among aesthetes, it's called ugly.

The Desktop Icons sliding control enables you to adjust the spacing between icons. The default value is 77 pixels between each icon and its neighbors to the right, left, above, and below. To tighten up the spacing without crowding your Program Manager windows, try 70 pixels instead. (Go much below a setting of 65, and your icon descriptions will overlap, and your screens will start to become too cluttered to use effectively.) Click on OK and switch back to the Program Manager again. Select Window, Arrange Icons one more time to judge whether that improves the layout.

Put the Squeeze on Your Upstairs Neighbor

The Desktop Icons Spacing control doesn't own up to this, but it adjusts only the *horizontal* spacing between icons. Slide the figure down as small as you like, and the space between an icon and its upstairs or downstairs neighbor will remain a constant 77 pixels—that is, unless you feel like editing WIN.INI again.

Buried in WIN.INI's [DeskTop] section (which corresponds, predictably, to the settings in the Control Panel's Desktop section) is a line that reads *IconSpacing=77* (or some other number if you've changed the setting). Windows will recognize another icon spacing line:

```
IconVerticalSpacing=n
```

but you have to insert it manually. Here's how to change the spacing to 65 pixels, which is just about right for maximizing your program group's icon space (as long as the icon captions are no longer than two lines):

1. Open Sysedit and switch to WIN.INI.

2. Select Search, Find. Then enter **IconSpacing=** and press Enter.

3. Beneath the *IconSpacing=* line, enter a new line reading **IconVerticalSpacing=65**. Select File, Exit, and save your change on the way out.

4. Quit and restart Windows. Click in any Program Manager group to highlight the title bar, and then select Window, Arrange Icons.

The spacing between icons will tighten up. If you previously had a vertical scrollbar for accessing hidden icons in your window, it may have disappeared. If your icons already fit in the screen beforehand, you'll have more space at the bottom of your window, which enables you to either fit in more icons or reduce the window's size.

■ Plug In a New Group Icon

So much for the Windows alternatives for changing your icons. Conspicuously absent is a Windows alternative to the drab group icons you get when you minimize a group in the Program Manager. After a while (certainly after you read about program mismanagement in Chapter 8), you'll have more program groups than you'll ever want open at any given time, which will force you to run many of them minimized. And all Windows offers is the crummy white rectangle with a few dots in it that crops up too much in Figure 5.3. You'd never believe there are 11 colors in this bland thing, but there are—and 8 of them are practically invisible.

What's to be done? Plug Plug-In into your Startup group and never take it out. This masterly piece of shareware uses a different generic group icon created with only ten colors that are so much better used that you'd swear it's more colorful. In addition, special groups have different icons assigned to them. Not only do these make the Program Manager look better, they also make the job of finding certain groups much easier.

Horror of horrors! Plug-In is a productivity tool in time-waster's clothing. Need to edit the Startup group? Click on the coffee cup. Want a gander at the Character Map or Terminal from the Accessories group? Click on the gang of four icons with a red phone. It couldn't be easier—or look much better, as you can see in Figure 5.4.

But that's just the beginning of what Plug-In does for Program Manager's appearance. In the true spirit of experimentation, Plannet Crafters threw in the ability to change your Program Manager's group icons to whatever suits your fancy. The process is as simple as it could be, easier even than changing a program icon. Simply highlight the minimized icon of the group in question, and either press Alt+I or select File, Change Icon from the Program Manager menu. (This option is available only when Plug-In has been installed over Program Manager—the shareware program mutates the Program Manager menu structure to give you access to all of Plug-In's capabilities.)

Try this out on Accessories, since the default Plug-In icon for this group could stand a little improvement. Select the icon, press Alt+I, and you'll be presented with a scrolling gallery of icons like that in Figure 5.5. These are the graphics incorporated into PLUGIN.EXE. (You'll even see a few familiar faces from the cursors section.) This provides some variety, but nothing much better than the current Accessories group icon.

To assign a better choice, select the Windows directory in the Directories box. In the File Name list box, select PROGMAN.EXE and scroll through

Plug In a New Group Icon 77

Figure 5.3

You'd never guess that there are more than 11 colors in this screen, would you? The Program Manager wastes many opportunities with its group icons…

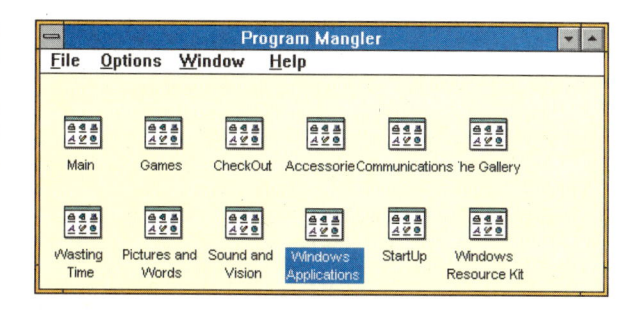

Figure 5.4

…which Plug-In picks up on. Not only does the default icon look more colorful (see the Windows Resource Kit icon here), it can be replaced by any icon you like with a simple menu choice.

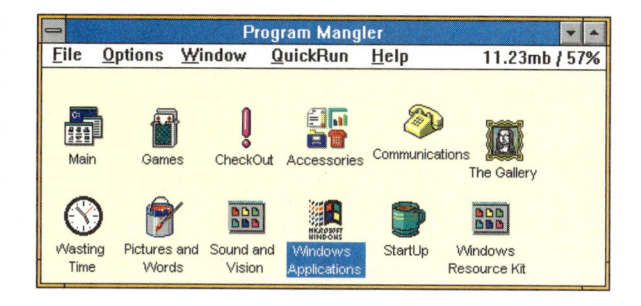

Figure 5.5

Want to replace a Program Manager group icon? Plug-In makes it possible and provides a few icons to choose from. Don't like any of them? Just click on Browse.

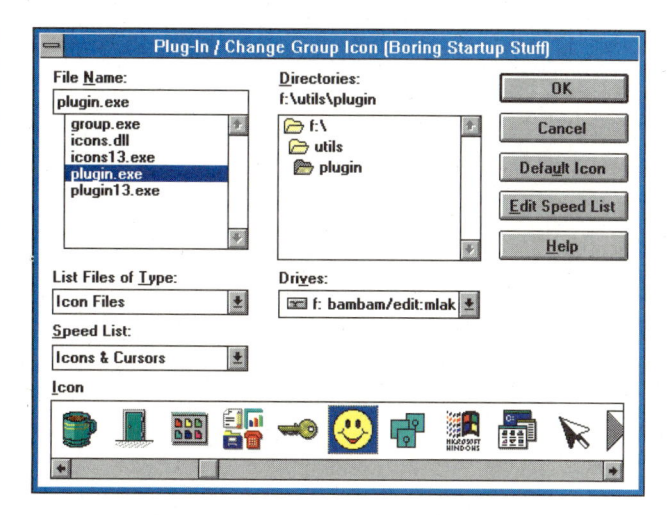

the gallery until you're about halfway through. You'll see a red Swiss Army knife icon. What could be a better fit for your Accessories group? (If you have time—and of course, you do—try out a few other applications and .DLLs and see if you can find a better match. I couldn't.)

■ Build Your Own Icons

Take a second look at the contents of MORICONS.DLL and PROGMAN.EXE, and ponder that this is the pinnacle of variety, as far as Windows's own icon offerings go. All told, it's rather pitiful. Though better than most of the Windows defaults, the selection hardly enthralls: You have to plow through a lot of mediocrity and program-specific icons to find something you can actually use. And sometimes an otherwise perfect icon is spoiled by one element, such as a program name or a vile color scheme.

This is where a good icon editor comes in handy. Any tool that enables you to either make your own icons or take existing ones and make them better (or even worse) is essential for anyone who wants to accessorize Windows stylishly.

Icon editors are such a hot property that even otherwise responsible companies like Symantec make them. Norton Desktop for Windows packs a pretty good icon editor alongside all its backup, antiviral, and productivity enhancement tools. But even if you already have an icon editor, the one bound into the back of this book is worth putting on your system for a trial. It's one of the best I've seen.

The Right Tool for the Job: AZ Icon Edit

Icon editing programs don't come a lot better than AZ Computer Innovations's Icon Edit. Like any icon editor, AZ Icon Edit has an editing window, a color palette, and various drawing tools. That much is obvious from Figure 5.6. But unlike many editors, AZ Icon Edit has a handy toolbar composed of easy-to-read icons and a roving screen capture window 32 pixels square, just the right size to bring in icons or other graphics to use as icons. If you need to scale the window up and down, all the elements on it will scale up and down, too, with the single exception of the icon preview, which stays a consistently iconic 32 pixels square (all the better to preview with, my dear).

The first time you run the program, it generates its own .INI file, AZICONED.INI, in the same directory as the program itself. The .INI file stores the window size and position when you quit the program, so that it will be restored in the same place the next time you fire it up. So find a place on your screen for the program, scale it up to a good size, and get familiar with AZ Icon Edit.

Figure 5.6

AZ Icon Edit should provide everything you need from an icon editor—from a strong suite of drawing tools to partial screen capture.

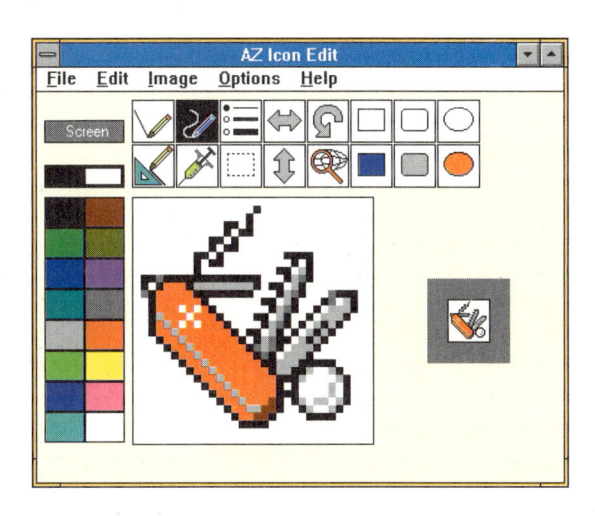

Pick a Color, Any Color

Along the left side of the program's window is a color palette of the sixteen colors you can choose from. Above the palette are two boxes that show the currently selected colors—one for each mouse button. Selecting new colors is easy enough: Place the cursor over the color you want in the color palette, and click on it with either the left or right mouse button.

Having two active colors at any given time makes it easy to undo minor errors—just make sure the two current colors are selected, and then change back a pixel you discolored by mistake with a click of the right mouse button.

The third color option is harder to understand than the others, because it represents no color at all. The Screen button above the left and right color selections is the key to one of AZ Icon Edit's nicest features—transparency. If you choose to make a portion of the icon transparent, click on this button, select another color, and start drawing. Anything you lay down here will take on the background color of the window you place it in—which makes for pretty intriguing effects if you play around much with the colors in the Control Panel.

Screen color is disabled when you have the left and right color selections active (a state you'll recognize because the active option has a heavy black border). To change between the two modes, just click on the one you want with either mouse button.

Slap on Colors Like Crazy

Want to dabble in the noble art of filling 1,024 pixels with color? Use one of the two straight-line drawing tools on the leftmost part of the toolbar. Select either one and move the cursor onto the editing area; the cursor will change to a cross hair.

The straight-line drawing tool in the upper-left corner can draw a straight line of the selected color from any point on the image to any other point. The tool below it with the set-square snaps its straight lines to one of five angles: 0, 45, 90, 135, or 180 degrees.

The regular Pencil tool changes the color of the pixel on which it's clicked. Hold the mouse button down, and it becomes a freehand drawing tool—something ol' Ham Hands finds a tad unwieldy.

The thickness of the line that all these tools use is controlled in one of two ways, either with the Line Thickness icon or through the Options menu. Most everything you do can be done from icons, so stick with that—the highlight changes anyway to show you which thickness is currently selected.

The syringe-shaped Fill tool is there for you to apply a color (from a left or right mouse-button click) to a large area of your icon. Click on an area with this tool and all the adjacent pixels of the same color will change to whatever's assigned to the mouse button. This is particularly handy when you look at one of your creations and shudder at the color combinations you chose. (And believe me, you will.)

To the right of the Fill tool's syringe is a dotted box that represents the Select tool. Click on this, and draw a box around any element in the editing window, and you can cut it out, copy it to the Clipboard, and select another area to paste it back in—all using the regular combinations of Delete, Control, and Shift keys.

Draw Some Shapes and Move 'Em Around

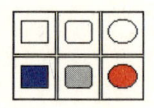

The rightmost tools on the toolbar pretty much resemble their functions. Use them to create perfect rectangles, round-cornered rectangles, and circles—either filled with your color of choice or just framed in it. Hold down either mouse key when the crosshair cursor is at the point where you want the shape to begin, and drag it to the shape's proposed end point. If you make a mistake (and it's easy to do), select Edit, Undo (or press Alt+Backspace) to return to the image as it was before you messed it up so appallingly. Then try again.

Once you have a shape in place, try switching it around a little. The two straight-arrow icons in the middle of the toolbar flip the contents of the window horizontally or vertically. The curved arrow rotates it at 45-degree intervals.

And Now, Mutilate Someone Else's Art

So much for creating your own art. We've already established that it's much easier and more fun to destroy somebody else's. That's the subversive side to the otherwise benevolently handy Capture tool. To use this to its best advantage, shrink AZ Icon Edit to a quarter or less of the screen, and run the Program Manager in the background. Click on the Capture tool, and move the capture cursor outside the confines of Icon Edit's window. Observe the edit window as you sweep across the screen—you'll see everything the cursor passes over magnified in there.

During a Capture tool sweep, check out some of the tricks professional icon designers use to make their icons work. Pick one or two of your favorites, and look at them in the magnifying edit window. You can learn heaps about icon design by poring over the tricks used by the Microsoft guys (even the Calculator monstrosity, which, as Figure 5.7 shows, uses a few neat tricks). Once you've mastered a technique, use it shamelessly.

Figure 5.7

Capture an icon in AZ Icon Edit by selecting the Capture tool and sweeping the square cursor around. The magnifying edit window reveals another side to icons you see every day.

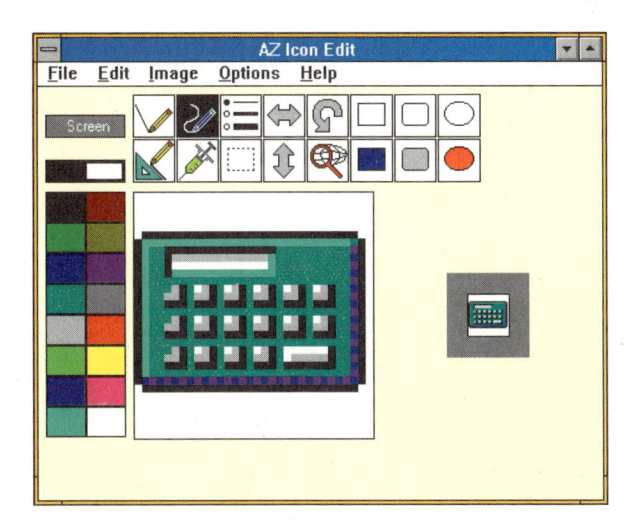

When you hit upon an image you want, abandon all hope of centering the cursor window over it precisely using just the mouse. Use the arrow keys to fine-align the sights over the target, looking all the time at AZ's editing window, not at the icon itself. When the image is as centered as you can get it, press the Enter key to capture the icon into the editing window. Then let the games begin!

The Right Job for the Tool

Want to do yourself a real favor? Change that Calculator icon to something of your own devising (almost). Tucked away in MORICONS.DLL is an icon that contains a little gray calculator that makes a more than decent substitute for the mucky green pastille that passes for a default Calculator icon. All you need to do is extract the new calculator from its resting place, and that's easy enough. Here's how:

1. Start AZ Icon Edit, resize its window as small as you can make it, and move it to the lower-left corner of your screen.

2. Press Alt+Tab to change to the Program Manager. Pick an icon at random, press Alt, and double-click on it.

3. In the Program Item Properties box, click on Change Icon. Browse through your Windows directory, and select MORICONS.DLL. Scroll to the end of the gallery.

4. Press Alt+Tab to bring up AZ Icon Edit, and click on the Capture tool.

5. Bring the capture cursor over the fourth icon from the right, and press Enter to capture it to AZ Icon Edit's editing window.

6. Switch back to the Change Icon dialog box, and click on Cancel to close it. Click on Cancel a second time to close the Program Item Properties box.

The image should now be in place ready to edit, as it is in Figure 5.8. Maximize the icon editor to give yourself more working room before rolling up your sleeves and starting the work of extracting the gray calculator from its current resting place, buried amongst other office clutter:

1. Click on the Select tool, and drag it roughly over the calculator. Don't worry if you include some background elements, but make sure the entire calculator is enclosed.

2. Press Shift+Del to cut the selection to the Clipboard.

3. Select Image, Clear to remove the rest of the pixels from the editor.

4. Select a large area of the icon editing window, and press Shift+Insert. In the Paste Options dialog box, ensure that the Stretch/Shrink Clipboard Bitmap option contains a check mark, and click on OK. A distorted but recognizable calculator will appear.

5. Select the background color from the palette and the pencil from the toolbar, and clear away any elements pasted in from the Clipboard that aren't part of the calculator.

6. Check the life-sized icon preview to the right of AZ Icon Edit's screen. If the icon's position looks all right, select File, Save, and name the icon CALC.ICO. If it needs to be repositioned, click on the Select tool, lasso the calculator, and follow steps 2 through 4.

Build Your Own Icons 83

Figure 5.8

The icon-editing window does more than just provide an area to make icons; you can capture and edit existing icons too.

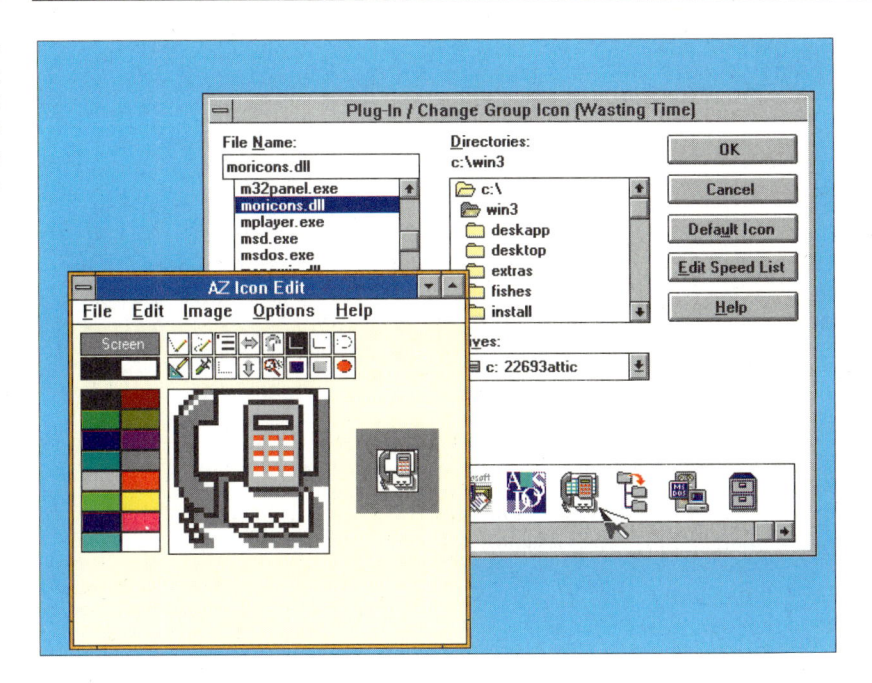

7. Press Alt+Tab to switch to the Program Manager, press Alt while double-clicking on the Calculator's icon, and select Change Icon. Browse through the subdirectory to which you saved CALC.ICO, select the icon file, and click on OK. Click on OK to quit the Properties box, which is shown in Figure 5.9.

Congratulations. You don't have to endure the default Calculator icon anymore. And remember: The Surgeon General says that quitting the Calculator icon now can significantly reduce your chances of serious eyestrain, headaches, and general malaise. Do yourself a favor. Don't wait any longer.

Figure 5.9

As the last step in replacing the regular Calculator icon, call up its Change Icon box (by way of File, Properties) and assign the icon you've made.

Gratuitous Tip: Mix-and-Match Icons

Want a quick way to incorporate elements from two existing icons? Since the Capture tool selects only full 32-by-32 pixel images, you can't do it directly. However, it's easy to juggle around images when you use the Select tool, too. Capture the first image, and with the Select tool, lasso the portion of interest. Press Shift+Del to cut it to the Clipboard. Now capture the second image. Draw a selection as close as possible to the size of the image you cut to the Clipboard, and press Shift+Ins. If you misjudged the dimensions, a dialog box will pop up asking whether it should distort or clip the image it pastes in. The box provides the dimensions of both images—if they're close enough in size, pick either option. If they're not, cancel the operation, and try to get closer to the right size.

■ Hang Them in a Gallery

So what are you going to do with all these spiffy icons you're making? Leave them on your hard disk until you feel like assigning one to a program? No! Your icon collection will gather virtual dust if the only way you can see them in a group is to check out their file names in the File Manager. Set up a display gallery in the Program Manager. Not only will this make it easy for you to make the right choice when you come to assigning a new icon to a new application, it will give you a chance to admire your handiwork.

This icon management technique requires a small additional effort at the end of each icon editing session, but it will pay off in spades when it comes to enjoying your handiwork. Here's how to set up your gallery:

1. Switch to the Program Manager and select File, New, Program Group. Name the Group "Icon Gallery" or something equally descriptive (MoMA, Le Louvre, or whatever).

2. From the active new group, select File, New, Program Item. In the Program Item Properties box, click on Browse and navigate through your hard disk to locate AZICONED.EXE. Select it, and in the Working Directory box, enter the drive and directory where your icon files are stored.

3. Click on Change Icon, and in the Change Icon dialog box, click on Browse. Then navigate to the directory that contains your icons.

4. Select an icon name, and click on OK. In the Change Icon dialog box, click on OK a second time.

5. In the Program Item Properties box, select the Description box and enter the name of the icon file. At the end of the Command Line box, after the word AZICONED.EXE, add a space followed by the icon's file name (and the drive and directories that lead to it, if they're different from the ones that lead to AZ Icon Edit). Click on OK to save the program item.

6. If you have more icons to display, hold down the Control key and drag the program icon to make a duplicate in the same program group.

7. Select the duplicate, and press Alt+Enter to bring up its Properties dialog box.

8. Repeat steps 3 through 7 for each of the duplicate program items until your entire collection of icons is in the gallery. Remove any excess duplicates by selecting them and pressing the Delete key.

Now you have a working gallery of icons that you can bring up from the Program Manager with two clicks of a mouse's button. Straighten them up a little if necessary by selecting Window, Arrange Icons. There, that's better. Sit back and admire your handiwork.

Any time you create a new icon, Ctrl-drag one of your icons to duplicate it (as shown in Figure 5.10), press Alt+Enter to bring up the Properties box, and go through steps 3 through 7 to assign the new icon to a place in the gallery.

Figure 5.10

Now keep your icons in a gallery—Ctrl-drag icons to duplicate them, and replace the existing icon with one you've just made.

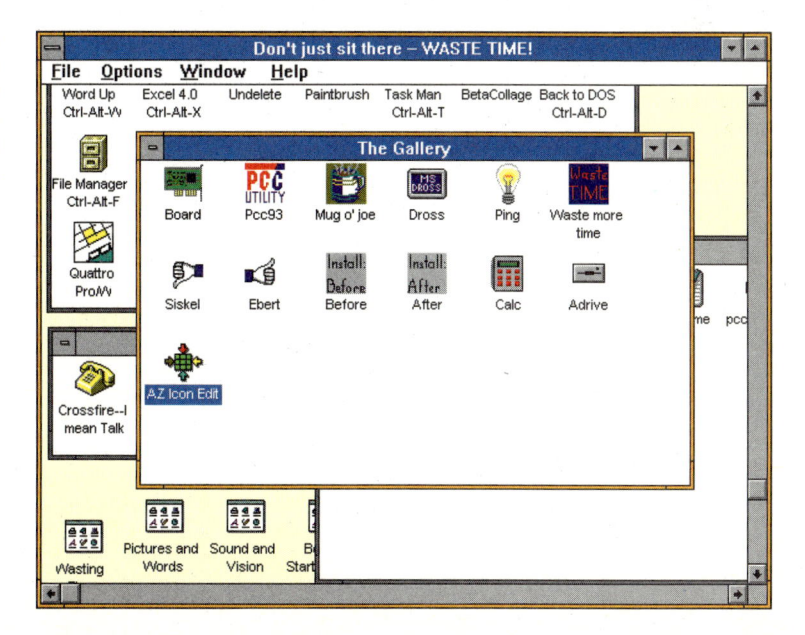

Retouch the Rough Edges

It's only when your icons are in the Program Manager that you see your work in its proper context. And although the icon you see in the Program Manager is identical to the one in AZ Icon Edit's preview, it's usually only now that you notice something that needs to be changed. Don't worry. It's easy to bring up the editor to do a little post-facto cosmetic work.

With your gallery set up as described in the previous section, all you need to do is double-click on the icon to bring up AZ Icon Edit. If you entered the correct path of drive and directory names that house the icon file at the end of the Command Line entry in the Properties box, the icon file will load automatically into AZ Icon Edit's editing window. If you missed that step, just load the icon file manually.

Now do your editing work on the file. When you're finished, select File, Exit, and save your changes on the way out. When you look at the icon on screen, you'll see, horror of horrors, that it hasn't changed a bit. Don't let that worry you. Just highlight it and press Alt+Enter (or press Alt and double-click on the icon with the mouse). Make no changes to the Program Item Properties box, but just click on OK or press Enter. The icon's changes will now show up on screen.

Install an Icon in a Permanent Collection

Want to bring one of your gallery icons into service in one of your "live" Program Manager groups? No problem. Open both the gallery and the other Program Manager group, and follow these steps to copy the icon and assign a new program to it:

1. Resize the gallery group and the group to which you want to add the new icon.

2. Hold down the Control key and drag the icon you want from the gallery to the new group. The icon remains in place, but a ghost image of the icon moves as you do this. The ghost indicates that you're copying and not moving the original icon.

3. Once the icon is in place in its new program group, select it and press Alt+Enter (or press Alt and double-click on it) to bring up its Program Item Properties box.

4. Change the description to the name of the program you want to assign to the icon.

5. Click on Browse, and navigate to the drive and directory that contain the program in question. Select the program and click on OK.

6. Make the necessary adjustments to the Working Directory, so that it reflects where you'll be storing the program's files.

7. Click on OK to save the changes. That's all.

The gallery arrangement is an ego-boost for budding pop artists whose medium is Windows. But it's not just icon-oriented Lichtensteins who benefit from it. Ignore this technique if you will, but next time you're wading through directory after directory of file names looking for the perfect icon, remember—it's better to waste time when you have it than when you don't.

■ What Was the Point of This Chapter?

In "I Think Icon, I Think Icon," you learned how to:

- Trade in your default program icons for spiffy new models
- Find spiffy new models
- Move icons closer together and push them apart
- Use Plug-In to change group icons
- Use AZ Icon Edit to create, capture, modify, and mangle icons
- Banish the default Calculator icon forever, HA HA HA HA!
- Store your icons in a Program Manager gallery and call them into service at a moment's notice

- *Give Your PC Its Voice*
- *Catch a WAV*
- *Replay with the Sound Recorder*
- *More Sound Ideas*
- *What Was the Point of This Chapter?*

CHAPTER 6

Disturbing the Neighbors

Turn your PC's beige box into the White Album

NOT TOO LONG AGO, PC SOUND WAS LIMITED TO AN ANNOYING BEEP whenever you did something wrong. Atari and Macintosh users—their hard disks laden with sound bites from feature films and rock albums—snickered at the paucity of the PC's audio offerings. The best a PC devotee could hope for? The work of a few DEBUG nerds and BASIC jockeys, who had programmed the PC's feeble internal speaker to beep out "Happy Birthday" (and not even the version from the *White Album*). Those were dark days indeed for the DOS-based world.

One of the big draws of Windows 3.1 was the promise of multimedia support, meaning that sound would finally have its place on the PC. Of course, you had to buy extra hardware to do it, which many people did. But for the many who didn't, the sound component of Windows wasn't worth the bytes it was encoded on. Most sensible, disk-conscious people without sound hardware either didn't install the Windows Sound Recorder and .WAV files at all or removed them when space got tight.

And that was that, except for one fact: Microsoft produced a Windows 3.1 driver for the PC's internal speaker. They even made it available on bulletin boards and CompuServe forums, but they did so only with effusive and un-Microsoftly apologies for its shortcomings. Why? While the sound is being played, Windows can do nothing except pump bytes through the internal speaker. This shortcoming discouraged Microsoft from including the speaker driver in the finished Windows product. If you have access to sound hardware—and there's plenty to be found—install and use it. If you don't want to spend another penny but want to use sound anyway, read on.

■ Give Your PC Its Voice

Despite its limited capabilities, the Microsoft speaker driver included on this book's disk is pretty good. For the reasonable price of nothing at all, it has the other sound alternatives beat on the price/performance curve, to say the least. But like a cassette tape, it's only as good as the hardware it's played on, and—in the case of PCs—that's usually not too good. Many PC builders stuff their systems with 25-cent speakers capable of emitting only an annoying beep clear and true (but obscuring everything else with static). Clearly, the driver for a PC's internal speaker only makes the best of a bad job.

Once you've copied the archived sound file from the floppy disk at the back of this book to its own sound subdirectory (according to the instructions in the Appendix), use WinZip to unzip the archives. Apart from various .TXT files that describe the software, there are two active files, namely OEMSETUP.INF and SPEAKER.DRV. The latter is obviously the driver itself; the .INF file contains data needed by the Control Panel to install the driver. Here's how you do it.

Installing the PC-Speaker Driver

The ubiquitous Control Panel is in charge of Windows's drivers and sounds (and pretty much everything else). To activate your PC's internal driver, begin by bringing up the Control Panel and selecting the Drivers icon. Then follow these instructions to install the driver:

1. The Control Panel's Drivers dialog box lists drivers that were installed when you installed Windows. To add the internal speaker driver, click on the Add button.

2. Under List of Drivers, select Unlisted or Updated Driver, as shown in Figure 6.1, and click on OK.

Figure 6.1

Here's the chorus of dialog boxes that make Windows sing. Starting from the Control Panel's Drivers option, navigate through the four dialog boxes to find the unlisted sound driver. From then on, it's a snap.

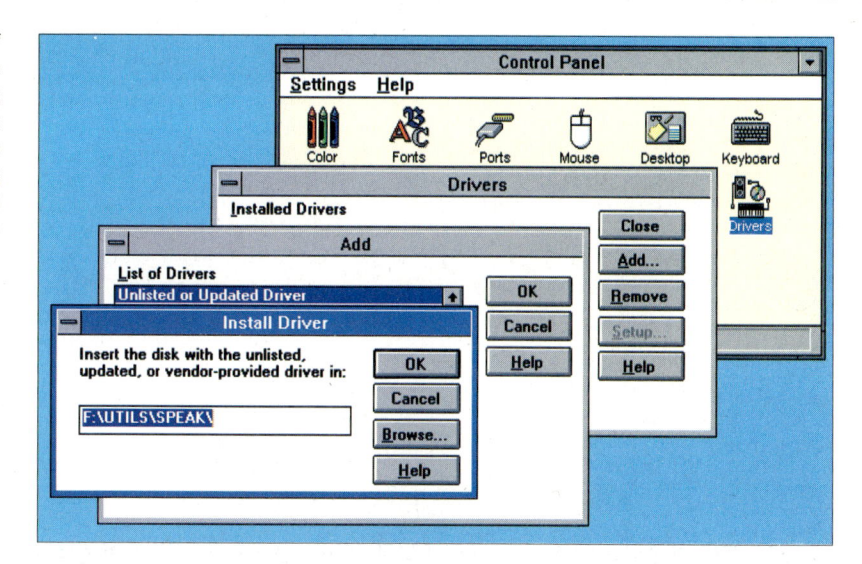

3. Click on the Browse button, and navigate to the drive and directory where you expanded the driver and OEMSETUP.INF files. Select the directory and click on OK.

4. Click on OK in the Install Drivers dialog box. In the Add dialog box, you'll see Sound Driver for PC-Speaker highlighted. Click on OK again.

5. You'll hear a two-tone sound from your PC's internal speaker, and a dialog box entitled PC-Speaker Setup appears, similar to the one in Figure 6.2.

6. If the test beep's volume was either too loud or too soft, adjust the volume bar. Check out your new setting using the Test button, and adjust the levels until they sound just right.

7. While you're still in this dialog box, slide the Seconds to Limit Playback bar all the way to the right.

Figure 6.2

Except for adjusting volume, the only change you should need to make to the PC speaker's settings is to increase the length of playback to None.

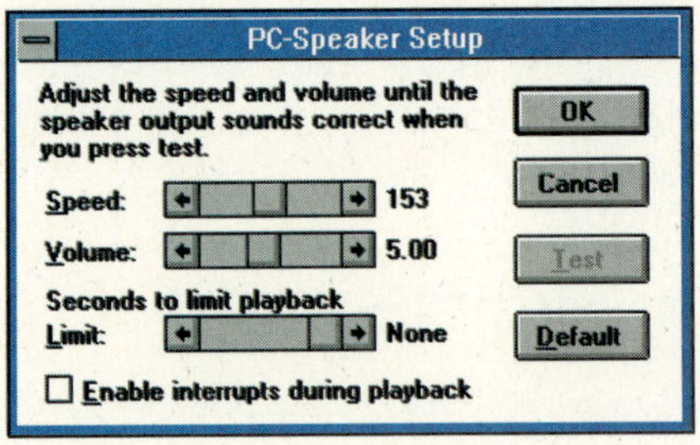

8. Click on OK. A dialog box will appear, asking whether you want to restart Windows. Click on the Restart Now button if you want the new driver to take effect immediately.

CAVEAT. *Read my glyphs: Don't check Enable Interrupts During Playback in the PC-Speaker Setup dialog box. The sound quality will deteriorate so drastically you'll wish your PC were mute again.*

As Windows starts up, you'll hear a fanfare—TADA.WAV, to be exact—that signals you're in business. If the sound seems too quiet or too loud on reflection, select Control Panel, Drivers, and click on the Sound Driver for PC-Speaker option. Select Setup, and adjust the sound accordingly. When everything tests out all right, click on OK to save the changes, and get ready to waste time with the *real* business of Windows sound.

■ Catch a WAV

If you were the kind of PC user who was satisfied with the Windows defaults, you'd never have read this far in the book. Obviously, you won't want to keep the feeble fanfare as your Windows start-up sound or the weedy farewell chimes. And the annoyingly high-pitched ping that greets any serious interference with a program's operation is frankly unbearable—worse than the DOS system beep. Minor infractions of a Windows program's etiquette are greeted with a similarly irritating chord—also to be devoutly avoided.

Each of these sounds is created by one of four files that ships with Windows, namely TADA.WAV, CHIME.WAV, DING.WAV, and CHORD.WAV. But with the requisite hardware (a sound board or sound box that plugs into the parallel port, and a microphone or stereo jack), it's easy enough to make your own .WAV files. For those without such luxuries, I've included a few sample files—just enough to get you started. Make sure you've installed the .WAV files from the disk bound in the back of this book. They're archived in the file SOUNDS.ZIP. Then switch to the Program Manager, and read on.

The Big Event (and What It Actually Means)

The first step in changing the sounds allocated to various system events is to determine the current settings. You'll find this information in WIN.INI's [Sounds] section. Just fire up Sysedit and either scroll down or perform a search. [Sounds] will be toward the end of WIN.INI if you've just installed a sound driver for the first time. In it, you'll find the lines in Figure 6.3, which show the location and name of the files associated with various system functions.

Figure 6.3

Every sound setting in Windows is listed in WIN.INI's [Sound] section. Just don't expect to understand the meaning of the sound events described in it.

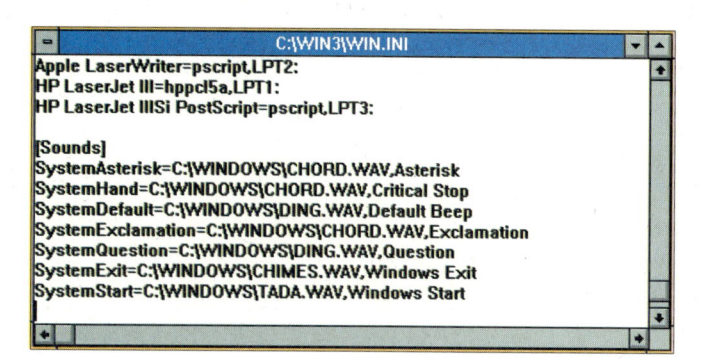

```
                          C:\WIN3\WIN.INI
Apple LaserWriter=pscript,LPT2:
HP LaserJet III=hppcl5a,LPT1:
HP LaserJet IIISi PostScript=pscript,LPT3:

[Sounds]
SystemAsterisk=C:\WINDOWS\CHORD.WAV,Asterisk
SystemHand=C:\WINDOWS\CHORD.WAV,Critical Stop
SystemDefault=C:\WINDOWS\DING.WAV,Default Beep
SystemExclamation=C:\WINDOWS\CHORD.WAV,Exclamation
SystemQuestion=C:\WINDOWS\DING.WAV,Question
SystemExit=C:\WINDOWS\CHIMES.WAV,Windows Exit
SystemStart=C:\WINDOWS\TADA.WAV,Windows Start
```

Except for the lines that end with Windows Exit and Windows Start, there aren't many clues as to what each of the events means. What are system questions and system exclamations, for example? The answers are in Table 6.1. Once you know what they are, you're a lot better equipped to reset your sounds.

When an Unstoppable Sound Meets an Immovable Event

You're now ready to stick a sound to a system event. To do so, turn to our old friend the Control Panel. First, call up a dialog box like the one in Figure 6.4 by starting the Control Panel and clicking on the Sound icon. Then follow these guidelines:

1. In the Events list, select an event that's assigned to a sound you don't like. The Default Beep is a good place to start.

2. If you don't want to assign a sound to the event at all, select None from the Files list. Otherwise, select the drive and directory that contain the .WAV files from this book's disk, and select the sound file you want to use.

3. To hear the sound you've assigned, click on the Test button or double-click on the event or file name.

Chapter 6: Disturbing the Neighbors

Table 6.1

Windows Sounds (and When They Occur)

System Event	What It Means	Default .WAV File Played
Asterisk	Accompanies an error message that varies depending on the application.	CHORD.WAV
Critical Stop	Accompanies an error message that varies depending on the application.	CHORD.WAV
Default Beep	Sounds when you use keyboard shortcuts that aren't allocated, click outside a dialog box, and so on.	DING.WAV
Exclamation	Accompanies dialog boxes that contain exclamation points.	CHORD.WAV
Question	Varies depending on the application. Often accompanies dialog boxes asking if you're sure you want to do something.	CHORD.WAV
Windows Exit	Plays when you quit Windows.	CHIMES.WAV
Windows Start	Plays when Windows loads.	TADA.WAV

Figure 6.4

Once your sound driver's installed, use the Control Panel's Sound dialog box to marry system events to specific sound files.

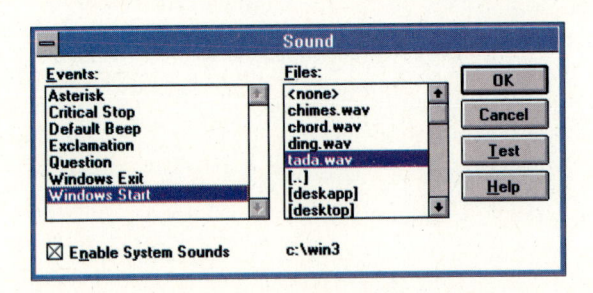

4. To turn off the warning beep and all sounds except for those assigned to Windows Exit and Windows Start, clear the Enable System Sounds check box.

5. When you're satisfied with your sound choices, click on OK to save your new assignments.

Gratuitous Tip: Events That Make Sense

What's the likelihood you'll remember what a system exclamation is? If you wind up resetting your sounds often, don't leave anything to chance—make the Control Panel's Sound option describe what each event really means, in terms you understand. It's easy to do. First, run Sysedit and select WIN.INI. In the [Sounds] section, edit the ends of each of the lines to something more mnemonic. For example, if the exclamation sound turns up most often when you hit the Escape key in Word for Windows (which it does for me), add a description that fits the action:

```
SystemExclamation=C:\WINDOWS\CHORD.WAV,Escape Key in WinWord
```

Use this example as a starting point, but feel free to use any description up to 23 characters long (you won't see longer descriptions in the Sound Control Panel's Events window, which lacks a horizontal scroll bar).

When you next start up the Control Panel's Sound selection, the new descriptions will appear in the Events box. Note that the events will be sorted in alphabetical order, so their order will most likely be different than they originally appeared.

■ Replay with the Sound Recorder

Using the Control Panel's Sound section to listen to and compare sounds is like using a brick to hammer nails. Sure, you can do it, but that's not what it was designed for. Instead, acquaint yourself with the Sound Recorder utility that Windows plops into the Program Manager's Accessories group during installation. (If you're anything like me, you'll have trashed this default arrangement long ago, but that's where Microsoft decided to put it.) Start it up, and you'll see a small dialog box like the one in Figure 6.5.

When you use the Microsoft driver for the PC's internal speaker, the Sound Recorder isn't a recorder at all, but merely a player. The microphone button at the lower-right corner of the screen will remain grayed until you properly install hardware capable of recording sound. It's also impaired by the sound driver's tendency to monopolize CPU time: The rectangular Stop button next to the microphone serves as a pause key for systems with special sound cards or plug-in sound boxes, but not for systems which use the internal speaker.

Chapter 6: Disturbing the Neighbors

Figure 6.5

When you're using the PC speaker for your Windows sound device, the Sound Recorder can play any .WAV file, but it can't record one. It also can't pause a sound file unless you've enabled interrupts in the PC-Speaker Setup box, which makes replayed files sound dreadful.

That much aside, there's plenty you can do with the Sound Recorder and the .WAV files on your hard disk. First, use the File, Open dialog box to locate and load a .WAV file. Now click on the Play button. You'll hear the .WAV file play, and while it's playing, everything else stops. The hourglass cursor will appear and won't go away until the sound is over. The waveform window, Position status box to its right, and sliding scrollbar beneath it will also stay put, and then suddenly zip to their end positions.

The way sounds *look* is a constant obsession of everyone who watched oscilloscopes in science (and science fiction) shows as a kid. The Sound Recorder has the same blips on its green line as the ones you see on oscilloscopes, but you don't see them in action when you're running the PC speaker driver. Don't let that hold you back. Take a look at the waveform pattern that makes up the sound you've just heard. Click on the Rewind button at the lower-left corner of the Sound Recorder. The Position status box will show 0.00 seconds, and the scrollbar's slider will be located underneath it. Drag the slider slowly to the right and watch the green line in the waveform window. If any pattern of blips grabs your interest, stop dragging and click the Play button to hear what that pattern actually represents.

The Wall of Sound

Remember listening to the overproduced sound salad that passed for music in the late sixties and early seventies? Ever wished you could indulge yourself half as much as the addled performers and producers of that bygone age? No problem. Microsoft threw its own special effects pedal into the Sound Recorder. With them, you can turn familiar sounds into "Revolution Number Nine Revisited." All you need is a few .WAV files and too much time on your hands.

Most of the Sound Recorder's special effects are available, predictably, under the Effects menu, but there's some mileage to be gleaned from the Edit menu also. To see just how far we've regressed (about 25 years, by all music production standards), open up DING.WAV, one of the more mundane sound files in your Windows directory. There it will stand, looking like Figure 6.6, 0.52 seconds of high-pitched digital sound.

Gratuitous Tip: Short Is Beautiful

When you have a .WAV file open in the Sound Recorder, check out the wave pattern at the beginning and end of the file. If you see a straight line that goes on for a while at either end, you'll probably be able to shorten the file without affecting the sound you hear. Shorter sound files return control of your mouse cursor quicker, so they're worth aiming for.

To shorten a .WAV file, slowly drag the scrollbar's slider to the right from the beginning of the file, and stop when you hit a blip in the waveform window's green line. Move back so the blip isn't showing, and select Edit, Delete before Current Position. A dialog box will appear to warn you that all the data before the position you marked will be deleted. Click on OK, and then click on the Play button. If the file sounds OK, save it, move the slider to the end of the scrollbar, and locate any slack time at the end of the file. Once the slider is in position, select Edit, Delete after Current Position, and click on OK. Check that the results are OK before saving the file. If they're not, select File, Revert, and try again.

Figure 6.6

Ever wondered what the sound "Ding" looks like? Wonder no more. The attack (the first part) looks like this screenshot. The decay (the sound as it fades out) looks the same, but smaller.

The challenge: To make a dull sound interesting. The solution: Use the entire arsenal of Windows sound effects. The ingredients: DING.WAV and Sound Recorder. The technique: Read on....

Play It Again

The Sound Recorder's Edit, Insert File option makes it possible to insert a sound file into the current sound file. Since the Sound Recorder loads sound files into memory and doesn't look back at the disk, you can load multiple iterations of the same sound file at once. Invoke Edit, Insert File and load DING.WAV twice into the current iteration of DING.WAV. You'll now have three dings in one file and since the Sound Recorder is always prepared to play the last sound loaded, it's set to play only one ding. Don't play the sound yet.

Mix It In

Selecting Edit, Mix with File enables you to blend the sound of a file on disk with the one loaded in the Sound Recorder. The sound files will play simultaneously. The first step is to cue up the sound file in memory (which you did by opening it).

From the Edit menu, choose Mix with File, and select DING.WAV to mix in. Click on OK. Now play the sound file. You'll hear a single tone. Play it again, and you'll start from the beginning—you'll hear three tones. The last one will be louder, since it's actually two dings playing together.

Say That Again—Only Slower

Did you ever get a kick from playing singles at 33 RPM or LPs at 45? (OK, so it was just me.) [*no it wasn't—Ed.*] Try the same effect on your .WAV files with Effects, Increase Speed (by 100%) or Effects, Decrease Speed. In the case of the three dings, faster is nerve-shatteringly high. Slow down the sound, and it lowers the pitch and doubles the playing time—which for DING.WAV is an unequivocal benefit. If you like the effect, do it again for an even slower rendition.

Don't care for the effect? Return the sound to its previous speed. Choose the Increase Speed command right away. To increase the speed of a sound, choose Effects, Increase Speed. Think this sounds worse? Undo your changes by immediately choosing the Decrease Speed command.

Just Say It Again

Want to re-create that church-bell-in-the-village-in-the-south-of-France effect? Select Effects, Add Echo. This bounces DING's bell tone back and makes for a pleasant effect. In other .WAV files, you may not notice any effect from the echo menu option—it tends to be most effective when used on short sounds, especially those that get to the point quickly (or, in sound engineer's parlance, have a "sharp attack") and don't take long to fade out (or "decay").

Paul Is Dead

Some sounds benefit from being played backwards—though not on songs recorded after the psychedelic rock era. To reverse a .WAV file's sound, select Effects, Reverse. Play the new DING.WAV again to hear what havoc you've wreaked. If you like the result, save it under a new name. Try out SGNID3 for a file name. You figure out why.

Gratuitous Tip: When Sounds Go Bad

Added a few too many effects to a sound file? Restore it to its former glory. Select File, Revert, and you'll be prompted with a dialog box that asks if you're sure you know what you're doing. Of course you do, so click on Yes. The file will revert to the last version you saved.

After you've saved a file, you can no longer undo the changes you've made to it. For this reason, when you're finding your way around in the Sound Recorder, keep an audit trail of your experiments. Use File, Save As during your sound mixing sessions, and save your working sounds in their own directory. When you get the PC equivalent of the Wall of Sound, switch to the File Manager and delete all the versions you saved. You can even delete the version you currently have open, since the Sound Recorder keeps the live file in memory. Then switch back to the Sound Recorder and save the file as you leave it.

■ More Sound Ideas

It won't be long before you are losing yourself in Windows sound. You'll be wondering why you can't label more system events to sound files. You'll find yourself repeatedly making the same mistake just to hear its event sound. Before long, you'll be finding excuses to edit WIN.INI just so you can quit Windows and restart it to hear two sounds in less than a minute.

You may even sink into File Manager obsession: Your View, By File Type box will be set to *.WAV, you'll be double-clicking on all the .WAV files and running ten or more iterations of the Sound Recorder behind a maximized "front" application.

Don't let it come to this! There are better ways of wasting time. The Golden Rule: Waste your time constructively. Learn how *object linking and embedding* (OLE) can save you effort in playing sound files—and help you set up a scrapbook of all your sound files. Remember, even though you're tinkering with advanced technology in OLE, it's all for a frivolous cause.

OLE Smokes! All Your Sounds in One File

Your .WAV file library is now as small as it will ever be—Windows's minimal offerings, a few more from the disk at the back of this book, maybe some downloads from an on-line service. This is the perfect time to catalog your files. Even if you don't care about keeping them in order, plugging sound files as

OLE objects into a document is the only way to get your entire collection into a single scrapbook document, like the one in Figure 6.7, ready to be played at a moment's notice.

Figure 6.7

Use OLE to group all your files into a single file (like this Excel worksheet) ready to play at a moment's notice.

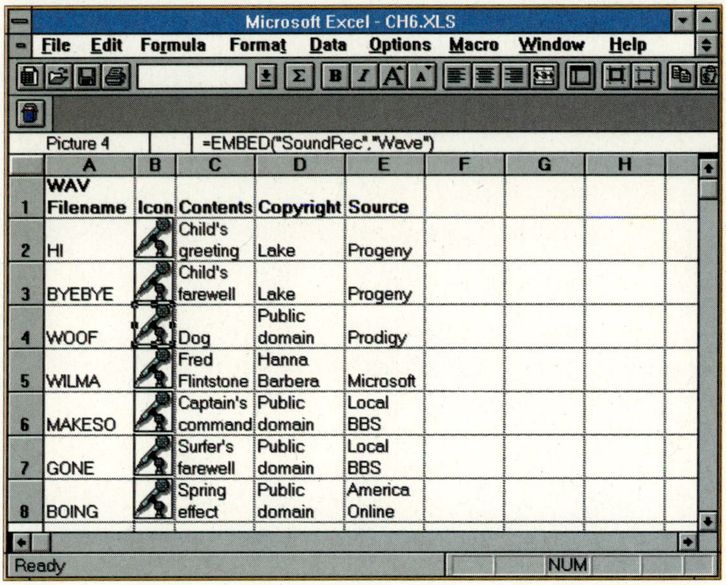

Before getting down to business, here's the technical background of what we're about to do. The Sound Recorder belongs to a class of Windows applications called *OLE servers*, which provide files that can be linked or embedded in the composite documents of an OLE client application. OLE servers are the unsung heroes of the object embedding world—they don't get much glory, but they make the whole thing work.

The ranks of the OLE clients are populated by programs you use all the time—Word for Windows, Ami Pro, Excel… basically any program with a Paste Special and/or Insert Object option under its Edit menu. Any one of these applications could be the creator of your sound scrapbook. It's best to use one that can manage tables easily, so you can fit as many sounds into the available space as possible. Also, each sound object is embedded as an icon that you'll probably want to position carefully next to descriptive text.

An audio scrapbook is compiled the same in any OLE client, but since Windows ships with its own OLE client—namely Write—I'll use that to describe how the process works, as follows:

1. Open the Sound Recorder and load a favorite .WAV file that you want in your scrapbook.

2. Select Edit, Copy. A copy of the sound will shift into the Clipboard.

3. Press Alt+Tab to switch to the Program Manager and open Write (or another OLE client). Open the file you'll be using for your sound scrapbook.

4. Enter a description of the file you've just copied to the Clipboard. Then move the insertion point cursor to the position you have in mind for the sound icon.

5. Select Edit, Paste Special, and press Enter to select the Paste option. A Sound Recorder icon will appear in the document.

6. Double-click on the icon. After a short pause, the file will play.

7. Save the document once you're satisfied the sound is pasted in properly.

That's all there is to it. Repeat this process for all your favorite sound files, and you'll have a one-stop shop for all your sounds.

That's the quick-and-dirty way of gathering a collection of sounds in a composite document that contains words and pictures, too. But all it takes is a glance at Figure 6.7 to see that the pictures are repetitive, and there's no easy way to distinguish the sounds. That's where the versatility of another Windows OLE offering comes in.

A Better-Packaged Sound Scrapbook

The trouble with regular OLE is that you can't change the icons the way you can in most other Windows venues. If you're throwing just one or two objects into a document, that's actually an advantage, but if the medium is the message—as it is with a sound scrapbook—variety is everything. The solution? A neat little end-run using the OLE server and facilitator, Object Packager.

To make this technique work, you need to run three applications and patiently work through more steps per sound than with a straight embedding job. The results, however, are more visually arresting and well worth the additional wasted time. Just compare Figures 6.7 and 6.8 to see which looks better.

Here's what you need to do:

1. Open the Sound Recorder and load one of the .WAV files you want in your scrapbook.

2. Select Edit, Copy. A copy of the sound will shift into the Clipboard.

3. Press Alt+Tab to switch to the Program Manager, and open Write (or another OLE client). Open the file you'll be using for your sound scrapbook.

4. Move the insertion point cursor to the position you have in mind for the sound icon.

5. Select Edit, Insert Object, and scroll down to highlight Package. Click on OK. An Object Packager dialog box will appear.

Chapter 6: Disturbing the Neighbors

Figure 6.8

Vary the icons and labels of your sound scrapbook file. Use the Object Packager to set up the OLE link.

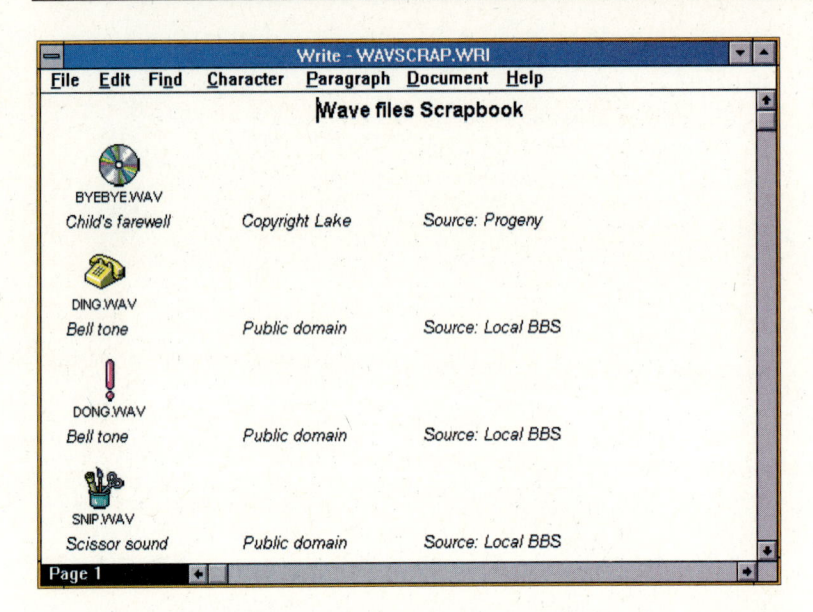

6. In the Object Packager dialog box, select Edit, Paste. A Sound Recorder icon will appear in the window on the left, like the one in Figure 6.9.

7. Click on the Insert Icon button. Select Browse, and navigate to the appropriate drive and directory for your icon of choice. (If appropriate, select another file extension under List Files of Type.) From the Insert Icon box, pick an icon and click on OK.

8. Back in the Object Packager box, select Edit, Label, and enter a new description of up to 39 characters to go under the icon. (Use as few characters as possible, since the labels won't word-wrap, and carefully consider including the file name.) Press Enter, and you'll see a window like Figure 6.10.

9. Select File, Exit, and click on OK to the Update warning.

10. Double-click on the new object, and as soon as you're confident that it's working, save the document.

Either of these methods of creating and maintaining your own library of sound bites should work fine. If either the Sound Recorder or one of the sound files gets deleted, the icon in your scrapbook will be there for decoration only—it will become mute. If you lose interest in a sound file, don't delete it and go through the ten-step process of re-embedding another one. Instead, edit it into another file altogether, as follows:

1. Highlight the object you want to change, and select Edit, Package Object, Edit Package.

Figure 6.9

The Object Packager offers the same lame default icon for its objects as plain OLE does, but you can change both the icon and the dull description…

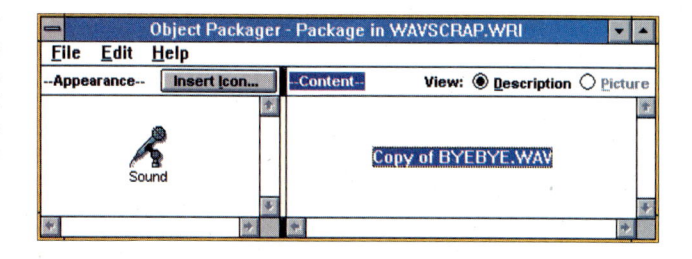

Figure 6.10

…to look more like this. The added steps in creating a link in the Object Packager pay dividends in the final appearance of the object in the file.

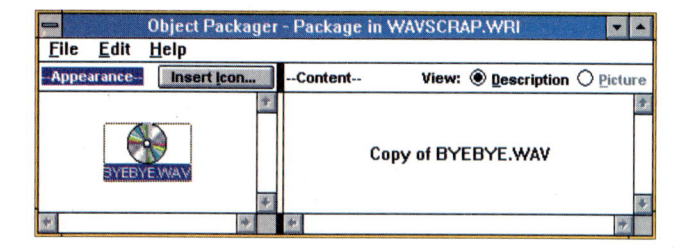

2. In the Object Packager dialog box, select Edit, Sound Object, Edit. A Sound Recorder window will appear.

3. Click on the fast-forward button to zip to the end of the sound file. Select Edit, Insert File, pick a new file, and click on OK.

4. Now get rid of the original sound by selecting Edit, Delete Before Current Position, and then click on OK.

5. Select File, Update, and File, Exit.

6. In the Object Packager, select Edit, Label, enter a new description, and then select File, Update, and File, Exit.

And that's about all you need to know about operating the sound driver and maintaining a sound library. Other sound software and hardware provide more choices. The list of events to which you can tie sounds using Wired for Sound, Mr. Sound FX, and other sound utilities is as long as the most demanding time-waster's wish list. With the purchase of a sound card or parallel-port sound unit like Digispeech's Port-Able Sound or Logitech's AudioMan, you can record your own voice or sound effects to use as .WAV files, and open the sound options even further. In the meantime, there's plenty of time to waste mixing away the files you already have on your system.

■ What Was the Point of This Chapter?

In "Disturbing the Neighbors," you learned:

- That, like the brain, the PC's internal speaker is used to less than 10 percent of its peak capacity
- How to install and operate Microsoft's PC-Speaker driver
- How to choose sounds and control when you hear them
- How to make sense of the Event list in the Control Panel's Sound option
- How to play, edit, and overproduce sounds with the Sound Recorder
- How to use OLE and the Object Packager to create your own library of sound bites

- *Windows Typecasting*
- *In Your (Type)Face Font Trivia*
- *The Uses and Overuses of Fonts*
- *Fonts 101 and More*
- *Putting a New Face on Windows*
- *What Was the Point of This Chapter?*

CHAPTER 7

Font Mania

Never tell a typesetter that your favorite font is Baskerville. The best response you can hope for from this kind of announcement is an indulgent smile that lets you know you're in the presence of a professional and that you shouldn't be trying this at home. This has nothing to do with professional opinion of Baskerville itself—it's been a well-respected typeface ever since it was designed in the mid-1700s in Birmingham, England, by John Baskerville. But it isn't a font. It's a typeface, and the two words—to the professional, at least—don't mean the same thing.

The difference between a font and a typeface is slight but fundamental: A font is a typeface in a specific size, weight, and style. Baskerville, therefore, is a typeface; Baskerville bold italic, 12 point is a font. To put it another way, a typeface is created by a typographer on a drawing board—it's the archetype, some might say the Platonic form, of which the font is a concrete example. By contrast, prior to the dawn of the computer age, a font was created in a foundry by pouring molten lead into a mold.

FONT TRIVIA. *The words* font *and* foundry *come from the same root word, the Latin verb* fundere—*to pour. Don't you wonder how you got by without knowing that?*

Back in the glory days of hot lead type, each font—with its fixed point size and style—was shipped to typesetters, who stored the type in two wooden cases—one for the capital letters and one for the rest. Typesetters used to store the capital letters at a raised level at arm's length, and they kept the non-capitals, which they used much more frequently, near at hand. Hence, capitals are called uppercase letters, and the others, lowercase letters.

But enough of the William Safire routine. Electronic typesetting has eroded the meaning of font from its original and more precise definition. When digitized fonts first appeared, they were fonts in the true sense of the word—typefaces in one style (italic, bold, or whatever) and in one size (10 point, 12 point, and so on). These were beautifully crafted, professional, and expensive; they also had to be installed one size at a time.

For a professional typesetter, this was staggeringly convenient. (Remember, the alternative for them was slotting blobs of molded lead into a wooden frame, trusting that they could mirror-read well enough to prevent errors.) To everyone else, dealing with fixed–point-size type was a pain. When Adobe Systems and Apple Computers started to provide digital typefaces that you could scale from 6 points or so to just about any size, the pulse of the amateur type-diddler quickened—here was a chance to *experiment*. This technology was referred to generically as scalable type, but it didn't take long for a term that chilled the blood of typesetters to take hold: *scalable fonts*. With apologies to typesetters, I'll be using this term freely from now on.

PC users had to wait a while before they could share the bounty of scalable type. Adobe Type Manager and Bitstream's FaceLift provided Windows 3.0 with scalable fonts, and both systems can still be used to great effect with Windows 3.1. But when Windows 3.1 came out, it included a built-in scaling technology—a joint Microsoft and Apple venture called TrueType—and a selection of five fonts. This was it. Font mania had arrived in Windowsville, and the town was never the same again.

In Your (Type)Face Font Trivia

Like any trade that has been plied for more than a couple of centuries, typography has its share of impenetrable jargon and professional secrets. By the end of this section, most of the important terms will no longer be secrets.

Fonts are measured in units called *points*, which doesn't mean much to the layperson. As a rule of thumb, think of the point as $1/72$ of an inch—but don't assume that any 72-point character is a full inch tall. The point size is equal to the total height of the font, not its individual parts. For example, set in a 72-point font, the word Hop measures about an inch from the top of the H to the bottom of the p.

The common parts of each letter in a font have their own names—all of which make sense when you hear them in context. The stem of the p, y, q, and g is called a *descender* because it dips below the font's *baseline*—the imaginary line on which the majority of a font's letters lie. The twin towers of the capital H (called *ascenders*) and other tall letters rise above the font's *x-height* (so called because it's the height of the font's lowercase x). All these elements are shown in Figure 7.1.

Figure 7.1

Don't let typographers' jargon cloud font issues. This diagram explains most of the commonly used and little-understood argot from the type trade. Wow your friends.

Fonts fall into four basic categories: serif, sans serif, script, and symbol. Although there are many subcategories, we won't get bogged down in discussing them here. Windows has examples of all four.

Courier New and Times New Roman belong to the clan of serif fonts, which means that little flourishes called *serifs* appear on pretty much any straight line, including: the ascenders on lowercase letters d, b, and others; the descenders on p, q, and those like them; and the tops and bottoms of the letters m and w. *Sans serif* fonts, as any French person could tell you, are fonts without serifs. Arial is the dominant example in Windows.

Script fonts mimic handwriting and are represented in Windows by Script (no surprises there). Symbol fonts replace readable characters with symbols, and include WingDings and (predictably) Symbol.

That covers about all the font jargon and measurements you need to know, except the space between lines of type. Word processing and desktop publishing programs variously refer to this as line-spacing (original, no?) and leading (pronounced *ledding*). The software that aspires to professional use favors the term leading, because it's a throwback to the days of lead type, in which the space between printed lines was adjusted by inserting lead strips of a given width. That's positively the last casual piece of font trivia I'll drop (he lied).

■ Windows Typecasting

Windows is full of fonts. They're in your application title bars and menus, they're in dialog boxes and beneath icons, and yes, they're in the documents you create, too. It's a snap to change the appearance of any text you type in your applications—you simply go through the Text, Character, or Format menu option and scan for the word Font. Later in the chapter, you'll learn to change the fonts Windows uses for title bars and menus.

But for now, let's concentrate on the ones you can use in documents. Your choices are five native TrueType fonts (Arial, Courier New, Times New Roman, Symbol, and WingDings) and several non-TrueType fonts (Courier, Modern, MS Sans Serif, MS Serif, Roman, Script, Small Fonts, System and Terminal)—some of which you can see in Figure 7.2.

Figure 7.2

Here are some of the fonts Windows provides for your formatting pleasure. Use them at will (except for the impenetrable Symbol and WingDings).

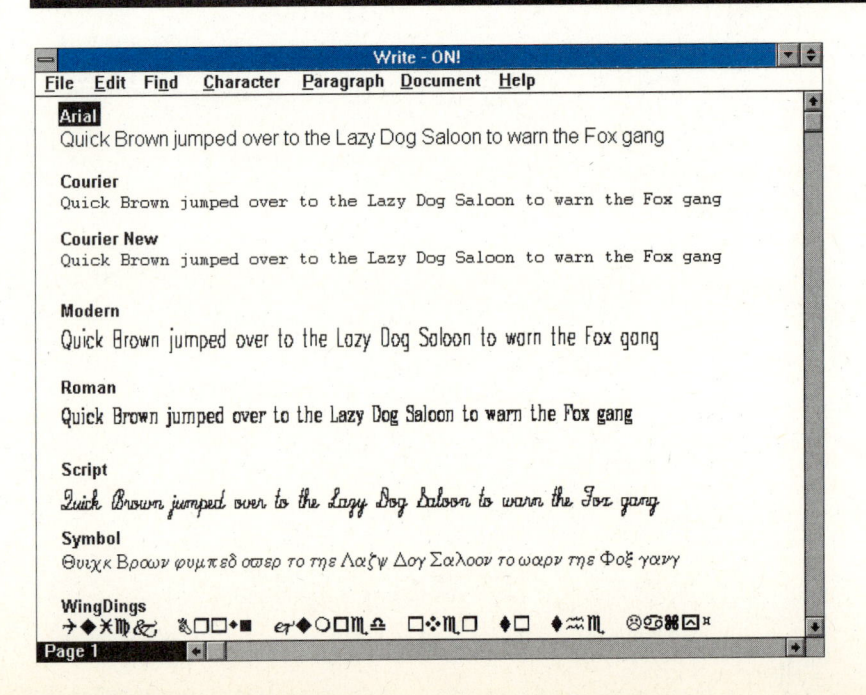

Although they're outnumbered, the TrueType fonts are the most appealing of the selections. Don't believe it? Check out Terminal and System—then tell me I'm lying. Even though the other non-TrueType fonts look considerably better than those two examples, they still have their limitations. Take MS Sans Serif, for example. It's limited to specific point sizes (8, 10, 12, 14, 18, and 24). Small Fonts comes in one size only, and it's *tiny*, but I gather that's the point.

Enough theoretical talk. The best way to experience your font collection is to look at it, and the quickest (if not best) way to look at it is via the Control Panel. Fire up the Control Panel, click on the Fonts icon, and check out the list of installed fonts. Click on the first font that takes your fancy, and a sample of it will appear in the Sample box. Beneath it, you'll see an indication of how much disk space the font files take up.

Lose a Font

Scroll down each of the fonts listed in the Installed Fonts list, and take in the fonts and their respective sizes. If you surmise that one just isn't worth the disk sectors it's monopolizing, you can easily delete it. Here's how:

1. In the Installed Fonts list box, click on the name of the font you want to deep-six. If the font comes in several styles (bold, italic, bold italic, and so forth), press Control and click on each of them.

2. Click on the Remove button.

3. In the Remove Font dialog box, click on the Remove Font File from Disk check box.

4. Click on Yes to All, and say hello to your salvaged disk space.

You should delete fonts only if you're really short of disk space or tolerance for a particular typeface. After all, font futzing is one of the world's finest timewasters. But if you delete a font you want later, you can always restore it from your Windows installation disks.

Gain Seven Fonts

In keeping with the "more is better" ethos of the 1980s, it's better to add fonts than take them away. To that end, you'll find several public domain fonts culled from various online services on the disk bound in the back of this book. To press them into active service, first check out Figure 7.3 and see which ones you like. Then copy the archived font files from the floppy disk into a new subdirectory on your hard drive, and unarchive them as described in the Appendix. Then read on:

1. Start the Control Panel and select Fonts.

Chapter 7: Font Mania

Figure 7.3

Fancy a change from Microsoft's own font offerings? Try out some of these fonts from this book's disk. They are all public domain TrueType fonts.

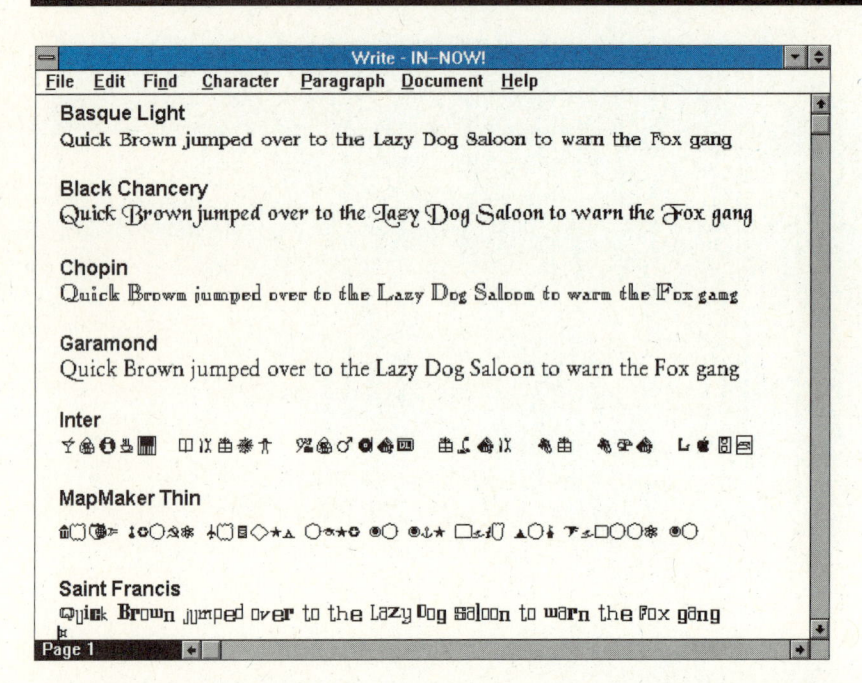

2. Click on the Add button, and if necessary change to your Windows System directory.

3. In the Add Fonts dialog box, you'll see a running percentage of fonts being read, which is labeled Retrieving Font Names. When all the fonts have been checked, the List of Fonts box will fill with their names, as shown in Figure 7.4. Either press Control and click on the fonts you want or click on the Select All button to highlight them all.

4. Click on the Copy Fonts to Windows Directory check box to remove the *X*. This will prevent Windows from duplicating files on your hard disk by having it refuse to copy the files to the Windows System directory.

5. Click on OK.

6. You'll be switched directly back to the Fonts dialog box, and you'll see each font name as it's added to the Installed Fonts list. When they are all in place, click on each in turn to ensure it has been properly installed.

7. Finally, click on Close to quit the Fonts option.

You're now fully prepared to flood your system with any font that happens to come your way (and you can find some excellent examples both in stores and online). Then simply dispose of them when you're tight on disk space.

Figure 7.4

The Control Panel's Font utility makes adding fonts as easy as clicking on names, but unless you want several copies of a font file on your disk (trust me, you don't), keep the Copy Fonts box unchecked.

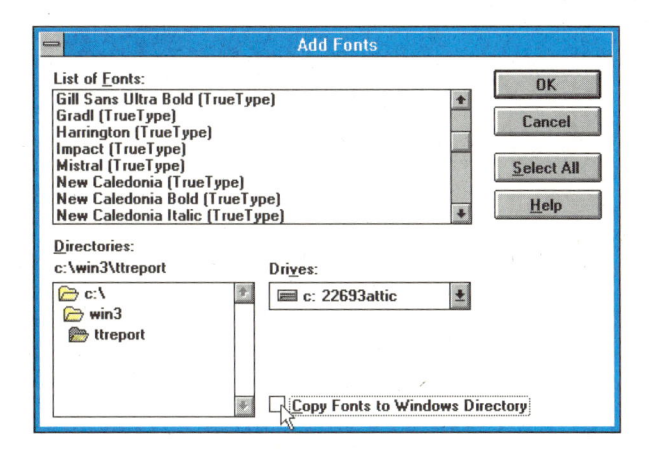

But addition and subtraction of fonts is considerably less than half the story. The real business of fonts comes in using them at every opportunity.

■ The Uses and Overuses of Fonts

When the microcomputer world gained access to a wide variety of fonts, the response was one of orgiastic indulgence. A minor revolution called desktop publishing began that turned wireheads with no training in design into an army of Charles Foster Kanes (at least in their imaginations).

No longer was a document containing less than seven typefaces considered worthy. Text had to be set in bold, italic, bold italic, and varying point sizes for emphasis. In some cases, all these variants appeared in the same line. Print professionals shuddered at the results, and after a while, so did everybody else. The popular mood has now swung away from the "ransom note" school of desktop publishing—and aesthetes the world over are now breathing a heavy sigh of relief. But there's no reason to swing too far in the other direction. With a little knowledge and a lot of fonts, you can improve the look of your documents and Windows itself. You need only waste a little time examining ten little rules to see how much you can get away with (see sidebar).

■ Fonts 101 and More

The standard PC keyboard has 101 keys, including a few duplicates. Most fonts that ship with Windows have more than 220 characters. The characters you can't get directly from the keyboard are called the *extended character set*,

Ten Ways to Use Fonts without Looking Stupid

1. *Don't overuse italics.* It's hard to follow more than a few consecutive words in italics. Limit the use of italics to foreign words and phrases, captions, the names of books or other publications, and short phrases you want to emphasize.

2. *Never underline.* Underlined type was invented for typewriters that couldn't produce italics. Use either italics or boldface for emphasis instead.

3. *Use the right font for the job.* Use serif fonts for body text (the text that makes up most of the document). Serif fonts are easier to read in large blocks than sans serif fonts. Use sans serif fonts for headlines and for anything you'll be looking at onscreen.

4. *Pick the right point size.* To make a document readable, stick to text between 9 and 12 points for body text. Unless your readers are very young or myopic, larger text makes reading harder.

5. *Avoid gray blocks of text.* Scan your document before you give it out. If the text looks too dense, it's probably because your linespacing is too tight. Many Windows applications let you increase this, so give it a try.

6. *Don't over-hyphenate.* If you use hyphenation to split words at the end of a line, don't do so more than three times in any paragraph. And don't end more than two consecutive lines in hyphens.

7. *DON'T USE TOO MANY CAPITALS.* Sentences in shout mode, as uppercase letters are called in online services, are very difficult to read. If you must use a lot of uppercase letters, determine whether your software has a small caps option that reduces the size of most uppercase characters by a point or two.

8. *Use typefaces sparingly.* Don't use more than two or three typefaces in a document, and check that those you use go well together. This takes practice, but bear in mind that often, similar fonts don't go together as well as dissimilar ones. Times Roman and Arial are an example of a pair that do work well together.

9. *Use emphasis sparingly.* The point of increasing your type size or using a decorative typeface is to draw attention to one thing you're writing. Don't make every element you format vie for the reader's eye—decide what's worthy of the most attention, and format only that.

10. *Always use typographer's quotes.* Look font-savvy with almost no effort by replacing typewriter-style quotation marks and apostrophes with curled typographer's quotes (also called smart quotes), like those you see in books. Turn on NumLock, and enter the following key combinations with keystrokes on the number pad. Replace an opening single quote with the character generated by Alt+0145, a single closing quote or apostrophe with Alt+0146. Generate double opening and closing quotes with Alt+0147 and Alt+0148.

and they include such niceties as the British pound sign, the registered trademark and copyright symbols, and typographical characters such as smart quotes and em dashes—long hyphens like the one that separates the words *dashes* and *long* in this sentence.

MORE FONT TRIVIA. *The em dash gets its name from a typographer's measurement, the em, which is the width of the lead block that housed the letter M in a given font. Any guesses where the en dash, a slightly shorter hyphen, gets its name from?*

Until Windows 3.1 came along, inserting extended characters into your documents was a real pain. You had to turn on the Num Lock key, hold down the Alt key, and pound out a four-digit number on your keyboard's numeric keypad. The routine itself was easy; remembering the four-digit number was the tricky part. If you know the numbers for the extended characters (or at least the ones you need most often), this technique is still the quickest way to insert something like the copyright symbol © (the code for which is Alt+0169, by the way). If you have trouble remembering your own zip code, forget extended ASCII characters. Just read the next section.

Strength of Character (Map)

Whenever you need a weird symbol fast, press Alt+Tab to switch to the Program Manager and fire up Windows 3.1's Character Map. Found in the Accessories group (or as CHARMAP from a File, Run menu), the Character Map provides a quick visual reference of a font's entire character set—even the spacebar character—in a 7-by-32 grid, as shown in Figure 7.5.

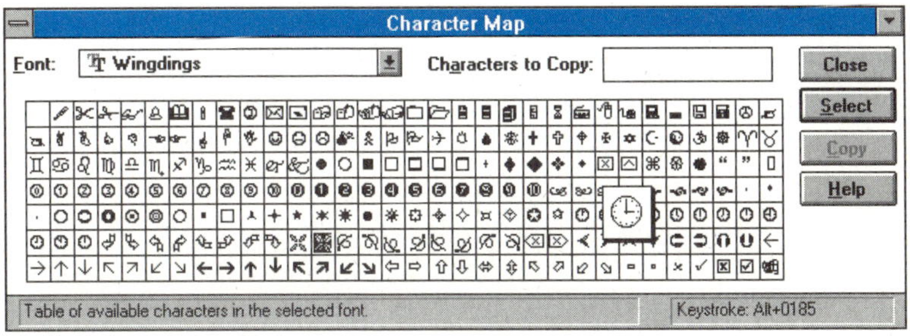

Figure 7.5

The Character Map is the prime Windows tool for the font futzer. It provides two-click access to all of a font's 255 characters. All you do is select one, copy it to the Clipboard, and paste it into your working document.

This many characters in one small dialog box means one thing: The characters are illegible. That's why when you click on a square in the grid, the character blows up to four times its original size, which is enough to see the character clearly and its style passably well. If you're not seeing the characters in the right font, the drop-down Font box makes changing the selection a three-click operation.

Once you've located the character you want, click on it twice, and it's selected in the Characters to Copy box. Click once on the Copy button, and it's in the Clipboard ready to paste in your application. And for the numeric keypad jockeys, there's a handy readout of the Alt+*number* combination for the highlighted character in the lower-right corner of the dialog box. What more could you ask for?

Gratuitous Tip: Build Your Own Font Checklists

Get this straight: Neither the Font Control Panel nor the Character Map shows enough for you to make an informed choice of a font for a given task. To get a good idea of what a font will look like, create a sample file in Write that contains text formatted in all your fonts in several font sizes. Label each line of text with the font's name and size.

Save the document and close it. Then change to the File Manager and the document's directory. Press Ctrl and drag the Write program icon to copy it. Press Alt and double-click on the duplicate, and enter a description like "Font Comparison." In the Command Line box after WRITE.EXE, enter the name of your font document (and the path to it, if you saved the file in a remote directory). Finally, click on Change Icon and pick something suitably fontly.

Now whenever you need to pick a font, press Alt+Tab to reach the Program Manager and click on your Font Comparison icon. Use the Write document to make your informed font choice.

Fonts in Folders Make Windows Faster

You can't have too many fonts, that's true, but you *can* have too many active at once. The five TrueType fonts that come with Windows and the seven you've installed from this book's disk won't make too much of a dent in your system's performance, but if you download a few shareware fonts or buy one of the many TrueType font packs on the market, you'll notice Windows creaking under the burden.

As with every element that Windows uses, fonts are loaded one by one when Windows starts up. Check the BOOTLOG.TXT file you made in Chapter 1 for font references. Now consider what happens when you double or triple the number of fonts on your system. You've got it—really slow loading.

If you happen to have Ares Software's FontMinder or the Font Assistant utility that comes with the Microsoft TrueType Font Pack 2, you'll already know the benefits of maintaining groups of TrueType fonts. They're convenient and minimize clutter in your font dialog boxes. They also make Windows and font-conscious Windows applications fly open. If you don't have these utilities, never fear.

Though it's easier with a font manager, maintaining your own font groups is pretty straightforward using the tools that come with Windows. It's not usually necessary to sort fonts into groups unless you have more than fifty (or if your PC is really slow or short of RAM), but if Windows is noticeably slower since you added some TrueType faces, it's time to manage those fonts.

Anatomy of a TrueType Font

Every TrueType font has two elements. The actual font metrics and details are stored in a file with a .TTF extension. This can be stored anywhere on your hard disk, but for Windows to recognize it, it must be installed using the Control Panel's Font utility. When you install a TrueType font (even if you don't copy the font file to the Windows directory), Windows generates a second font file with the extension .FOT. Among other things, .FOT files point to the location of their corresponding .TTF files.

To check out the font file names installed on your system, open Sysedit and check the [Fonts] section of WIN.INI. The fonts are listed in the order in which they were installed, in this format:

```
Courier New Bold (TrueType)=COURBD.FOT
Courier New Bold Italic (TrueType)=COURBI.FOT
Courier New Italic (TrueType)=COURI.FOT
```

The three elements that tell Windows a TrueType font is available are

- A listing in WIN.INI's [Fonts] section
- A .FOT file in the Windows System subdirectory corresponding to that listing
- A .TTF file in a directory the .FOT file knows about

These three elements make it easy to maintain font folders for Windows to use only when you need them. All you need is a little patience and a plan.

Planning Font Folders

The first step in setting up several groups of working fonts is to have a clear idea of which fonts belong in which group. Sift through your fonts, decide which go together for particular projects, and make a note of their names. It's fine to have a font in more than one group—certain fonts like Arial are perennial favorites. Once you've settled on a scheme, here's how to break them out:

1. Start the File Manager and change to the Windows system subdirectory.
2. Select View, By File Type, and enter *.**TTF**.
3. Select File, Create directory, and make subdirectories for each of your groups of fonts.
4. Hold down Ctrl and click on the file names of each font that belongs in a group. When you've selected them all, keep holding down Ctrl and drag the files into their group's new subdirectory.
5. Repeat step 4 until all your groups are allocated to their folders.

This much work has set the scene for your font management routine. These next steps remove all the TrueType fonts from Windows. They also delete the .FOT and .TTF files from your Windows System subdirectory, but don't worry about this—you'll have made copies in all your font group subdirectories, and these will take their place during font group installation (described later).

1. From the Program Manager, select the Control Panel and the Fonts applet.
2. In the Installed Fonts list box, press Control and click on each of the TrueType fonts.
3. Click on the Remove button.
4. In the Remove Font dialog box, click on the Remove Font File from Disk check box.
5. Click on Yes to All.

Congratulations. You just cleared a load off your Windows start-up routine. Of course, you also waved goodbye to all your TrueType fonts, so pick one of your font subdirectories for the next stage—installing a font group.

1. Start the Control Panel and select Fonts.
2. Click on the Add button.
3. In the Add Fonts dialog box, change to the appropriate font group's subdirectory. Click on the Select All button to highlight every font in the directory.
4. Click on the Copy Fonts to Windows Directory check box to remove the X, and then click on OK.

5. Back in the Fonts dialog box, wait until each font name has appeared in the Installed Fonts list, and then click on Close.

This system is a bit of a pain to run, as it involves repeated installation and deinstallation of fonts from various directories on your hard disk. It is, however, a proven timesaver. Ooops. Better find something to do with that saved time.

■ Putting a New Face on Windows

New and better fonts are all very well for your documents, but they don't really count as configuring Windows. They are using Windows to configure your documents. This is a good end in itself, but it's not the limit of font use in Windows. Words appear everywhere in Windows—from icon bars to Notepad's text, from dialog boxes and menus to Program Manager icons—and all of them can be changed. Check out Figure 7.6 to see just how far you can take the madness.

The Windows system font rejoices in the euphonic name VGASYS.FON (ah, how it must feel to live on the same disk as Bodoni Poster or Caslon). But there's no reason for you to retain this blocky little font if you don't like it. There are two ways to change the fonts Windows uses for itself, and both involve editing .INI files, so prepare to fire up Sysedit yet again.

More Fonts for Menus and Title Bars

The Windows distribution disks contain several system fonts, but install only one of them. If you find the one on your system too small, too large, or too square, try out the others for size. First, check out your Windows System directory in the File Manager.

Select View, By File Type, and check out the *.FON files. You'll see all the non-TrueType fonts on your system represented there. Assuming you have a VGA system, you'll see two in particular, VGAFIX.FON and VGASYS.FON. These fonts are the ones you see on title bars, dialog boxes, Notepad and Sysedit editing windows, and menus. Hate this font? You can replace it, but only with another system font—either larger or smaller. If you see either EGASYS.FON or 8514SYS.FON lying about your system subdirectory, you'll be able to increase or decrease the size of your system font without further ado. If you don't find these files, you must first expand these fonts from your Windows floppy disks.

The trusty EXPAND program we looked at in Chapter 1 will serve well in the quest for different system fonts. First, find your system fonts on the Windows distribution disks—they'll be somewhere on the first two floppy disks. Need a larger system font? It's on the disk as 8514SYS.FO_. Want a

Figure 7.6

Don't let your Windows desktop look like a "before" picture. The font used in title bars, menus, dialog boxes, and the Notepad can be any .FON file on your hard disk. The font under your Program Manager icons can be any font at all.

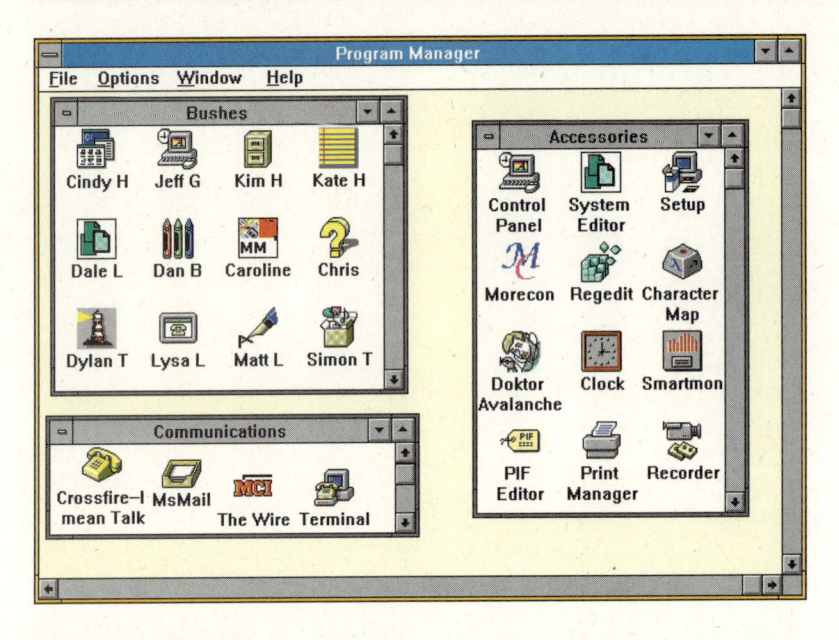

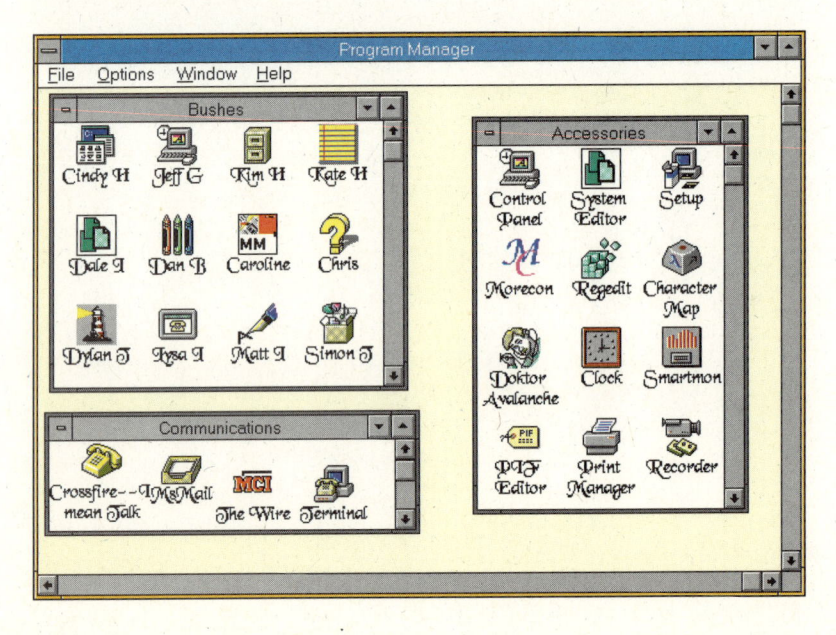

smaller one? Try EGASYS.FO_. Want to try them both? Good! Get to a DOS prompt, use CD to change to the Windows System subdirectory, and then use these lines (assuming the right disk is in your A drive):

```
EXPAND A:\8514SYS.FO_ 8514SYS.FON
EXPAND A:\EGASYS.FO_ EGASYS.FON
```

Thus armed with new system fonts, return to Windows and fire up Sysedit. Click on the SYSTEM.INI window, and read on:

1. Locate the line beginning *fonts.fon=* in the [boot] section. Precede it with a semicolon to comment it out.

2. Under the original line, add a replacement. For a larger system font, enter the line **fonts.fon=8514sys.fon**. For a smaller system font, enter the line **fonts.fon=egasys.fon**.

3. Select File, Exit, and save your changes on the way out.

4. Exit and restart Windows. The new font should be in place in title bars, menus, and dialog boxes.

5. If you encounter a system error message and cannot enter Windows, use the DOS line COPY SYSTEM.SYD SYSTEM.INI to restore your SYSTEM.INI settings. Then try again.

Even More System Fonts

There's not much variety in the designated system fonts. Three choices, and that's your lot. And don't even think of using any other kind of font in your SYSTEM.INI's lines—that's the way to GDI.EXE errors that won't even let you start Windows. Fortunately, there's a little trick for editing WIN.INI that puts more fonts at your menus' and title bars' disposal. It involves adding a new line to WIN.INI that makes any font file with the extension .FON available to your title bars and text editors. It's also possible to make some—but not every—TrueType font into a new system font. You're more likely to fail changing to TrueType system fonts, but that shouldn't stop you if you follow these instructions closely:

1. Open Sysedit and change to WIN.INI's listing.

2. Anywhere in the [Windows] section, add the line **SystemFont=**.

3. To select another font, scroll down to the [fonts] section. Pick any font with a .FON extension, and highlight the name that appears *after* the equal sign (such as SERIFE.FON, SMALLE.FON, or ROMAN.FON). Press Ctrl+Ins to copy the name to the Clipboard.

NOTE. *This technique also works with* some *TrueType fonts (with the extension .FOT), but it won't work with all of them. When you experiment with TrueType system fonts, proceed with caution, and be prepared to reinstate the original WIN.INI in a heartbeat.*

4. Scroll back up to the *SystemFont=* line and press Shift+Ins to paste the exact font name after the equal sign.

5. Select File, Exit, and save your changes on the way out.

6. Exit and restart Windows to implement the changes.

So much for your system font. Now let's get to work on the other fonts Windows uses.

A Change of Icon Label

The font that's used in your Program Manager groups to name each of your program icons is 8-point MS Sans Serif. However, you aren't stuck with that choice (thank goodness). A quick edit of WIN.INI—a process that involves adding two lines that don't exist in the file by default—can put a different font in a different size under your icons. Here's how:

1. Open Sysedit and change to WIN.INI's listing.

2. Scroll down to the [Desktop] section and add these two lines anywhere in the section:

   ```
   IconTitleFaceName=
   IconTitleSize=
   ```

3. To select another font, scroll down to the [fonts] section. Pick any font with a .FON extension, and highlight the name that appears before the equal sign (such as MS Serif, Small Fonts, or Symbol). Press Ctrl+Ins to copy the name to the Clipboard.

4. Scroll back up to the *IconTitleFaceName=* line, and press Shift+Ins to paste the exact font name after the equal sign.

5. If you wish, add a number after *IconTitleSize=* (the default is 8) to increase or decrease the icon title's point size.

6. Select File, Exit, and save your changes on the way out.

7. Exit and restart Windows to implement the changes.

■ What Was the Point of This Chapter?

In "Font Mania," you found out

- The difference between a font and a typeface
- How to remove fonts (or typefaces) from your system
- How to add typefaces (or fonts) to your system
- The best ways to use fonts (or typefaces)
- How to lose your eyesight with the Character Map
- How to waste time managing groups of fonts to save time when you load Windows
- How to change the fonts on title bars, menus, Notepad, and Sysedit, and under Program Manager icons

You also learned more than you ever wanted to know about fonts *and* typefaces.

PART 2

Mismanaging Your Time
Keep Busy without Actually Getting Anything Done

- *Program Mismanagement ... **126***

- *File Mismanagement ... **146***

- *Recorder Macrocosm ... **164***

- *Trash the Program Manager's Settings*
- *Five Steps to a Better Program Manager*
- *Two-fisted Program Management*
- *Shuffling the Program Deck*
- *Five Ways Plug-In Improves Program Management*
- *Cram the Most Icons in the Smallest Space—
  A Button Bar*

- *Manage Program Installations with (gasp!) Batch Files*
- *What Was the Point of This Chapter?*

CHAPTER

8

Program Mismanagement

Waste time with your programs now, save time with them later

YOU'VE ALREADY LEARNED HOW TO RENAME THE PROGRAM MANager's title bar, change its fonts, change its start-up group, put screen-saver icons on its desktop, and alter its icons. What more could you possibly want to know about the Program Manager? Take a deep breath, because there's plenty more. And since the Program Manager (the Windows shell) is your primary contact with Windows, it's your bounden duty to learn all you can. It's the only way to bend Windows to your will.

Chapter 8: Program Mismanagement

Get one thing straight in your mind before you continue: The Windows default settings don't make sense, except to some sheltered programmers in Redmond. They must have realized this, because they provided all the tools for easily rendering the Program Manager unrecognizable. Remember: It's *your* desktop. Nothing about the way Windows programs are arranged is cast in stone, so don't knuckle under to any arrangement you don't like.

■ Trash the Program Manager's Settings

When you first install Windows, it has five program groups: Main, Accessories, Games, Startup and Applications. Each group has its own file in the Windows directory (its file name is a truncated version of the group name, with the extension .GRP), and each group's file is recorded in the Program Manager's initialization file, PROGMAN.INI. The .GRP files are not text files, so you can't fiddle with their settings; PROGMAN.INI is text, and we've already seen in Chapter 1 how to edit it to change the Startup group. Stay tuned for more tricks like this. But first, look at Figure 8.1 and contemplate reasons for destroying and rebuilding the screen.

Figure 8.1

If you can think of three good reasons for retaining this default Program Manager arrangement, retain it. The rest of us will dismantle it in the course of this chapter.

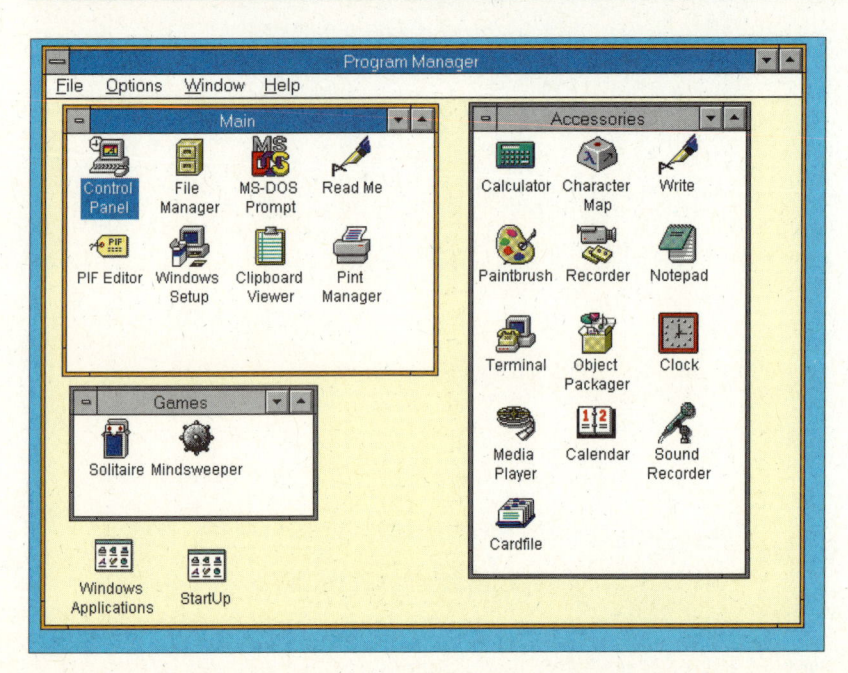

The Main group contains Control Panel, File Manager, Print Manager, Clipboard Viewer, PIF Editor, MS-DOS Prompt, Windows Setup, and Read Me icons. The Main group doesn't contain Solitaire or Minesweeper, the mainest of most people's main applications, which are relegated to their own group (cunningly labeled "Games"). The Accessories group contains Notepad, Write, Terminal, Paintbrush, Recorder, Object Packager, Cardfile, Calendar, Character Map, Clock, Calculator, Sound Recorder, and Media Player. It doesn't contain the crucial accessory Sysedit, which you have to create by selecting File, New, Program Item, and entering SYSEDIT in the Command Line box. The remaining groups contain whichever application icons you choose to set up or have allowed Windows to set up from your hard drive.

Why should you trash this arrangement? The same reason George Leigh Mallory cited for climbing Mount Everest: Because it's there. And unlike Mount Everest, the Program Manager's default setup actually gets in the way of what you want to do. (I'll concede that Everest does this, too, if you're traveling from Shekar Dzong to Bhaktapur, but I suspect more people call up Solitaire during the average work week.)

Gratuitous Tip: Don't Save Changes on Exit

Whenever you quit Windows, one of Windows's final chores is to save all the settings to PROGMAN.INI—whether you've changed anything or not. This can steal five or more seconds every time you quit. A much more efficient method of getting in and out of Windows is to deselect the Program Manager's Options, Save Changes on Exit menu option, so that it isn't marked with a check. Better yet, open PROGMAN.INI using a text editor, and create a section at the end by entering **[Restrictions]** and under it, type the line

```
NoSaveSettings=1
```

Of course, this means that certain settings (including icon arrangement and minimized program groups) aren't automatically saved. After making these additions, saving settings becomes a conscious decision, and it's one that isn't an obvious menu selection (unless you're running Plug-In). To save settings under straight Windows, hold down the Shift key and select File, Exit Windows. Windows will chug away, saving your settings, but your session won't end. Using Plug-In, save settings by checking the exit dialog box's Save Settings button or by selecting Options, Save Settings Now.

■ Five Steps to a Better Program Manager

The idea behind "program mismanagement" is to spend a lot of time now so you don't have to waste time later doing mundane things. The general technique is to put everything you need most where you can get to it and hide the stuff you don't need immediately somewhere you can find it quickly. Unfortunately for all you time wasters, doing this really doesn't take that much time. In just five steps, you too can have the ideal desktop:

1. Get the size of the main Program Manager window right. It should be large enough to show the maximum number of icons, but there should be enough space at the bottom to show the minimized icons of running applications. It should look something like Figure 8.2. See the Gratuitous Tip "Instant Program Manager Settings" for how to do this automatically.

Figure 8.2

This Program Manager arrangement is a little more human than the plug-ugly and random default arrangement. The maximum number of icons available are showing, minimized group icons are accessible, and you're only a click away from minimized applications, too.

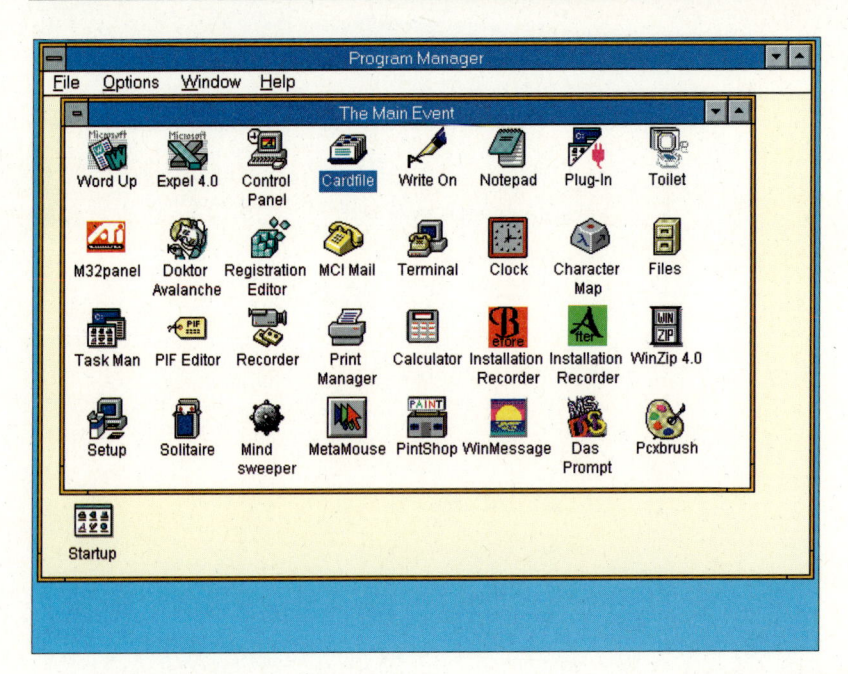

2. Abandon Microsoft's arbitrary distinction between Applications, Main, and Accessories. Pick or make a large group for everything you use regularly, and drag each significant icon into it.

3. Sort the remainder of the icons into "shoebox" groups—either retaining the original name or lumping them into some other group name—and minimize them.

Five Steps to a Better Program Manager

4. When you're done, size your main group's window to fill most of the main Progman window, but leave enough space to show the minimized icons of other Program Manager groups.

5. Sort icons into task specific groups, duplicating icons where necessary, as described in the section "Toolkit Groups—A Place for Everything and Everything in Its Place," below.

Gratuitous Tip: Instant Program Manager Settings

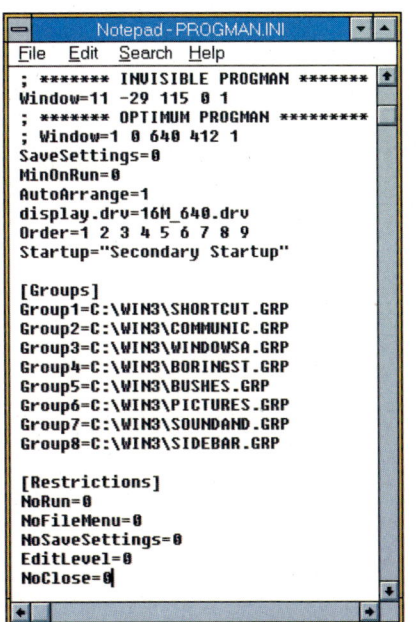

Note. This tip works only when the Program Manager's Options, Save Settings on Exit is not selected, and the changes take effect only when you restart Windows.

```
; ****** INVISIBLE PROGMAN ******
Window=11 -29 115 0 1
; ****** OPTIMUM PROGMAN ******
; Window=1 0 640 412 1
SaveSettings=0
MinOnRun=0
AutoArrange=1
display.drv=16M_640.drv
Order=1 2 3 4 5 6 7 8 9
Startup="Secondary Startup"

[Groups]
Group1=C:\WIN3\SHORTCUT.GRP
Group2=C:\WIN3\COMMUNIC.GRP
Group3=C:\WIN3\WINDOWSA.GRP
Group4=C:\WIN3\BORINGST.GRP
Group5=C:\WIN3\BUSHES.GRP
Group6=C:\WIN3\PICTURES.GRP
Group7=C:\WIN3\SOUNDAND.GRP
Group8=C:\WIN3\SIDEBAR.GRP

[Restrictions]
NoRun=0
NoFileMenu=0
NoSaveSettings=0
EditLevel=0
NoClose=0
```

You don't have to use a mouse to resize the Program Manager. A less obvious way is to edit PROGMAN.INI's *Window=* line. To resize and position the main window to allow the maximum amount of space while still leaving room to show minimized application icons at the bottom of the screen, adjust the line to read:

`Window=1 0 640 412 1`

These settings translate into the pixel measurement of the offset from the left and top, the width and depth of the image, and the offset from the right. Why use this technique instead of the easier mouse dragging? Because this way you can keep several precisely defined settings (commenting out the ones that aren't active) and position the Program Manager window where the mouse alone can't place it—including off screen altogether. This line shrinks the window and hides it just off the upper-left corner of the screen:

`Window=11 -29 115 0 1`

With this setting in place, the only way to access the Program Manager is through the Task List—and even then simply clicking on the Program Manager task won't bring it up. Only Cascade or Tile will do the trick.

Toolkit Groups—A Place for Everything and Everything in Its Place

People work and recreate best when the tools they need are easy to find, and tools are easiest to find when they've been thoughtfully arranged. One of the best arrangements for your Windows tools is in task-specific toolkits. Let's say you need a spreadsheet, a word processor, a database, a calculator, and Solitaire to prepare a budget. (Solitaire is an imperative tool for retaining your sanity during the process.) Get into the Program Manager; select File, New, Program Group; click on OK; name the group Budget, and press Enter. Minimize the group and rearrange the Program Manager until you can see its icon.

Now hold down Control and drag the icons for every program appropriate for doing your budget. Keep the group minimized until your budget cycle begins, and then you'll have everything you need in one place, just two clicks away.

How about those program icons you almost never use or will probably never use? There's no reason to waste valuable screen real estate on icons you won't use, so make a special group for them, too. Call it something suitably forbidding, like Icon Graveyard, Rejects, or Useless. The prime candidates for this group are the Main group's Read Me and Print Manager icons. Yes, it's nice to be able to check out information on networking, memory management, and hardware configurations, and to examine your print queue, but to most people, they aren't worth the hundred pixels square occupied by each icon and its surrounding space. But they might be useful someday…so keep 'em, but keep 'em hidden.

■ Two-fisted Program Management

So you're in your pristinely arranged Program Manager. What's next? Something to do with programs, perhaps? Maybe load one? OK, but first, ask yourself whether double-clicking on an icon is the quickest and easiest way to do it. Most of the time, the answer will be yes, but if you have two hands on the keyboard, and you don't happen to have a third hand (a more common happenstance than most GUI boosters are prepared to admit), there's a quicker way to load a program.

If the program you want to launch happens to be in the active program group, just tap on the first letter of the program's name (as it appears under the icon). The "selected program" highlight will zoom to the first program icon that starts with the letter. If you want the Control Panel, but the highlight jumps to the Calculator, press C a second time. OK, so this gets you to the Clipboard, but another C will send the highlight to the Control Panel. Press Enter, and it'll load. Unless you have seven or more programs with the same initial letter, it will always be quicker and more efficient to load a program using the initial letter trick.

Oooops! Sorry, this is a book about *wasting* time. OK, here's a way to waste time now (though it will save time *later*): Assign keyboard shortcuts and label the icons with them. The technique is easy:

1. Hold down Alt and double-click on the icon of one of your frequently used programs.

2. In the Properties box, click once on the Shortcut Key box.

3. Press any key. In the Shortcut Key box, the characters *Ctrl + Alt +* will appear, followed by the letter you pressed. Press Shift and a letter, and *Ctrl + Alt + Shift +* will appear, followed by the letter.

4. When you've decided on a permanent shortcut key, select the Description box, and after the program's name, copy the shortcut key combination from the Shortcut Key box.

5. Click on OK or press Enter. In the Program Manager group, the caption under the program's icon will show up. If the caption word-wraps strangely, return to the Properties box and enter extra spaces.

Note. This technique works fine until you attempt to assign a shortcut key that's already assigned. You won't be allowed to assign the same shortcut to two programs in the same group. You can for programs in different groups, but you'll be warned first.

Now you're set. Keep your hands off the mouse, and launch the program using just the shortcut keys. This launching technique works as long as the Program Manager is the active application and the program group containing the application is maximized.

Once you've loaded an application that has a shortcut key combination assigned to it, you can switch to it directly from any other application by pressing the key combination again.

■ Shuffling the Program Deck

Now that you've got several applications running, take the time to show off your Windows prowess. Don't ever confess that you always swap between open Windows applications by minimizing the one you're running and maximizing one of the ones behind it. And don't admit that you always use two clicks on the mouse to launch a program. Only those who haven't spent long enough wasting time in Windows always take the same dull route. The other means to the same end are legion. They are also more interesting.

Let's take switching between applications, for example. The fastest way is to press Alt+Tab. When you do this under Windows 3.0, and in certain circumstances under Window 3.1, you'll see the title bar and outline of the next window in line appear. Keep Alt pressed down and hit Tab again, and another window's outline will appear. Want to reverse? Simultaneously press Shift+Alt+Tab (if you can manage this feat of digital Twister), and the last window shows up. Release the Alt key, and the outline window will fill in. Presto! You're in another application.

But this is only the second-quickest method of window swapping. The quickest is the Windows 3.1 default, wittily entitled Fast "Alt+Tab" Switching—an option in the Control Panel's Desktop. When this option is checked off, pressing Alt+Tab kicks up a nicely bezeled box in the middle of your screen containing the name and icon of the next application. It's an object of beauty and a joy forever. And it's faster than the other way. In fact, there's no earthly reason for using the other way. That's why the Microsoft programmers chose the name of the WIN.INI line that the Fast "Alt+Tab" Switching box changes—*CoolSwitch=1*. It is indeed a cool way to switch.

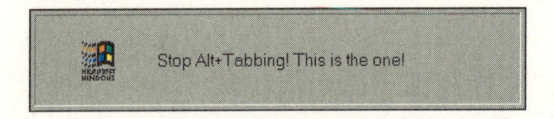

> Stop Alt+Tabbing! This is the one!

Of course, cool is the way of hippies and programmers—neither of which I and most people would ever confess to being. The goal-oriented, strictly business way to switch applications is using the Task List—a term that reeks of corporate efficiency. The technique itself isn't too corporate or efficient, but it has one or two benefits over Coolswitching.

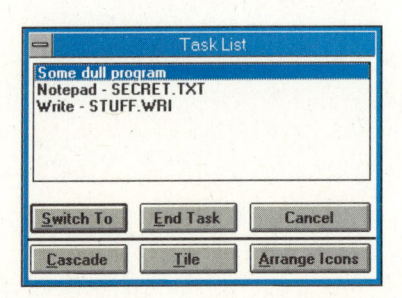

> Task List
> Some dull program
> Notepad - SECRET.TXT
> Write - STUFF.WRI
>
> [Switch To] [End Task] [Cancel]
> [Cascade] [Tile] [Arrange Icons]

Press Ctrl+Esc and the Task List will appear. In its window is an alphabetical list of the active applications you're currently running. (If you renamed the Program Manager as shown in Chapter 1, the changed name is the one that appears on the list.) To switch between applications, just click twice on the name of the running application in the Task List—or press its initial letter followed by Enter. This is not much of an advantage over Alt+ Tabbing through open applications, but the advantage to Task Listing lies in its handling of open windows. Three Task List buttons are key in this.

The End Task button doesn't need much explanation. If you're running short of memory or other Windows resources, call up the Task List, click once on an application you don't need to have running, and click on End Task. Then say hello to the resources you wanted.

The other two key buttons are Cascade and Tile, as shown in Figure 8.3. Both change the shape and position of the application windows you're running. Cascade makes each application window fairly large and stacks them so their title bars and upper-left corners are all showing. If you've not already cascaded your windows, you'll still find it familiar: Sysedit uses a cascade arrangement to display its four files.

Note. Cascading and tiling are not merely options in the Task List—they're also available for the windows in the Program Manager. But don't use them there unless you've first turned off Options, Save Settings On Exit—otherwise your pristine arrangements will get messed up.

The Tile button divides up the screen, allocates a space to each application, and resizes the windows to fit in the space. If you have any more than two applications running (including the Program Manager), don't think about tiling them. Unless you're cutting and pasting objects between applications or using drag-and-drop to move things between the File and Program Managers, tiling makes application windows too small and weirdly shaped to do any meaningful work in them. You can regain a little space by minimizing a few applications before you tile, but it's still less than optimal. You know what they say: A miss is as good as a tile.

Time-Wasting Tip: Use Solitaire as Task List

Does pressing Alt+Tab meet all your program switching needs? Why not reassign the Ctrl+Esc key combination to another application that you use often—such as the Program Manager, Sysedit, or, more likely, Solitaire? First, check the exact name of the program (SOL.EXE for Solitaire, for example). Then fire up Sysedit and switch to SYSTEM.INI. In the [boot] section, look for the line that reads

```
taskman.exe=taskman.exe
```

Change the name after the equals sign to the name of your chosen application. Now whenever you click twice on the wallpaper or press Ctrl+ Esc, you can indulge in a different kind of task management.

Figure 8.3

Want to know the difference between tiled and cascaded windows? The screen on top shows tiled windows; the one below shows cascaded windows.

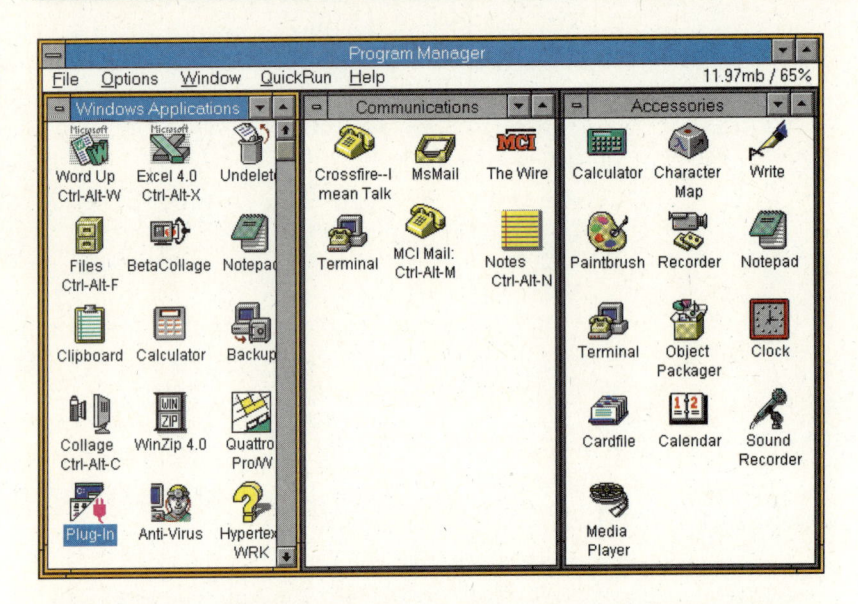

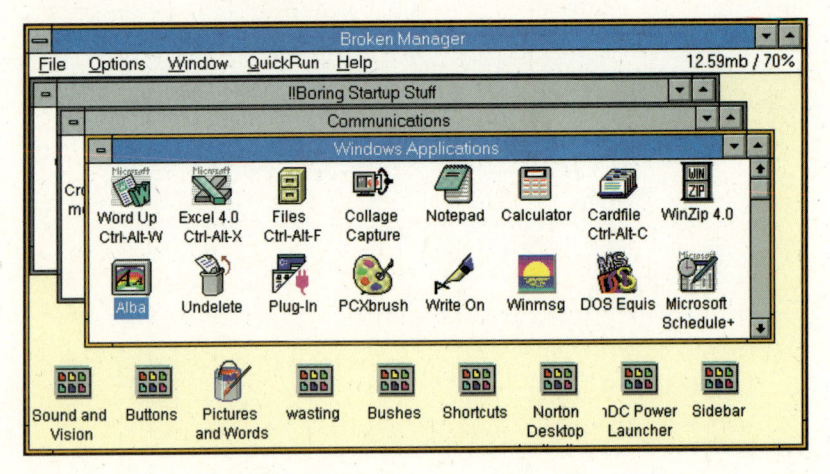

■ Five Ways Plug-In Improves Program Management

Once you've exhausted the possibilities of Program Manager (which should take a while), the next step is to try out Plug-In's offerings. Plannet Crafters's add-in for the Program Manager does for program management what the Control Panel does for changing the appearance of your Windows desktop—namely, makes it fun and easy to experiment with.

But unlike the Control Panel, Plug-In can do things you just can't do with the Program Manager alone. Here are five improvements Plug-In provides over plain Progman—each one of which is an addition to the Program Manager's own menu system. Plug-In has more than these five tricks up its sleeve (some of which you can read about in the chapters on cursors and icons), but these are the killer program management functions that you'll wonder how you did without.

See How They Run

Tired of typing command lines in the Program Manager's File Run dialog box? Plug-In adds a command line history to the File Run dialog box that takes the typing out of command reruns. Select File, Run, and click the down arrow next to the Command Line box. You'll see all the command lines you've run while Plug-In was active. To rerun one, click on it.

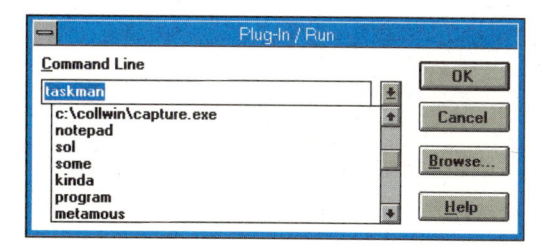

The default length of the command history pick list is 25 items—but you can increase that to any number up to 99. To effect the increase, use the Notepad to open PLUGIN.INI, and under [Settings], change the *History-Count=* line to read whatever number you want. If you want to keep the number small, you can also reduce the number to as little as ten.

See How Quickly They Run

Using File Run is all well and good, but for *really* fast access to a command or program, use the QuickRun menu. There are six offerings by default, but nothing is set in stone. You change any of the default offerings and increase

138 Chapter 8: Program Mismanagement

the list to 25 selections using the Options, Configure Plug-In menu option. In the Plug-In / Configure box, click on the QuickRun Menu button. In the dialog box that pops up, you can either add or modify a QuickRun menu item.

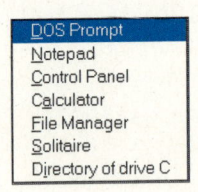

```
DOS Prompt
Notepad
Control Panel
Calculator
File Manager
Solitaire
Directory of drive C
```

The first step in adding an item is to click on the Insert button, and the first step in modifying one is to select it in the QuickRun menu box. After that, the steps are the same for both processes: Add a name in the box, preceding the active letter with an ampersand. &Minesweeper, for example, would appear in the menu as <u>M</u>inesweeper, and you'd load it by pressing Alt+Q to activate the QuickRun menu, and then pressing M. Enter a command line and working directory in the appropriate boxes, and click OK.

Incredible Shrinking Program Groups

Mired down in open program groups that you can't get through by pressing Alt+Tab? Reduce them all to a manageable state in a single move: Press Alt+N (or select Window, Minimize All Groups), and all the groups will shrink into icons. On a hectic Monday morning, this simple function makes all the difference.

Group Management

Now that you've been adding to your collection of Program Manager groups, you'll need a hand in managing them—and each of the File, Group menu's options lends a hand. These four options—Copy, Reposition, StartUp, and Manage—each bring a particular skill that Program Manager lacks.

The Copy option makes a duplicate of any group, which is very hand for creating task-specific groups, like the ones discussed in the section "Toolkit Groups—A Place for Everything and Everything in Its Place." It's also easy: Select a group, name a new group, and click on OK.

The Reposition option reverts the program group arrangement to the last-saved version—a handy little "undo" function for when you get bogged down in shuffling groups.

The StartUp option changes or disables the designated Startup group. It's easier to use than editing the PROGMAN.INI line, as you can see from the illustration—you just pick a name from a list box. Alternatively, you can disable all Startup groups by selecting <<No StartUp Group>>.

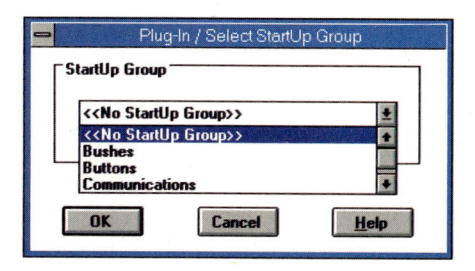

NOTE. *You can also change the Startup group by adding a line to the end of PROGMAN.INI's [Settings] section. At the* Startup="Group" *line, add the exact name of a group, as it appears in its title bar.*

The Manage option is really handy for those who create far too many groups (and we all do). You use Manage to disable groups temporarily and bring them back into commission easily when you need them. It's a self-explanatory process, accomplished by a deceptively simple technique: Plug-In disables a group by renaming it (with the extension .G_P) and by removing the PROGMAN.INI line that identifies the group. The inactive groups list box (see the illustration below) is created from a file listing of all files with the extension .G_P. Since group files contain all the icon and program information, restoring them is as simple as renaming the file and letting PROGMAN.INI know where they are.

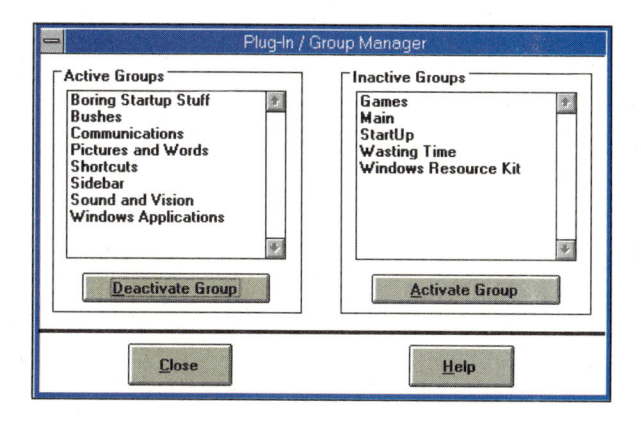

Installation Made Absurdly Easy

Install many programs? Don't numb your typing fingers or wade through unnecessary steps. Select File, Install Application, and let Plug-In do the work. It will check both floppy drives for programs called Install or Setup, and offer to show you any Read Me files first.

■ Cram the Most Icons in the Smallest Space—A Button Bar

The techniques we've covered cram a lot of programs into a little space. On a VGA monitor, you can fit 32 icons into the program group described in "Five Steps to a Better Program Manager" (assuming your icon spacing is set to 70 with vertical spacing at 65), and you'll still have space to spare for minimized program icons. That's plenty for most people, but if you find yourself short on space and long on applications, cram in more icons per square inch by crunching the icons tightly together and discarding their names.

To do so, pick a few applications that you use so often you don't need to show their names or keyboard shortcuts. Then follow these steps:

1. First create a new group in the Program Manager: Choose File, New, select Program Group, and click on OK. Name the group, call the file BUTTONS.GRP (or something else you'll remember), and click on OK.

2. Move or copy the programs you use most often into the new group. To move them, click once on their icons and drag them into the new group; to copy them, hold down Ctrl and drag them.

3. Clear all the icon titles from the new group: Hold down Alt and double-click on a program's icon. In the Program Item Properties dialog box, press the spacebar to replace the title, and then click on OK.

4. Start up Sysedit and select the window containing WIN.INI. In the [Desktop] section, set the *IconSpacing=* and *IconVerticalSpacing=* lines to 35. (Add an *IconVerticalSpacing=* line if it isn't already there.)

5. Quit Sysedit, saving your changes. Exit and restart Windows.

6. Resize and position your new group to suit your arrangement, and then choose Window, Arrange Icons to tidy up its icons. Then hold down Shift while selecting File, Exit Windows to save your Program Manager desktop.

Gratuitous Tip: Keep Many Groups in Order

Maintain more than nine groups? If you look for them under the Program Manager's Window menu, you may need to go into a supplementary list—Progman's list goes no further than group number nine. But you can bring any group to the head of the list by editing PROGMAN.INI's [Settings] section. There, you'll find a line reading something like this:

```
Order= 1 2 3 4 5 6 7 8 9 10 11 12
```

Under the [Groups] section, you'll see a list of group names with their numbers, in this format:

```
Group2=C:\WINDOWS\GROUP.GRP
```

To bring group 12 to the head of the menu, for example, select it and the space before it in the *Order=* line, press Shift+Del to delete it, and then move the cursor to directly after the equals sign. Press Shift+Ins to paste the number in, double-check that there are spaces on either side of the number, and then save the file. The next time you load the Program Manager, the group will be where you want it.

---

7. Open File Manager and select the BUTTONS.GRP from the Windows subdirectory. Press Alt+Enter to bring up its properties, put an *X* in the Read-Only box, and click on OK.

8. Still in the File Manager, select WIN.SYD (the Sysedit backup of WIN.INI), press F7, and enter **WIN.INI**. When you click on OK, the WIN.INI file with your old icon spacing settings will be restored.

9. Exit and restart Windows.

Because the button bar group is read-only, you can't move or rearrange it—which means that you can always depend on it to look the same. To change its layout, first select it in the File Manager and remove its Read-Only attribute. Then add or remove icons, change the spacing, or perform some other operation. Remember to reset the Read-Only attribute again when you're done.

Manage Program Installations with (gasp!) Batch Files

Windows programs are your worst enemy when it comes to maintaining the orderly desktop you've spent hours creating. Not only do they make arbitrary changes to your Program Manager by slapping on full-sized program groups (containing a mere three or four icons) but they also change settings and file structures beneath the surface, so that you don't know what effect they are having. Practice the old school of program management. Take control of installation programs—or at least be aware of what they do behind the scenes.

No matter how diligent you are, you'll never be able to track everything an installation program does. However, you *can* see the results in plain text using two DOS batch files. (Don't panic! Once they're set up, they're a breeze to use.) *PC/Computing* Help editor Dylan Tweney's Before and After batch files are included on the disk in the back of this book, and they work fine under Windows using the .PIF files included. Follow the instructions in the Appendix to install them, and then read on.

Before and After are pretty obvious to use. Before installing a program, double-click on the Before file. It will open a dull DOS window and periodically throw up a line explaining what's taking so long. It's making a series of text files in the WINDOWS\INSTALL subdirectory, each of which is either a backup of an .INI or other configuration file or a listing of the contents of directories. This record covers most of the important areas that Windows installation programs tend to alter—AUTOEXEC.BAT, CONFIG.SYS, and the Windows .INI files, including those for the Control Panel, Program Manager, and File Manager. It's also recording the directory structure of all the hard drives and partitions it can find, and exhaustively listing the contents of the root directory and your Windows and System subdirectories.

When Before has completed its work, you install your program in the usual way. After installation is done, click on the After icon. AFTER.PIF prompts you for a parameter, which is its prosaic way of asking for an eight-character description of the program you've just installed. Press Enter, and AFTER.BAT starts its work. It creates directory listings in temporary text files. It then takes these and the configuration and .INI files, and compares them to the versions BEFORE.BAT created. The results are written into a text file with the same name as the parameter you entered. When AFTER.BAT is finished, open the text file and check it out.

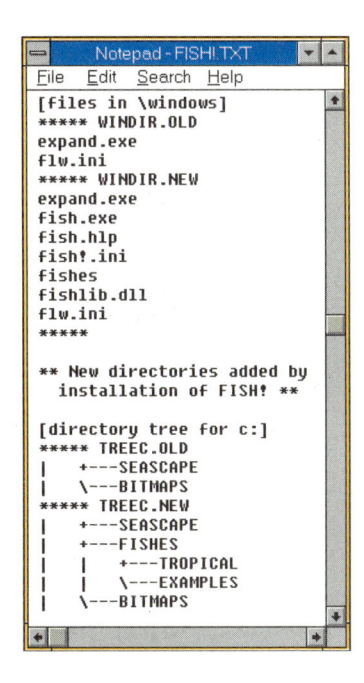

```
            ┌─────────────────────────────┐
            │ ─  Notepad - FISH!.TXT  ▼ ▲ │
            ├─────────────────────────────┤
            │ File  Edit  Search  Help    │
            ├─────────────────────────────┤
            │ [files in \windows]       ↑ │
            │ ***** WINDIR.OLD            │
            │ expand.exe                  │
            │ flw.ini                     │
            │ ***** WINDIR.NEW            │
            │ expand.exe                  │
            │ fish.exe                    │
            │ fish.hlp                    │
            │ fish!.ini                   │
            │ fishes                      │
            │ fishlib.dll                 │
            │ flw.ini                     │
            │ *****                       │
            │                             │
            │ ** New directories added by │
            │    installation of FISH! ** │
            │                             │
            │ [directory tree for c:]     │
            │ ***** TREEC.OLD             │
            │ |    +---SEASCAPE           │
            │ |    \---BITMAPS            │
            │ ***** TREEC.NEW             │
            │ |    +---SEASCAPE           │
            │ |    +---FISHES             │
            │ |    |   +---TROPICAL       │
            │ |    |   \---EXAMPLES       │
            │ |    \---BITMAPS          ↓ │
            │ ←                         → │
            └─────────────────────────────┘
```

Let's say you installed a program that made no changes to WIN.INI or SYSTEM.INI. In the file, under the heading "Changes made to INI files by installation of *program name*" you'll find headings [win.ini] and [system.ini] with nothing under them. If the installation program has reset a line, the text file created by After will contain a comparison of both versions, like this:

```
[win.ini]

***** WIN.OLD
shb=D:\CORELDRW\SHOW\corelshw.exe ^.shb

***** C:\WIN30\WIN.INI
shb=D:\CORELDRW\SHOW\corelshw.exe ^.shb
oaf=D:\OAF\cretin.exe ^.oaf
```

After the section dealing with changes to .INI files, there's a record of the changes made to directory structures. These also show changes made in the specific context.

If you ever need to remove an application from your hard disk, the text file created by AFTER.BAT is the first thing to turn to. Either print it out, or load it into Notepad and tile it next to the File Manager. The file lists every addition or change to the directory structure made by installing the application—so to remove every trace of the application, remove all the changes listed. Then load Sysedit and restore each of its four files to the way it appears in the Old line. When you're done, it will be as though the program were never there.

> ### Gratuitous Tip: Before and After—Better and Faster
>
> Before and After check for the existence of drive letters up to drive F:. If you install applications to drives beyond F:, you'll need to add references to them. If you won't be installing Windows applications to a given drive, you can speed up Before and After incrementally by excluding such drives from the recording and comparison. In Notepad, open *both* batch files in turn, and look for lines beginning:
>
> ```
> for %%d in (c d e f) do if
> ```
>
> Change the letters in parentheses to include or exclude drives. To ensure you've edited them correctly, double-click on the Before icon. Immediately after BEFORE.BAT finishes, click on the After icon. When asked for a parameter, enter **NOTHING** and press Enter. When After is finished, check out NOTHING.TXT from the WINDOWS\INSTALL subdirectory. This should show no changes anywhere if you edited correctly.

Just as there's a thin line between management and mismanagement, the distinction between managing programs and managing files is a thin one. In Windows terms, the distinction is one between two applications—cunningly entitled Program Manager and File Manager. In this book, the distinction is even thinner—paper-thin, in fact. Turn the page for more mismanagement—of files, this time.

What Was the Point of This Chapter?

In "Program Mismanagement," you learned:

- What to do with the default Program Manager setup (that is, change it beyond recognition)
- How to arrange program groups for maximum usability

What Was the Point of This Chapter? 145

- How to start applications and switch from one to another with grace and efficiency
- The advantage of using Plug-In for Program Manager
- How to find out what havoc program installations wreak behind the scenes

- *Bend the File Manager to Your Will*
- *An Aside: File Management Made Incredibly Difficult*
- *A Sensible Arrangement*
- *Dragon Dropping Your Way to Cleaner Windows Directories*
- *An Association of Files, Desktop, and Printer*

- *Space Case: Too Many Files Spoil the Disk*
- *What Was the Point of This Chapter?*

CHAPTER

9

File Mismanagement

Forcing your hard disk into line the Windows way

Neither DOS nor Windows tells you when or how to sort your files. This is a good thing because you're free to make your own decisions. And it's a bad thing, because nobody does filing unless they're forced to. And while these operating environments seem so laissez-faire, they enforce an absurd restriction: File and directory names can be no more than eight characters long, with an optional extension of three additional characters.

Such is the cross we bear for using a system based on DOS. But like any rigidly structured task that you aren't forced to do unless you're in the mood, file management can be a very creative process. It's not like writing sonnets or sonatas, but there's still room for a little style and a lot of wasted time.

■ Bend the File Manager to Your Will

Fresh out of the box, the File Manager is fussier than the prissiest person you've ever dealt with. When you attempt to do practically anything, it asks if you're sure you want to go through with it, which gets irritating after the third reminder.

The very first file management task, then, should be getting the File Manager to lighten up. Only then can you turn your attention to making the File Manager look the way you want it to. Under the Options menu, select Confirmation and pause for reflection. The options that face you are File Delete, Directory Delete, File Replace, Mouse Action, and Disk Commands.

Does your blood pressure rise every time you're asked whether you really intend to go ahead and delete a file? Do you find yourself muttering "No, I selected that file and hit Delete to hear the keyboard clicking"? Chill out, be happy, live longer: Uncheck the File Delete option in the Confirmation box. With DOS 6.0, Norton Desktop, and much of the time with DOS 5.0, you can undelete a file you deleted by mistake, so go ahead…uncheck it.

Directory Delete and File Replace are a different matter. You don't delete directories often, so the reminder isn't too annoying. And you never want to overwrite a newer file with an older version of the same file. And in both cases, it's next to impossible to undo a mistake, so leave that check mark where it is unless you're rabidly against Windows solicitations—and you're utterly convinced that you won't make mistakes.

The most irritating confirmation dialog box occurs when Mouse Action is checked. This dialog box indicates that Windows doesn't trust you to drag and drop properly. With this box checked, every time you drag a file into another directory or disk, you must confirm that you're sure you dragged it to the right place. You can uncheck this option and never look back (unless you're hopelessly ham-handed with your mouse).

The odds that you'll do something hopelessly inept with Disk Commands is fairly remote, but before you make a decision you might regret, check out all the options in the Disk menu. See anything risky there? Any danger you might format the wrong disk? Have you done it in the past? No? Fine. Uncheck that box and wave good-bye to oversolicitous Windows. Now get on with the real business of file management.

Face-lift Your File Manager

Before doing anything too radical—such as using the File Manager to manage your files—decide whether the program looks as good as it might. If you like the way it looks, leave it as you find it. If you aren't so sure, read on for ways to change the font and other elements of the Winfile window. You too could have a File Manager like the one in Figure 9.1.

I'm assuming that the element you want to see the most of in the File Manager is files. (Call me old-fashioned.) But the way the File Manager is set up by default, you don't see that many files, and the ones you do see aren't very clear. Blame it on the display font—it's MS-Sans Serif, 8-point, uppercase. Sans serif fonts *are* the best for displaying lots of text on screen, but uppercase text is hard to read and takes up more space to boot. Try out lowercase for size: Select Options, Font, and in the dialog box that appears, click on the Lowercase box to put a check mark in it.

While you're still in the Font dialog box, try out another font. A good one to start with is 8-point Arial, but your choices are many. Bear this in mind: Serif and decorative fonts are tough to read on screen. Fonts smaller than 8 points will be unreadable on most screens, and much above 10, they take up too much space. And the cruelest trick to play on someone is to select 4-point Small Fonts Bold Italic on their machine with Options, Save Settings on Exit deselected—even if the unsuspecting victim knows how to change the font back, the illegible blobs of small font will return next time the File Manager's opened. (*Disclaimer*: I'm not suggesting you do this. Just daydream about it sometime.)

So much for changing fonts. There's more to avoiding real file management than a little cosmetic work—much more.

Files from Another Point of View

Want to change the face of the File Manager some more? Go to it. There's barely an element that you can't change in some way. Want to see fewer files with more details? Select View, and select an option from the menu section that contains Name, All File Details, and Partial Details. The Name option throws on-screen the names of files in a given directory and that's all. All File Details adds the file size in bytes, the date and time the file was last modified, and the file's attributes. Partial Details gives you the choice of any combination of these details.

NOTE. *Having just the name showing in the File Manager doesn't prevent you from quickly seeing all the details of a file. Press Alt+Enter with a file name highlighted, and a Properties box will appear. Here, you can see all you need to see and can assign any of the RASH attributes (namely, Read-only, Archive, System, and Hidden).*

150 Chapter 9: File Mismanagement

Figure 9.1

(a) The File Manager isn't the most attractive of programs by its very nature—but you needn't put up with vile uppercase 8-point MS-Sans Serif file names for a moment longer. (b) Squeeze more (and more legible) file names into the mix instead.

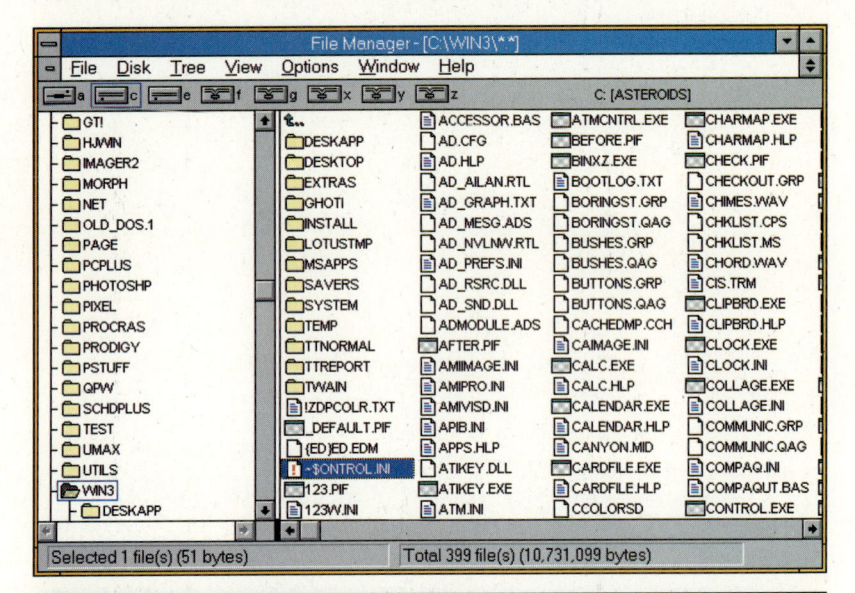

Not enough customization? Hungry for more? How about sorting the files in a different order? By default, the files are in ascending alphabetical order by file name, but that's not permanent. Under View, check out the Sort By options. Click in the file window, and select View, Sort By Extension. The files are thrown into alphabetical order by extension. Then there's Sort by

Size—handy if you're short of disk space and want to purge files. With this option checked, you can scroll to the top of the list and start axing the largest superfluous files. Finally, there's Sort by Date. This one's handy when you're looking through your Windows directory or any other one for files that other programs threw there, and for those that belong to Windows itself. It's also useful for digging up files you made or modified recently, but just can't find.

WINDOWS TRIVIA. *In both Windows and DOS, Microsoft uses a special code to show the version of the program—namely the time stamp. With View, Full Details enabled, check out the time column. Most Windows files (except WIN.COM itself, which you rebuilt in Chapter 1) have the date stamp 3:10:00, which means they are from the first release of Windows version 3.10. As minor upgrades are introduced, the seconds zone increases.*

The final set of file presentation criteria is hidden under View, By File Type. The primary use of this option is to filter extraneous files when you're looking for specific ones. Hunting for some .BMP files? Select View, By File Type, and type ***.BMP** in the Name box. (If you're doing a dedicated search across your disk, it's probably better to collect specific files by using File, Search and selecting the root directory—C:\, for example—as the Start From location.)

Here in the By File type dialog box, you can also choose whether directories will appear at the top of the file window and which types of files will show up there. Your file choices are

- Programs—files with the extension .PIF, .EXE, .BAT, .COM, and .SCR that are marked in the file window with squat gray icons

- Documents—any file that's associated as the document of a Windows application and marked with a piece-of-paper icon crossed with horizontal lines

- Other files—those marked with a blank piece of paper icon

Which Files Would You Like?

You've already altered how the File Manager displays its wares. Now it's time to work on which wares it displays. Like any program that supports the infamous *multiple document interface* (or MDI, if you prefer), the File Manager has a Window menu that enables you to switch between and arrange several open views. Unlike other MDI programs, you don't use File, Open to open a window. Instead, click twice on a drive icon in the ribbon between the menu bar and the file window proper. To change the current window into the new view, click on it once.

Gratuitous Tip: A Miss Is As Good As a Tile

Notice how when you select Window, Tile, all your open windows are stacked one on top of the other, as below? Well, it doesn't work the same way when you press the keyboard shortcut Ctrl+F4. That command stacks the open windows side by side across the screen—which can show a lot more of your files, as you can see on the facing page. If you keep forgetting the keyboard shortcut, you can always make Window, Tile do side-by-side tiling: Hold down Shift when you select Tile, and the windows will line up shoulder-to-shoulder.

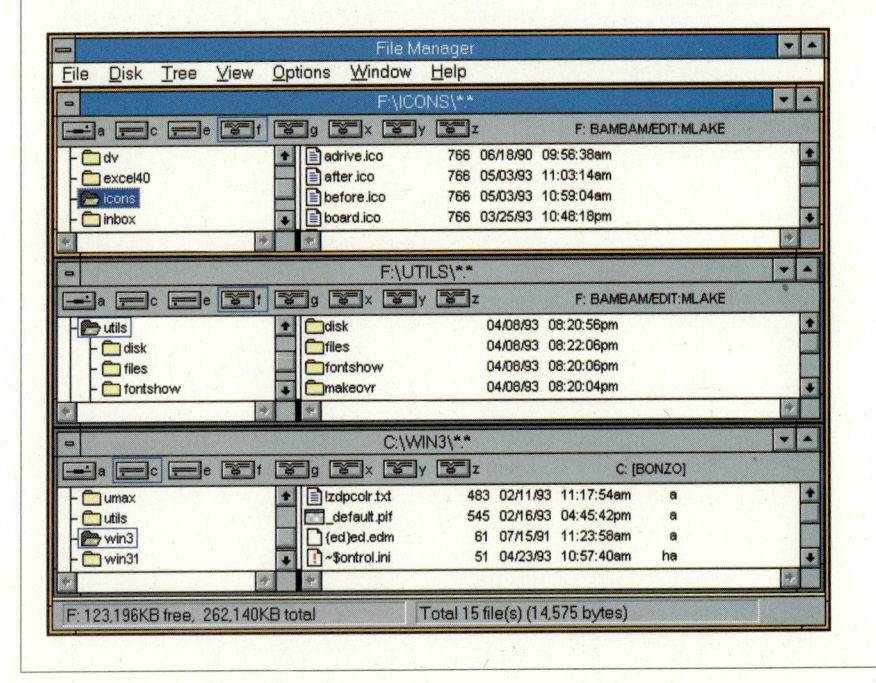

That's all most people know about how to open File Manager windows, but in fact, there are several other ways. The first and fastest is to hold down Ctrl and enter the letter of the drive you want to open. This changes the current window into a view of the drive you're looking for. Then there's Ctrl+Shift, plus the drive letter. This changes the current window into a view of the drive with every subdirectory showing (which takes a while longer than Ctrl and the drive letter alone). And if you're a vertical kind of person instead of a horizontal one, click twice anywhere on the drive letter ribbon

Bend the File Manager to Your Will   **153**

> ### Gratuitous Tip: A Miss Is As Good As a Tile
> *(continued)*
>
> [File Manager screenshot showing three tiled panes: F:\ICONS*.*, F:\UTILS*.*, and C:\WIN3*.*]

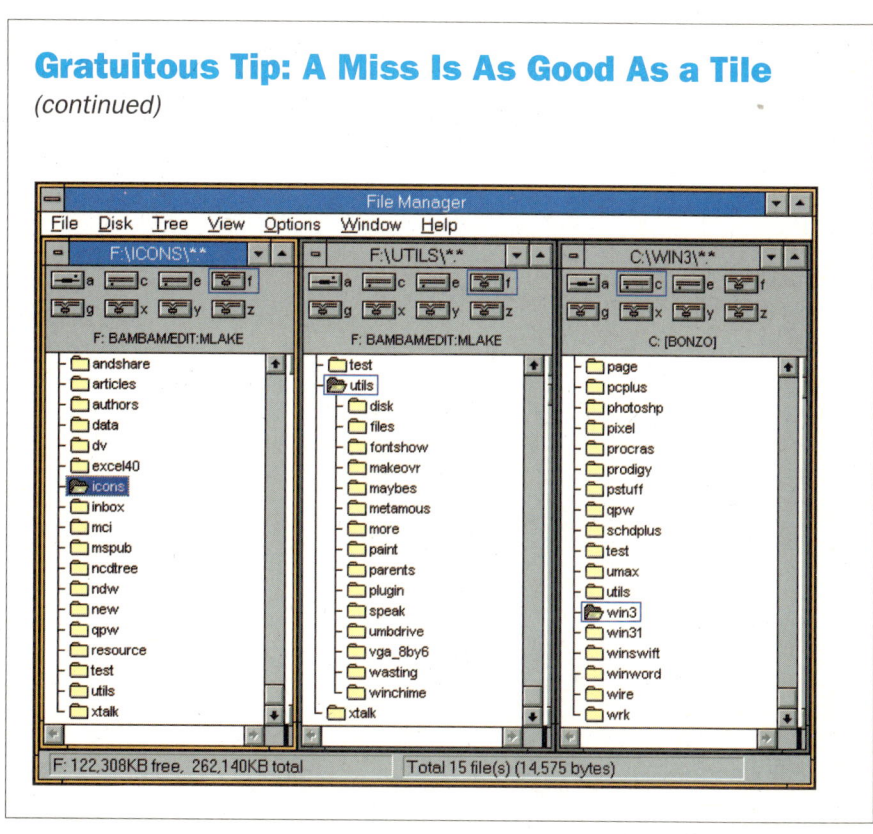

(except on a drive letter), and a vertical scrolling list of drives will appear, from which you can make your selection. This technique shows you all the drive names as well as their letters, and looks uncannily like Figure 9.2.

Figure 9.2

You too can name your hard drive—and after you do, pick your disks from the File Manager's Disk, Select Drive command to be regaled with the full roll call.

[Select Drive dialog box showing:
Drives:
A:
C: [OTIS]
D: [MARVIN]
E: [RAY]
G: [LOUIS]
with OK, Cancel, Help buttons]

Ah, yes, drive names. Giving pet names to your drives and disks is the kind of thing most people associate with the Mac, but Windows users can also waste their time at it. Of course, the File Manager is one of the only places you'll see them. The technique is in plain sight: Just use the Disk menu option Label Disk. The restrictions are hidden, but many. You can't use spaces, colons, periods, question marks, slashes, brackets, parentheses, ampersands, chevrons, carets, asterisks, or quotes. Apart from that, you can use anything you like, except that you have an 11-character maximum. Have fun.

■ An Aside: File Management Made Incredibly Difficult

I know what you're thinking. You have a book that's supposed to be about having fun in Windows, and you're being forced to read about the deadliest dull subject under the sun. You're feeling cheated. You're ready to skip on to the fun stuff and ignore this chapter. Well, this section's for you. I'm not going to sound like Pollyanna here ("No, really, file management can be fun!"). Instead, I'm letting you in on a deeper truth: Subversive tricks can be fun. Here's one such trick to play on a friend. Hey, you've read a few pages of information about file management—you deserve the break. The only drawback is that it requires the impressively ugly MS-DOS Executive that last shipped with Windows 3.0. If you installed Windows 3.1 into the same directory as 3.0, it'll be there. If you didn't, you must extract it from the Windows 3.0 distribution disks. Then, try this out for size:

1. In the Program Manager, select the File Manager icon and press Alt+Enter.

2. In the Command Line box, replace WINFILE.EXE with MSDOS.EXE.

3. Select Change Icon, and browse for WINFILE.EXE. Select the regular File Manager icon, and click on OK. Click on OK again, and you'll be returned to the Program Manager.

4. Click on the File Manager icon, and you'll see the monstrous MS-DOS Executive in all its monochrome splendor. Yes, it's a file manager, but without color, drag and drop, or any other redeeming factor.

This trick has one major drawback: The title bar, the minimized icon, and the About menu all tell the duped party about the switch you've made. It doesn't take much investigation to figure out that a program with MS-DOS Executive in its title bar isn't the File Manager. Don't worry. With a little bit of code hacking, you can remove that clue. Here's how:

1. While still in MS-DOS Executive, scroll over to MSDOS.EXE and highlight it. Select File, Copy, and create a backup called **MSDOS.BAK**.

An Aside: File Management Made Incredibly Difficult

2. Now scroll over to WRITE.EXE, highlight the file name, and press Enter to load Write.

3. In Write, select File, Open, and type in **MSDOS.EXE**.

4. Click on No Conversion.

5. When the file's open, select Find, Replace, and enter **MS-DOS Executive** in the Find What box.

6. Since this is code we're hacking, we need to replace the legend with the same number of characters to ensure that the program will run. In the Replace With box, enter two spaces followed by **File Manager**, followed by two more spaces, for 16 characters in all—the same number as in the name MS-DOS Executive.

7. Click on Replace All.

8. Still in Find, Replace, enter **A&bout MS-DOS Exec** in Find What and under Replace With, enter **A&bout Mismanager**, followed by a space.

9. Click on Replace, and when the replacement has finished, click on Close. Exit Write, saving the changes you've made.

There. That spiced up file management a little—and created the monster in Figure 9.3. Now it's time to get back to business.

Figure 9.3

Wouldn't you rather see this than the File Manager every time you click on the File Manager icon? Me neither.

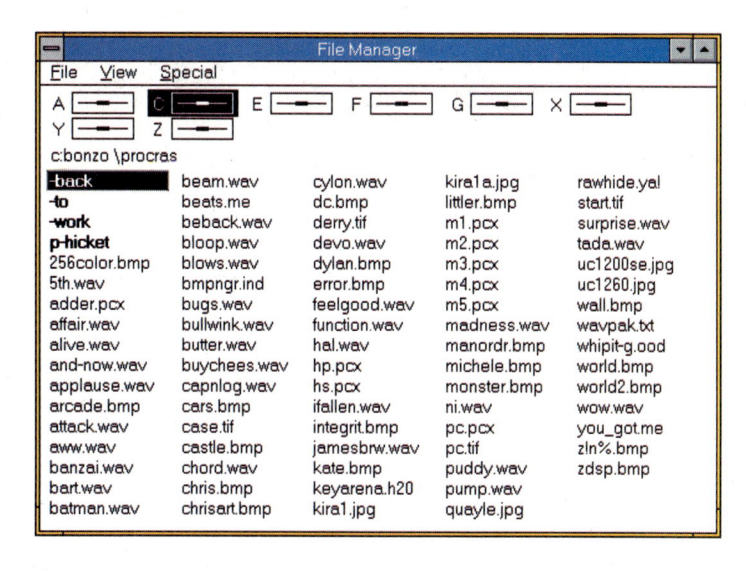

-back	beam.wav	cylon.wav	kira1a.jpg	rawhide.yal
-to	beats.me	dc.bmp	littler.bmp	start.tif
-work	beback.wav	derry.tif	m1.pcx	surprise.wav
p-hicket	bloop.wav	devo.wav	m2.pcx	tada.wav
256color.bmp	blows.wav	dylan.bmp	m3.pcx	uc1200se.jpg
5th.wav	bmpngr.ind	error.bmp	m4.pcx	uc1260.jpg
adder.pcx	bugs.wav	feelgood.wav	m5.pcx	wall.bmp
affair.wav	bullwink.wav	function.wav	madness.wav	wavpak.txt
alive.wav	butter.wav	hal.wav	manordr.bmp	whipit-g.ood
and-now.wav	buychees.wav	hp.pcx	michele.bmp	world.bmp
applause.wav	capnlog.wav	hs.pcx	monster.bmp	world2.bmp
arcade.bmp	cars.bmp	ifallen.wav	ni.wav	wow.wav
attack.wav	case.tif	integrit.bmp	pc.pcx	you_got.me
aww.wav	castle.bmp	jamesbrw.wav	pc.tif	zln%.bmp
banzai.wav	chord.wav	kate.bmp	puddy.wav	zdsp.bmp
bart.wav	chris.bmp	keyarena.h20	pump.wav	
batman.wav	chrisart.bmp	kira1.jpg	quayle.jpg	

■ A Sensible Arrangement

Having read the chapter thus far, you have the File Manager's individual parts looking just the way you want them. Now you're ready to get ergonomic and design a quick-and-easy structure to work with—and make the arrangement permanent.

You've been managing files for a while now. You've probably noticed that you play around with a few drives and directories most of the time. You'll want these to show up every time you open the File Manager. First, open separate windows for each of your favorite drives and directories. Minimize all of these window directories, and arrange the minimized icons along the right or left side of the File Manager window. Click on the one (preferably) or two (if you can't decide) icons whose directories you use all the time. Now resize and position the active windows so that they show the minimized icons along the side. This arrangement combines the fastest way to open common directory windows with the fastest File Manager startup, and looks like Figure 9.4.

Figure 9.4

You can keep your pristine file window arrangement by deselecting File, Save Settings on Exit. No more tidying up after yourself!

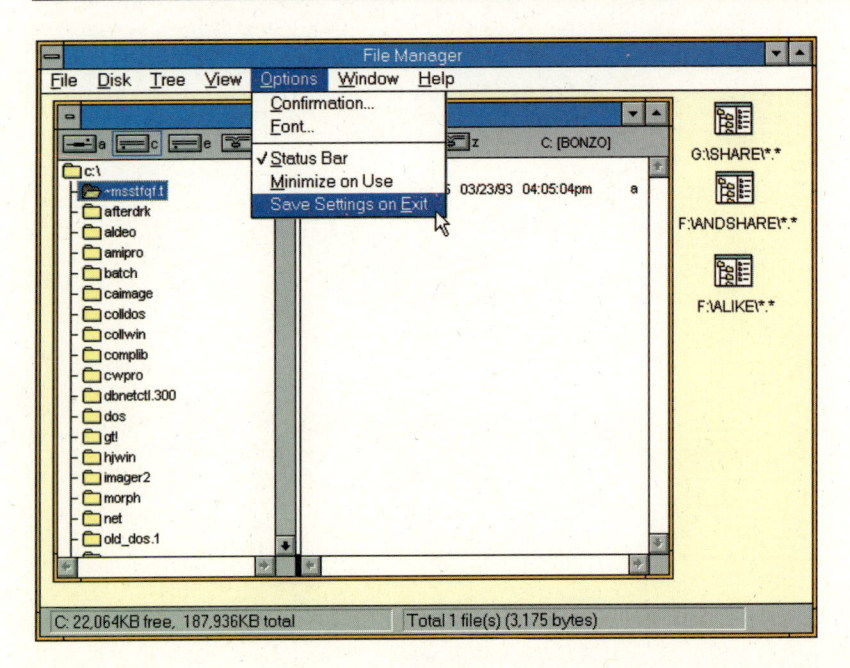

To save this arrangement and ensure that it appears identically every time, first check that Options, Save Settings on Exit is selected, and then close the File Manager. Open the program again, and this time click on Options,

Save Settings on Exit so that the check mark is deselected. Bingo. Now the File Manager will look the same every time you start it up.

NOTE. *Any time you improve upon the original layout, select Options, Save Settings on Exit, and then close and restart the File Manager. Finally, deselect Options, Save Settings on Exit to keep your layout pristine.*

Gratuitous Tip: Sensible Spacing

Notice how the tree window and the file window are roughly the same width? This arrangement makes very little sense. Unless you habitually view subdirectories seven or eight layers deep, you'll always need more space for the files than the directories. But that's easy enough to change.

Move your mouse cursor to the white strip just to the right of the directory window's scroll bar. The pointer will turn into a bar with a double arrow. Now hold down the left mouse button, drag the strip to the left until you can see enough of the file details in the right-hand window, and then release the mouse button. Alternatively, select View, Split, move the cursor and strip together, and click once to fix it in place.

■ Dragon Dropping Your Way to Cleaner Windows Directories

The Windows directories are a mess. The Windows installation routine makes only one concession to keeping your hard disk tidy—it limits itself to two subdirectories, \WINDOWS and \WINDOWS\SYSTEM. However, it piles files into those directories, and as you install more Windows apps, the files in your Windows directories swell to the hundreds. All this makes file management tricky, but not impossible. To make finding files and backing up data files quicker and easier, you need to get drag-and-drop fever.

Start with the PIF Editor, which is easy to fix. It lives in and drops its files into the Windows directory, but there's nothing to stop you from moving them all into a subdirectory off the main Windows directory. Setting this up is a little time-consuming, but it yields rewards in ease of access later on. To set this up from File Manager, follow this procedure:

1. Select the Windows directory, choose File, Create Directory, make a directory called PIF, and press F5.

2. While still in the Windows directory, select File, Select Files, and in the File(s) box, enter *.**PIF**.

3. Click on Select and then on Close. Then move the cursor to one of the highlighted PIF files. Hold down the left mouse button, and drag all the files into the PIF directory.

4. Move the PIF Editor to the new directory. Under View, File Type, change the file type to **PIF*.*** and click on OK. Back in the file window, press the slash key (/) to select all the files showing in the directory (which should be only PIFEDIT.EXE and PIFEDIT.HLP), and drag them into the PIF subdirectory. Then change View, File Type back to *.*.

5. Next, press Alt+Tab repeatedly to reach the Program Manager, and switch to your non-Windows applications program group. Starting with MS-DOS Prompt, press Alt and double-click in turn on each program that's loaded via a PIF—to bring up its Properties dialog box.

6. Change the Command Line box to reflect the file's new location, and click on OK to save changes.

7. Finally, change the PIF Editor's command line *and* working directory to the new location.

The PIF Editor and files aren't the only candidates for relocation. You can store your data files from Calendar and Cardfile in a PIM subdirectory—just move all the .CAL and .CRD files along with the two applications' executables and help files; then change the appropriate Program Manager icon properties to reflect the new command line and working directory.

Sound files with the .WAV extension can be called from anywhere on your hard disk with only a minor alteration to the directory listing in the Control Panel's Sound module. And if you're prepared to do a little juggling to load them, relocate .BMP wallpaper files from the Windows directory too. The only drawback to moving wallpaper files is that you must enter the full path and file name in the Control Panel's Desktop without any prompting from Windows.

■ An Association of Files, Desktop, and Printer

Remember how the icons beside the names in the file window look different for programs, documents, or other files? Want to know how the File Manager tells them apart? It's easy. Programs are defined in WIN.INI's *Programs=* line (the one you looked at in the chapter on screen savers). Documents are files whose extensions are listed in WIN.INI's [Extensions] paragraph, meaning they're associated with a program. The lines read something like this:

```
bmp=pbrush.exe ^.bmp
```

Association reaps big benefits in the File Manager. When you double-click on a file with a listed extension, the File Manager runs the associated program *and* loads the file into it. Magic! WIN.INI already has a few built-in associations from the Windows installation. The rest of the associations are put in place by application setup routines and by you. The command is right there under File, Associate.

Let's say you want to check out some mystery files direct from the File Manager. Let's say further that the files have the extensions .TMP, .BAK, and .CHK (the files that DOS's CHKDSK /F creates). These files might be formatted for use in any program, or none at all.

Since Write can import files without attempting a conversion, it counts as a kind of universal viewer. While not all files appear exactly as they should, Write can extricate some clue as to their contents and origins—unless they are graphics files. Here's how to associate files with Write:

1. Highlight a file with the desired extension; then select File, Associate.

2. In the Associate dialog box under Associate With, you'll see a scrolling list box. If a program has been associated with another extension, it will be listed here.

3. If you don't find the program name you're looking for, click on Browse and navigate your hard disk until you find it.

4. Click once on the program's name. With the name highlighted, click on OK. If your PC is slow enough, you'll see after a pause that the now-associated program's icon changes to a piece of paper with lines of writing on it.

In addition to the minor convenience of loading programs from the File Manager, there are other benefits to associating file extensions. For one thing, it means you can drag files onto the Program Manager desktop and load the parent program and the file in one go. This function is really handy for creating program groups with files you use often (such as to-do lists). It's also a way of increasing the 8-by-3 character descriptor of a file—just take a file in a Progman group, press Alt+Enter to bring up its properties box, and change the description.

The other argument for associating files is that in many cases, you can also drag a file onto the minimized icon of an associated program, and it will automatically load. Drag it onto the minimized Print Manager icon, and it will automatically print. This function is not enabled in some cases, but when it works, it's a very useful feature. Be aware that many programs don't support drag-and-drop printing—and the only way you can find out is when it doesn't work for you. So don't expect small miracles—just appreciate them when they happen.

■ Space Case: Too Many Files Spoil the Disk

No matter how carefully you manage your time and files, the day will come when your hard disk fills up. At that time, you need to make some serious decisions. What stays? What goes? How much can I afford to spend on a new hard disk?

But before budgeting for a new hard disk, consider the files you don't ever use: the wallpaper (.BMP) files, the screen saver (.SCR) files you don't like, the read-me files, sundry help files. These are your first points of attack. And if they were installed by Windows, they are the easiest things to purge from your hard disk. Don't tinker with the File Manager—use Windows Setup instead. When the Setup screen appears, select Options, Add/Remove Windows Components. The choices are set before you, complete with information about how much disk space you can recapture. Before removing any component whole, click on its File button to see what you might be kissing off. Then kiss it off. Don't panic about it—if you ever want it back, just use the same process to reinstall the element from your Windows distribution disks.

Zip 'em Up

If deleting files makes you nervous, you do have alternatives: compress them into archived files using Nico Mak's WinZip (a nifty shareware decompression tool) and Yoshi's LHA (a freeware DOS-based compression utility that WinZip calls from within Windows). WinZip contains its own algorithm for uncompressing archived files (without WinZip you wouldn't be able to extract all the other utilities on the disk accompanying this book). But when it comes to compressing them, WinZip needs outside assistance, which is something LHA is exceptionally good at (which is why it too is on the disk bound into the back of the book). (For more information about LHA, see the next section.)

Once you've installed these two programs according to the instructions in the Appendix, you need deal only with WinZip. It's already associated with the file extensions .ZIP, .LZH, .ARJ, and .ARC—so if you click on any file with one of these extensions in a File Manager window, the program will run and load that file automatically. In fact, this is how most of the files on the disk in the back of the book should be installed—and WinZip is also extremely handy for expanding files downloaded from online services such as CompuServe, Prodigy, and America Online. The alternative method for opening a file is the obvious way—launch the program, click on the Open button, and navigate your hard disk until you find the right file.

When you've opened an archived file, you'll see a list of all the files compressed in it. What you can do with the contents of a zipped file in WinZip is staggering: You can extract them into a directory on your hard disk, you can view the contents of most text-based files in an archive, you can open any single file straight from the archive, and you can temporarily check out the entire archive.

Extracting is a simple enough process—just select the files you want to extract, click on the Extract button, and select the target directory in the dialog box that appears. To bring specific files out of the archive, highlight one or more files (using Ctrl and a click to select files that aren't next to each other) before clicking on the Extract button.

Viewing a file is also easy—click on its name and click on the View button. By default, an internal ASCII text viewer (a kind of hobbled Notepad) will try to open it. If it can't handle the file, you'll get an error message—but since most files you'll want to view are read-me files, you should be OK.

NOTE. *If you want to use a more robust program than the ASCII viewer to view files, select WinZip's Options, Program Locations, and under Default Association, insert the name and path to WRITE.EXE.*

To open a single file, just double-click on it. Assuming the file is associated with an application, the application will load and open the file. If it's not associated, the default association file (as defined in Options, Program Locations) will have a go.

To try out the contents of an archive, click on the CheckOut button. This deposits the entire archive into a temporary file and creates a group in the Program Manager to display the associated icons. This feature alone is worth the program's shareware registration fee, and one trick will make it better. Assuming you have a large enough RAM drive, plonk the Checkout files there to make the process quicker and cleaner. Under Actions, Checkout, just enter the drive letter of your RAM drive, and you're set.

Putting the Squeeze on Your Files

So much for taking files out of archives. By the time your hard disk is sagging under the weight of applications, you'll want to be archiving stuff to free up a little space. This takes a little longer than extracting files, because WinZip operates by calling an external DOS application to do the archiving for you. Although it works faster with PKWare's PKZIP, I've included Yoshi's LHA on the disk in the back of the book because, among other things, it's freeware—copyrighted but distributed free of charge.

There are two ways to crunch down files into an archive—the drag-and-drop way or the direct way. With the direct technique, you load the program, either open an existing archive or create a new one, and click on the Add button. In the Add box, you select whether you want to add the file or move it (if you're saving disk space, choose Move; if you're sending a copy of a file to a buddy over a modem or on disk, go for Add).

Then under Compression, you decide whether to compress for size or speed. If you're really tight on space, go for Size, but this won't typically save you a lot more space. You probably won't lose out much by choosing Speed. Then select the files to compress. If you have a specific file criterion, replace *.* with it. If not, click on the Select button. An expanded Add box appears, much like the one in Figure 9.5.

Figure 9.5

Saving hard disk space may not be as hard as you thought. WinZip comes to the rescue—just remember to hit that Add button in the lower-left corner.

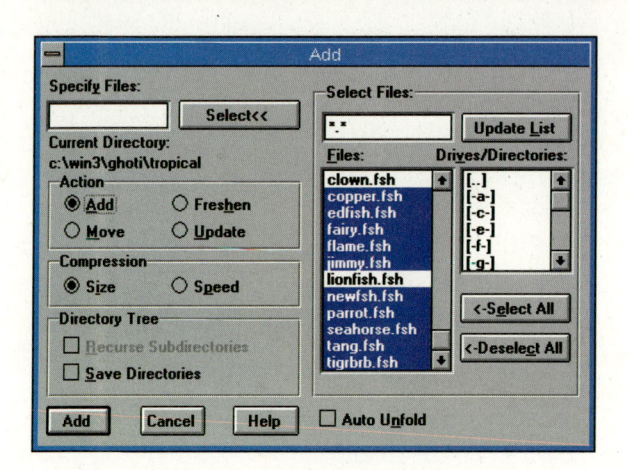

Select the directory and then the files you're after, and click on the Add button in the lower-left corner. LHA (or PKZIP if you have it) will do its compression thing, and you'll have a crunched set of files to show for it. Isn't technology wonderful?

Flushing Out Superfluous Files

Sometimes, archiving files isn't enough. Sometimes you want them off the face of your hard disk forever. But let's face it—the Delete key is the dullest way on earth to remove files. Make a big splash instead with the small shareware file-management utility, Toilet. Like the Macintosh trash can, Toilet runs as an icon—and it's best loaded as part of your Startup group.

When you're ready to get a load off your hard disk, drag file names from the File Manager and drop them in the Toilet icon. Any file so deposited will remain there until you either flush the toilet (click once on the icon and select Flush Toilet) or retrieve the file (a prospect that makes the toilet metaphor a tad less than tasteful). Any files in the toilet at the end of your Windows session will be purged from your hard disk.

To restore a file, click once on the Toilet icon and select Restore File. In the Un-Delete (Restore) File dialog box, either click on a file name and then click on Restore, or click on Restore All to retrieve every file you've so carelessly tossed in the can.

The possibility of restoring deleted files makes Toilet valuable. It's practical as well as fun, and it could set your mind at ease when operating without the safety net of deletion reminders (you remember, the annoying safety net we so blithely removed at the beginning of the chapter). And quite apart from the utilitarian angle, you've got to use this thing for its sound effects.

Now you have all the tools and information you need to manage your files and directory structure. All that remains is to impose the order on your hard disk that you've always wanted. On second thought, why not just move on to the next chapter and leave your hard disk in the mess that makes you feel at home? Time's a-wasting.

■ What Was the Point of This Chapter?

In "File Mismanagement," you learned how to:

- Make the File Manager lighten up on the fussy reminders

- Give the File Manager a makeover

- Ferret out files from around your hard disk

- Set up an ergonomic File Manager that reduces the amount of mousing around you need to do

- Drag and drop files for fun and profit

- Associate files with programs, and why it's a good idea

- Remove files from your hard disk or compress them to free up space

- *Aliens Ate My PC! The Daily Macro Tells All*
- *The File Manager's Friends*
- *Beating a Hasty Retreat Using Macros*
- *Cut! Print! Taking Pictures from the Silver Screen*
- *You Are Now a Professional. Attempt This at Home!*
- *What Was the Point of This Chapter?*

CHAPTER 10

Recorder Macrocosm

Take your good ideas, show them to the Recorder, and make Windows do the work.

THE WINDOWS RECORDER HAS A BAD REPUTATION, AND IT ALMOST deserves it. It looks promising but behaves forbiddingly—a bad combination. It has a cool camcorder icon, an enticing name, and the most disappointing function—recording macros. To make things worse, it has a learning curve so steep most people don't want to climb it. And worst of all, the few brave souls who do try it out find that macros often flake out on them, invoking mysterious error messages.

These drawbacks aside, the Recorder has the greatest potential of any Windows tool: Its scope is limited only by your imagination and available time. Now that you're into creative time-wasting, the Recorder is the place to waste time most creatively. Although it's tough to learn, once you're beyond the difficult parts (and most of these are in the early stages), it's extremely rewarding.

When you record with the Recorder, it looks over your shoulder, notes what you're doing, and saves the procedure as a macro in a file on disk. When you open the file and play back the macro, the Recorder repeats exactly what you did during the recording process. Most of what you need to know about the Recorder, then, is what you already know about other Windows apps. If you can find your way around Windows and its programs, the Recorder can take it from there. All you need is a few ideas and the time to practice.

This chapter will provide a little of both. We'll be working our way through a mouse-enabled demonstration macro and text-entry macro techniques. Then we'll be examining how to use a series of macros to augment a program—which involves loading macros from an icon. After these basics, we'll look at a few special techniques, including quitting Recorder using a macro and putting together your own application using macros. Ready? Strap yourselves in. It's going to be a bumpy ride.

■ Aliens Ate My PC! The Daily Macro Tells All

Teachers, documentation writers, and magazine editors give two stock reasons for using macros: on-screen demonstrations of Windows software and the automation of repetitive tasks. While this is a gross oversimplification, it's a good place to start—and in the process, it's a good place to highlight the other main purpose of running macros: to fool people into thinking their computers are related to the one in *2001: A Space Odyssey*.

Several of these macro purposes can be demonstrated in a macro in which, for example, you record yourself starting Paintbrush and drawing a smiley face. You could use this macro to introduce some of Paintbrush's tools or run it from the Paintbrush icon in the Program Manager to bewilder whoever opens the program (I'll show you how later, in the tip called "They Run from Command Lines"). To set this macro up, start from the Program Manager and load the Recorder. Then follow these instructions to set the program up:

1. Select Macro, Record. In the dialog box that appears, under Record Macro Name, enter **Draw a Smiley in Paintbrush.**

2. Enter **Shift+Alt+P** for a shortcut key. Set Playback to Same Application at Fast Speed. Set Record Mouse to Clicks and Drags. Then click on Start.

Aliens Ate My PC! The Daily Macro Tells All

[Record Macro dialog box showing:
- Record Macro Name: Draw a Smiley in Paintbrush
- Shortcut Key: P, with Shift and Alt checked
- Playback To: Same Application, Speed: Fast, Enable Shortcut Keys checked
- Record Mouse: Clicks + Drags, Relative to: Window
- Description: Purpose: Utter frippery. Reason: Why not?]

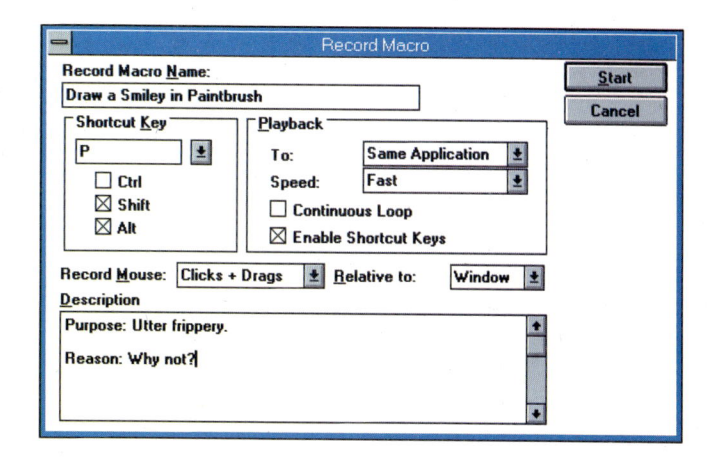

3. In the Program Manager, select File, Run, enter **PBRUSH**, and press Enter.

4. When Paintbrush comes up, press Alt+Spacebar to call up the program's Control menu, and press X to select Maximize. This will blow Paintbrush up to full screen size.

WARNING. *Whenever you record a macro that uses the mouse, always make it maximize the application's window at the start. If during replay the mouse moves where it did when you recorded the macro and the window is in a different position, the macro can't perform the same task and so will fail.*

5. Move the mouse to the toolbar, and click on the circle tool. Draw a large circle.

6. Select the filled circle tool, click on the blue color in the palette, and draw two smaller circles for eyes in the big circle.

7. Select the squiggly line tool, draw a line beneath the eyes, release the mouse button, and move the mouse to the center point of the line. Drag the line down until it forms a semicircle, and release the mouse button again.

8. Finally, press Ctrl+Break to stop recording the macro. Click on Save Macro and on OK in the dialog box that pops up. Then close Paintbrush, saving no changes on the way out.

9. Back in the Recorder, select File, Save, and save the file under the name **TEST.REC**. (*Note:* When you click on Save Macro in the dialog box, it does not save it to disk—remember to save the file after you're done.)

10. Now press Shift+Alt+P, and watch the macro work.

Assuming all went well, you'll now see your actions repeated, with a result resembling Figure 10.1. You'll also see several compelling reasons not to repeat certain steps in your next macro. The first mistake was using File, Run to start the program. It doesn't look right—it flashes dialog boxes that you don't want to see. Next time, we'll use keyboard shortcuts to make the process appear smoother. The macro will also run faster, since there will be no unnecessary screen drawing steps.

Figure 10.1

Wouldn't Paintbrush be much more entertaining if it came up with a screen like this every time you started it?

The issue of slow playback goes double—no, quadruple—for mouse actions. Even at the supposedly Fast Speed setting you checked off at the beginning, mouse movements crawl. If this is fast, just imagine what the other speed setting—Recorded Speed—would be like. And playback speed is only one reason for not using the mouse for Recorder macros.

The other issue is reliability. Bring up the Recorder, select the macro you've just recorded, and select Macro, Properties. Above the large Description box, you'll see the line

```
Recorded on a (compatible) 640 by 480 display.
```

This means that if you played the macro at a higher resolution, the macro would probably fail. The moral? Only when you're strictly controlling circumstances should you consider using the mouse. Canned demonstrations should be fine, as long as you rely on maximized screens, and you maximize the screens using the keyboard. Otherwise, stick to keystrokes only. (It's a good time to turn to those keyboard shortcut pages you've been meaning to memorize in the *Windows Users Guide*.)

And the most keyboard-oriented task of all is entering text. The classic example of when to use the Recorder for text entry is adding return addresses and standard "Yours sincerely" lines to letters. Of course, unless you write correspondence in programs that don't have their own glossary function (such as Write), you don't need this function. If, however, you want to simulate aliens talking to you through your PC, it's the only way to go. Let's say, for example, you want to read some cautionary text slowly unfolding before your eyes whenever you hit the Caps Lock key in any program. (Hey, some people do. None of us wants to meet them on a dark night, but they do exist.)

To do this, first, open the Recorder and another program—Notepad, for example. From Notepad, press Alt+Tab to return to the Recorder (without stopping at any other application on the way). Then follow these instructions:

1. In the Recorder, open the TEST.REC macro you just created, and select Macro, Record, and name the macro **Sorry**.

2. Click on the down-arrow in the Shortcut Key box, and highlight Caps Lock. Deselect the checked-off Ctrl box beneath it. In the Playback box, select Any Application and Recorded Speed. Under Record Mouse, select Ignore Mouse. Then click on Start.

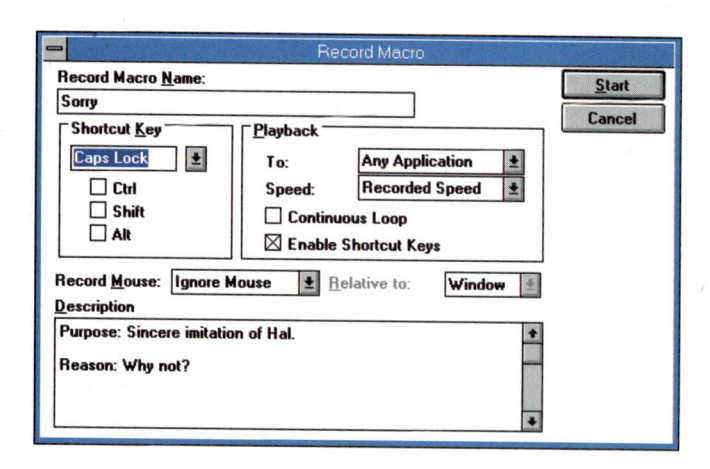

3. In Notepad, press Enter and type **I'm sorry, Dave, I'm afraid I can't do that.**

4. Press Ctrl+Break to stop recording the macro. Click on Save Macro and then on OK.

Not much new there. However, you can start a whole conversation chain by linking a series of macros together. These aren't quite like subroutines—once one macro starts another, the first macro won't resume after the second one is finished—but they do expand the horizons of your simple macro. Here's how to set it up.

1. From where you left off in Notepad, press Alt+Tab to return to the Recorder (no stops on the way).

2. In the Recorder, select Macro, Record, name the macro **Open**, and assign it to a shortcut key combination of Ctrl+Caps Lock.

3. Set the macro to play back to Any Application at Recorded Speed, and under Record Mouse, set it to ignore the mouse. Then click on Start.

4. Back in Notepad, type **Open the pod bay door, Hal.** Then press Caps Lock.

5. Press Ctrl+Break to stop recording the macro, and click on Save Macro and OK. You'll see a Recorder dialog box telling you that the macro playback has been aborted—which refers to the Caps Lock macro, not the one you just recorded.

6. Press Ctrl+Caps Lock and watch the dialog unfold.

If you don't see what you expect, try changing the shortcut key to something else. (Besides which, you'd have to be utterly insane to want a message from Hal every time you hit Caps Lock.) So here's how you can reassign the keystrokes, a little technique that will come in handy later, when you have so many key combinations that you can't keep track of them. First, open the macro file (if it's not still open) and highlight the macro in question. Select Macro, Properties, and simply click on the list box's down arrow and pick another key. (While you're there, you might want to increase the playback speed to Fast.)

So much for basic examples of macro recording. Now's the time to roll up our sleeves and get down to some serious macro making.

■ The File Manager's Friends

One of the most compelling reasons for using the Recorder is to add shortcuts to applications that don't have their own macro languages. The entire suite of Windows mini-apps falls into this category—from Cardfile to the File and Program Managers. The File Manager, with its burdensome weight of configuration options, is probably the best example of an application screaming for shortcut options. For that reason, we'll turn our attention to giving the File Manager the series of shortcuts it (and you) always needed.

Gratuitous Tip: They Run from Command Lines

You don't need to play Digital Twister to run Recorder macros from weird key combinations—macros can be assigned to icons and run from a command line. The technique is simple enough: Create a macro file in the Recorder, create a program item in the Program Manager, and in the Program Item Properties box, enter a command line. Let's say your macro file is called *MACRO.EXT,* and the startup macro's shortcut is Ctrl+Shift+Alt+X. This is the command line you'd use:

```
RECORDER -h ^+%X macro.ext
```

The command RECORDER loads the program. The last item, *macro.ext,* represents the name of your macro file. The -h parameter tells Windows that the keyboard shortcut of the macro you want to run is next in line. The ^, +, and % represent extended keys (Ctrl, Shift, and Alt respectively), and the X is the key in the shortcut. The illustration below shows the Program Item Properties dialog box for a macro called WASTING.REC.

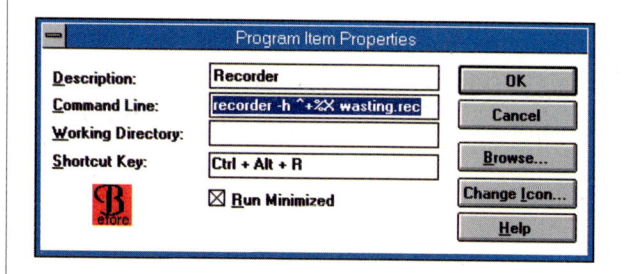

This technique enables you to open a program and a suite of Recorder macros at a stroke (see "The File Manager's Friends") or just play a trick on someone (perhaps something to do with Paintbrush and smiley faces).

A suite of macros recorded for a specific application belongs in its own macro file, and the first macro in the suite should load the program. So to begin, load the Recorder direct from the Program Manager, and open a new macro file. Select Macro, Record, and use the Ignore Mouse, Same Application, Fast Speed options. Name the macro "Open File Manager and Toilet," and assign a shortcut of Ctrl+Shift+Alt+F. Then click on Start, and when you return to the Program Manager, select File, Run, and enter **WINFILE** to load the File Manager. If you use Toilet alongside the File Manager for your file deletions, follow up by selecting the File Manager's File, Run command and entering the drive, directory, and file name **TOILET**.

NOTE. *This technique can be used to load multiple programs and multiple files from a single icon in a Program Manager group.*

When it has loaded, select Ctrl+Break and save the macro. Then press Alt+Tab to return to the Recorder, and select File, Save to save the macro file as **WINFILE.REC**.

With the macro file intact, you're ready to create a whole suite of shortcuts, like those in Figure 10.2. Pick a File Manager function, such as changing the font size for maximum legibility, and take a trial run at the task. Note each of the steps and menu options you need to go through (remember, you won't be able to use the mouse when you record the macro itself). (A little refresher: For every radio button and list box in a dialog box, there's a name with an underlined character. Press Alt and that character to move to that section of the dialog box. Alternatively, press Tab to move from one area to another.) Once you've noted each step, press Alt+Tab to return to the Recorder, and select Macro, Record to begin recording a new macro.

Figure 10.2

Once you've recorded a set of macros for a single application, you can start them either from their shortcut keys or by double-clicking on their names.

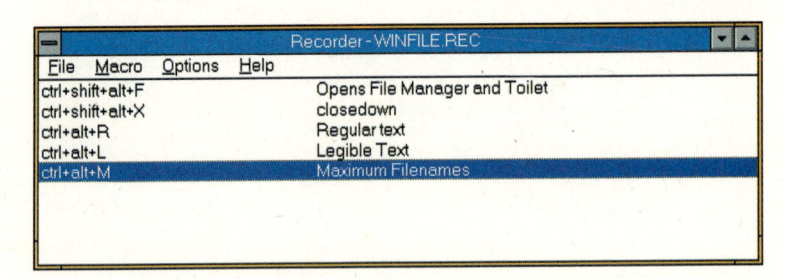

ctrl+shift+alt+F	Opens File Manager and Toilet
ctrl+shift+alt+X	closedown
ctrl+alt+R	Regular text
ctrl+alt+L	Legible Text
ctrl+alt+M	Maximum Filenames

Recorder - WINFILE.REC — File Macro Options Help

For each macro you record in a program-specific suite of macros, the settings should be pretty much the same: Playback should be to the same application (obviously); most of the time, the playback speed should be set to fast; most of the time, Shortcut Keys should be enabled and Continuous Loop disabled; and almost always, Record Mouse should be set to Ignore Mouse.

Some of the File Manager settings you might assign to macros include showing the maximum number of file names (press Alt+Spacebar, select X to maximize the window; select View, Directory Only and then View, Name) and providing more legible text (choose Options, Font, Alt+F Arial, Alt+Y Bold, Alt+S 10 or 12).

Gratuitous Tip: Tailor-Made Record Macro Settings

After a few macro recording sessions, you'll start to realize how dull resetting the options can be—and it's also unnecessary. Since the majority of the macros you'll be recording will have the same settings (and, of course, those aren't the default settings), just change the defaults in the Options, Preferences dialog box. Make it match the settings in this illustration, and you'll be able to jump straight into recording your macros after assigning a name and shortcut.

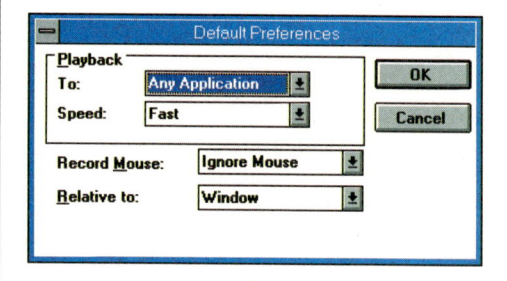

Default Preferences dialog box: Playback To: Any Application; Speed: Fast; Record Mouse: Ignore Mouse; Relative to: Window

Even if there are some minor differences between the Recorder settings and your final playback wishes, you can go back and edit most settings by highlighting a macro name in the Recorder window and selecting Macro, Properties.

Once you've recorded a macro, always test it out. The quickest way to do this before you're familiar with the keyboard shortcut is to press Alt+Tab to change to the Recorder and then double-click on the macro you're interested in. This technique is also good for everyday use—it's usually a lot quicker than going through several application menus.

When you've finished getting a few macros together, the next step is to ensure that the Recorder and the application always run at the same time. You've already recorded a macro to run the File Manager in this macro file, so note its keyboard shortcut (I'll use Ctrl+Shift+Alt+F as an example here). Hold down Alt and double-click on the File Manager icon in the Program Manager. Under Command line, replace WINFILE with

```
RECORDER -h ^+%f WINFILE.REC
```

Click on OK, and the next time you click on the icon or use its shortcut, the Recorder and the appropriate file will load, closely followed by the File Manager.

■ Beating a Hasty Retreat Using Macros

So far we've looked at how to open several applications with the Recorder, add commands to them, and perform unnatural tricks to boot. The missing factor is quitting. It follows that if you use the Recorder to make work easier, it's not doing its job if you have to close applications *and* their Recorder macro files when you're done. Fortunately, you can do the job easily enough with a Recorder macro and a little trickery.

Quit the Recorder Using a Macro

The first step is to write a Recorder macro that closes the Recorder. You can do this in a couple of ways, neither of which is entirely foolproof, but one of the two options should cover most eventualities. Like any macro routine that you're likely to use again and again, these macros should be recorded into their own macro file, ready to be merged into any macro file you use.

NOTE. *To merge macros from one macro file into another, open the multifunction client macro file, select File, Merge, and select the single-purpose server file (such as the one containing the Quit macros described here). Click on OK, and the macros will appear in the client file's roster.*

Like every macro recording project, the Quit macros need planning and preparation before recording and then need tidying up and testing afterward. Planning the macro involves breaking down the task into its constituent steps: You must first change to the Recorder, and then select File, Exit. This seems simple, but it isn't. Changing to the Recorder without using the mouse requires either using a keyboard shortcut or using the Task List. Neither technique will work all the time: You may load the Recorder from any program's icon (as with the File Manager in the previous section) using any keyboard shortcut, so no universal shortcut will get you to the Recorder every time. The alternative is to call up the Task List and press the letter R for Recorder, and then select End Task. The problem with this is if you're running another program beginning with R, or if you've renamed the Program Manager something like "Reasons to be cheerful, part 3.1." Press R in the Task List, and you'll go to the *first* listing that begins with R, which won't always be the Recorder. The other problem can occur when you're recording a macro and you bring up the Recorder, which pauses recording. To pull this one off, you have to trick the Recorder.

Now that the planning is done, the preparation steps begin. First press Alt+Double-click on the Recorder icon in the Program Manager. Remove any regular shortcut key assigned to the icon by tabbing to the right box and pressing the spacebar. Then press Alt and double-click on the icon of a simple application such as Notepad, and assign to it the shortcut you usually use for the Recorder. Then click on OK and double-click on the Notepad icon to load it. In the same Program Manager group, select File, New, Program Item, and enter **PROGMAN** for a command line. In the Description box, enter something beginning with R followed by a letter before E. "Rapid descent into confusion" is a good one. Click on OK, and you'll have a Program Manager icon with a new name. Click on it, and the title bar of the main Program Manager window will change. OK, preparation's over. Now for the recording phase:

1. Open the Recorder with a new file. Select Macro, Record, name the macro **Quit Recorder--Shortcut method**, and set playback to Any Application.

2. Click on Start, and from the Program Manager, press the normal Recorder keyboard shortcut, currently assigned to Notepad.

3. When Notepad pops up, select File, Exit.

4. Press Ctrl+Break and save the macro. Click on the Recorder icon to bring it up again, and select File, Save. Save the file as **QUIT.REC**.

5. Select Macro, Record, and name the new macro **Quit Recorder--Task List method**. Click on Start.

6. Press Ctrl+Esc to bring up the Task List.

7. Press R, and when the highlight pops to the name you gave to the Program Manager task, select Alt+E to end the task.

8. Immediately press Ctrl+Break to stop recording the macro. The Recorder will kick up its dialog box; you select Save Macro and click on OK.

9. Click on the running Recorder icon, and select File, Save to save the changes to the macro file.

The recording is now done: You have two macros with no shortcuts. Before you can test them, you need to tidy up the preparatory steps. Select the renamed Program Manager icon, press Alt+Enter, and give the icon a new description that doesn't begin with R—such as "Now I get it." Click on OK, and click on the icon so that the Program Manager title bar changes. Then bring up Notepad's Properties box by pressing Alt+Enter, change its shortcut back to whatever it normally is, and click on OK. Finally, select the Recorder icon and restore its shortcut key.

Now you're ready to test the macros you've just recorded. First, bring up the Recorder, and double-click on the Task List quit macro. If all has gone according to plan, the Recorder should be closed down by the macro.

Bring the Recorder back again by pressing the shortcut you assigned to it, and then select File, Open to call up QUIT.REC. Double-click on the macro called "Quit Recorder--Shortcut method" to start it. Again, the macro should close the Recorder.

With QUIT.REC fully tested, you're ready to use it. Open WINFILE.REC or some other existing application-specific macro collection. Select File, Merge, and pick QUIT.REC from the list box. This will bring the Quit macros into the macro collection. You're now ready to record another Quit macro—this time, one that quits the main application (File Manager) and the Recorder. Quit the Recorder, saving the additions to WINFILE.REC on your way out.

Quit Everything at Once

Let's try another macro and, in the process, cover the four stages involved in recording any macro: planning, preparing, recording, and testing.

The Plan: To create a Quit macro that will close the live application and then the Recorder. The Recorder part is already done, but currently has no keystroke assigned (and it should stay that way until later). The other part is simple—a macro that plays back to the application and ends with a key combination that will start the Recorder Quit macro.

The Preparation: First, decide the shortcut key combination you'll assign to the prefabricated macro that quits the Recorder. Start up the File Manager and WINFILE.REC combination by clicking on the icon you assigned to the macro.

The Recording Session:

1. From the File Manager, press Alt+Tab until you've switched to the Recorder. Select Macro, Record, and name the macro **Closedown**. Make sure the macro is set to play back to the Same Application.

2. Assign a shortcut that suggests leaving the application such as Alt+Shift+Q (or Ctrl+Shift+F12 for Word for Windows users). Click on Start.

3. In the File Manager, press Alt+F, X to quit.

4. Press the key combination you'll assign to the Recorder's Quit macro.

5. Press Ctrl+Break to break off recording the macro, and select Save Macro.

6. In the Recorder, highlight one of the Recorder Quit macros (try "Quit Recorder--Task List method" first).

7. Select Macro, Properties, and for a shortcut, assign the key combination you pressed as the last step of the general Closedown macro.

8. Double-click on "Quit Recorder--Task List method" to quit the Recorder, and save the changes you made to the file on your way out.

The Test: Open the File Manager and the Recorder macro file from the Program Manager icon. Press the Closedown key combination. If this technique closes everything down according to plan, celebrate. If not, open the Recorder macro file, and assign the keyboard shortcut that's called by the Closedown macro to the other Quit macro. Then try again. When you get it to work, celebrate hard.

Completely Useless Tip: Read Your Macros

Want to know what information is stored in a macro? It's easy to find out. Highlight the macro, select the Macro menu, and hold down the Shift key as you click on the Properties option. What appears is a scrolling list of the events—one to a line—that are recorded in the macro. If you are fluent in the language Windows speaks to itself, you can nod and smile knowingly at this list of gobbledygook. For the rest of us, this piece of trivia is useful only for impressing nerds at parties.

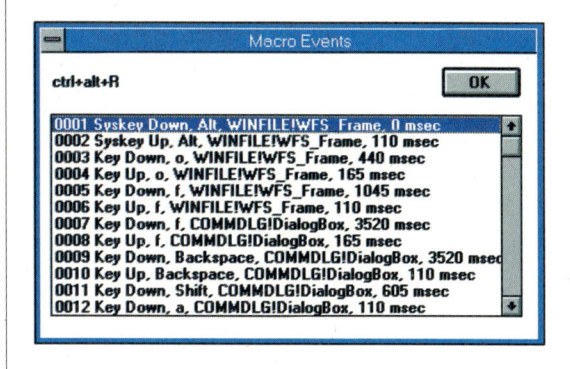

```
                    Macro Events
ctrl+alt+R                                    [ OK ]

0001 Syskey Down, Alt, WINFILE!WFS_Frame, 0 msec
0002 Syskey Up, Alt, WINFILE!WFS_Frame, 110 msec
0003 Key Down, o, WINFILE!WFS_Frame, 440 msec
0004 Key Up, o, WINFILE!WFS_Frame, 165 msec
0005 Key Down, f, WINFILE!WFS_Frame, 1045 msec
0006 Key Up, f, WINFILE!WFS_Frame, 110 msec
0007 Key Down, f, COMMDLG!DialogBox, 3520 msec
0008 Key Up, f, COMMDLG!DialogBox, 165 msec
0009 Key Down, Backspace, COMMDLG!DialogBox, 3520 msec
0010 Key Up, Backspace, COMMDLG!DialogBox, 110 msec
0011 Key Down, Shift, COMMDLG!DialogBox, 605 msec
0012 Key Down, a, COMMDLG!DialogBox, 110 msec
```

■ Cut! Print! Taking Pictures from the Silver Screen

Way back in the first chapter of this book, I wasted your time with a long description of how to make your Windows screen into a graphics file. It involves Byzantine contortions in Paintbrush's settings, and it was, I now confess, unnecessary. The reason? If you use a macro to do the work, screen shots take no more than three keystrokes. Sorry for keeping the process a secret, but you had to plow through all this Recorder information to master the necessary technique.

There are two options open to you with the Windows Print Screen function (the one that copies screen information to the Clipboard)—namely, copying the whole screen or just the active window. Once the screen or window is captured and copied into Paintbrush, you have more options: Print it out and return to work; mine it for interesting details to paste into other documents; or save it to your disk intact. Depending on how complex you want to get, you can handle all these options in a single macro file. Again, we'll proceed through the four basic macro recording steps (one day, this will be habitual.)

> *The Plan:* The macro file will start up from an icon and will run Paintbrush automatically as it loads. To capture screens, you'll press Alt+Tab from the screen you want to capture to the Recorder window, and you'll click on one of several macro options—or use keyboard shortcuts, if you prefer. The capture procedure comes in two parts: In the first stage, one of two macros captures the Windows screen to the Clipboard (one uses the Print Screen key and the other, Alt+Print Screen); in the second stage, another macro pastes the results into Paintbrush.
>
> *The Preparation:* Reserve a keyboard shortcut for the main macro that pastes the results into Paintbrush. We'll be using Ctrl+Shift+P in this example.
>
> Press Alt+Double-click on the Paintbrush icon in the Program Manager, and under Shortcut Key, assign a shortcut. In this example, we'll be using Ctrl+Shift+Alt+P. Then click on the Paintbrush icon to run the program.
>
> *The Recording Session:*

1. Fire up the Recorder and select Macro, Record. In the Macro Title box, enter **Capture a whole screen**. Specify playback to Any Application, and set the playback speed to Recorded Speed. Ensure the Record Mouse box is set to Ignore Mouse. Click on Start.

Cut! Print! Taking Pictures from the Silver Screen 179

2. Press Print Screen a couple of times (to ensure that the screen is captured to the Clipboard). Then press Ctrl+Shift+P. Finally, press Ctrl+Break and save the macro.

3. Return to the Recorder, and save the macro file as **CAPTURE.REC**. Then repeat step 1, but call the macro **Capture the active window**.

4. Press Alt+Print Screen a couple of times, followed by Ctrl+Shift+P. Finally, press Ctrl+Break and save the macro.

5. Return to the Recorder, and select Macro, Record. Name the macro **Open Paintbrush**, and assign it the shortcut Ctrl+Shift+Alt+B. Specify playback to Same Application, and set the playback speed to Fast. Ensure the Record Mouse box is set to Ignore Mouse. Click on Start.

6. Press Ctrl+Shift+Alt+P. Then press Ctrl+Break and click on Save Macro.

7. Return to Recorder, and select Macro, Record. Name the macro **Copy the Clipboard into Paintbrush**, and assign it the shortcut Ctrl+Shift+P. Specify playback to Any Application, and set the playback speed to Fast. Ensure the Record Mouse box is set to Ignore Mouse. Click on Start.

8. Press Ctrl+Shift+Alt+P (or whatever keyboard shortcut you've assigned to Paintbrush), and once Paintbrush has loaded, press Alt+Spacebar, X. Paintbrush will maximize.

9. Press Alt+O, followed by Enter, and in the Image Attributes dialog box, press Alt+D and Enter. This makes the image size equal to the resolution of the screen—640-by-480 for regular VGA, 800-by-600 for Super-VGA, and so on.

10. Press Shift+Ins to paste the Clipboard's contents into the new Paintbrush document. A hatch pattern will appear: Press Tab and then the Insert key to replace the pattern with the screen.

11. Press Ctrl+N to zoom in, and the image will appear life-sized and clear.

12. Press Ctrl+Break and select Save Macro. Double-click on the Recorder icon to maximize the application, and save the macro file.

The Test: After testing all the macros to make sure they do the job without a hitch, make this macro file a permanent fixture on your desktop. Select File, New, Program Item, and in the Description box, enter Screen Capture. Then enter this line in the Command Line box:

```
RECORDER -H ^+%P CAPTURE.REC
```

Click on OK. The icon that appears in the Program Manager group will run the macro to load Paintbrush (Ctrl+Shift+Alt+P) automatically when it opens the Recorder.

This macro file is pretty complete as it stands. To make quitting the application easier, merge the macros in QUIT.REC, record a Shutdown macro to close Paintbrush, and call a Quit macro to close Recorder in the same stroke.

When you're ready to capture screens later on, click on the icon to load Paintbrush and the macro file. Press Alt+Tab to switch to the program whose screen you want to capture, and press Alt+Tab again to return to the Recorder. Double-click on the option you want—full-screen or active window—and watch the Recorder do the rest.

■ You Are Now a Professional. Attempt This at Home!

Congratulations. You've passed through the Wasting Time Recorder Boot Camp with flying colors. You're now equipped to devise and record your own macros. Take it from one who has suffered long and arduous hours with the Recorder, revising procedures, suffering inexplicable macro failures, and staying up into the small hours muttering bitterly at Windows: It's a lot of fun. If you use the Recorder, you will suffer the same fate. The Recorder's a cussed monster of a batch procedure application. It doesn't behave how you'd expect it to. It can violate system integrity when (not if) you set up a macro wrong. You'll sometimes see general protection faults when you test out macros. But when you get a macro right, you can guarantee one thing: You'll never forget to use it.

So how do you approach the Recorder with the minimum of pain and the maximum likelihood of success? It so happens that there's a 10-step program that guarantees results with the same certitude as late-night infomercials on local TV channels. What's more, it's moderately more likely to deliver what it promises. Send no money! It's absolutely free! Read on.

1. Plan, Plan, and, Oh, Yes, Plan.

The best macros are ones that automatically do a task that requires a lot of effort to accomplish manually, but that you do often anyway. Before you try recording a macro, go through every procedure carefully, checking for keyboard shortcuts every step of the way.

2. Be Prepared.

Make sure that all the programs and supporting macros you will need are ready: Know their shortcuts and their quirks. Make sure that you arrange to have them in place every time you run the macro you're about to record.

3. Perform a Dry Run.

Load up the Recorder, but before actually recording, press Alt+Tab to get to the application window. From now on, pretend that the Recorder is running, and go through each step, making notes along the way. (Don't touch the mouse! Macros that rely on the mouse are too likely to fail and take too long to run even when they do work.)

4. Look for Pitfalls.

Once you've ironed out the procedure, try to second-guess Windows. What could go wrong? Do you change between applications using Alt+Tab? If so, make sure that the application you're going to will always be the next one down. Are you running applications from a shortcut key? Make sure the application's in an active Program Manager group. Are you duplicating shortcut keys? Did you leave the keys in the car? Did you turn the lights off? Make sure you know all these things before you trust a macro—and don't trust it even then.

5. Keep a Log of Shortcut Keys.

In a spreadsheet or a word processor that creates tables, make a grid with each of the keyboard keys on one axis except Ctrl, Shift, and Alt. On the other axis, add the seven possible combinations of the Ctrl, Shift, and Alt keys: each one individually, Ctrl+Shift, Ctrl+Alt, Shift+Alt, and Ctrl+Shift+Alt. At the intersection of each combination with a function assigned to it, put in the function and the program, macro, or Program Manager group it's assigned to. (For example, at the intersection of Alt and spacebar, enter **All Windows applications: Call up Control menu**; at Ctrl+Shift+Alt+P, enter **Main Program Manager group: Runs Paintbrush**, and so on. Armed with this list, you'll avoid assigning duplicate shortcuts.

6. Assign Shortcut Keys That Make Sense.

Since the default Program Manager shortcut key combination is Ctrl+Alt and the default Recorder shortcut is just Ctrl, maintain the distinction when you assign Recorder shortcuts. You can use any combination of the keys shown in the Macro Properties box, but limit yourself to Ctrl or Ctrl+Shift, and they'll be easier to remember.

When you're recording a macro to assign to a Program Manager icon, use a complicated or hard-to-type combination of keys, such as Ctrl+Shift+Alt+Z. These shortcuts don't need to be mnemonic or easy to type since you'll be entering them once only, and there's no point in wasting an easy shortcut on a function you won't be typing.

7. Proceed with Caution.

There are two main drawbacks to recording macros: They do everything you do; and you can't edit them. If you make a mistake in the middle of a long and complex procedure, you either stop recording (very frustrating) or you go ahead and undo your error—and then watch it play itself out every time you use the macro (very frustrating). You can avoid both frustrations with careful planning and careful recording.

8. Tidy up Afterwards.

Pay attention to the loose ends that hang off every macro recording project. Make sure all the shortcuts that need to be assigned are assigned. Make sure that each macro file you create is saved whenever a new macro is added to it. Merge every macro file you create with your QUIT.REC so that you can quit it with ease. Add your own Closedown macro to each macro file that loads another application on startup.

9. Test Thoroughly.

Before you trust a macro to do the job, test it immediately after recording it. Then close down the Recorder and all the attendant programs, and start them all up again. Try the macro a second time. Close down Windows and restart it. Try the macro a third time. OK. That's enough. If it still works as you expect, you can trust it.

10. Don't Be Surprised When Things Go Amiss.

The likelihood of your recording a perfect macro every time is zero percent. So don't be distressed when the Recorder doesn't behave as you expected. Just make sure you get the better of it more often than it outfoxes you.

Now close the book and get creative.

■ What Was the Point of This Chapter?

In "Recorder Macrocosm," you wasted time at:

- Learning the dos and don'ts of simple mouse-driven and text-entry macros (that is, making the Recorder draw pictures and write words for no readily apparent reason)

- Assigning macros to icons in the Program Manager
- Using macros to supplement Windows applications
- Creating macros that quit applications—including the Recorder—quickly
- Designing your own screen-capture utility using macros
- Learning how to plan and implement your own macros without undue pain

PART

3

Start Wasting Time
Windows Activities You Can't Pass Off As Work

- *Playing to Win ... **186***

- *Hunting for Easter Eggs ... **202***

- *Solitaire*
- *Minesweeper*
- *What Was the Point of This Chapter?*

CHAPTER

11

Playing to Win

Oh, yes, and Windows has games, too.

MOST PEOPLE'S INTRODUCTION TO WASTING TIME IN WINDOWS comes wrapped in the Program Manager's Games group. You already know how to play Solitaire and Minesweeper—you've probably wasted more time at it than I have. And even if you don't know all the rules, the on-line help gives you a pretty good outline of the basic procedures. (Check out any application's Help menu, select File, Open, and click twice on SOL.HLP or WINMINE-.HLP for the basics.)

Chapter 11: Playing to Win

But there's more to playing any game than a knowledge of rules and scoring. There's tactics, expertise, and above all, cheating. That's what this chapter's all about, so set aside the rest of the day, and put up a "Do Not Disturb" sign on your office or den door. Here's how to beat Windows at its own games.

■ Solitaire

The Windows version of Solitaire is one of the dozens of card games in the solitaire family. In living rooms and waiting rooms, the game is commonly called Canfield or Klondike. To play the game, you draw cards from the deck (in the upper-left corner of the window) and move them to suit and row stacks (respectively in the upper-right corner and center of the window).

In the row stacks, you count down, alternating between red and black cards, as shown in Figure 11.1. In suit stacks, you start with an ace and count up in the same suit. When you've arranged every suit from the ace to the king, you've won. If this happens once in a dozen games, you're either lucky or cheating. (Luck I can't guarantee, but I'll provide a few tips in the other department later.) This version of Solitaire is largely won by one or the other technique and seldom by skill.

Figure 11.1

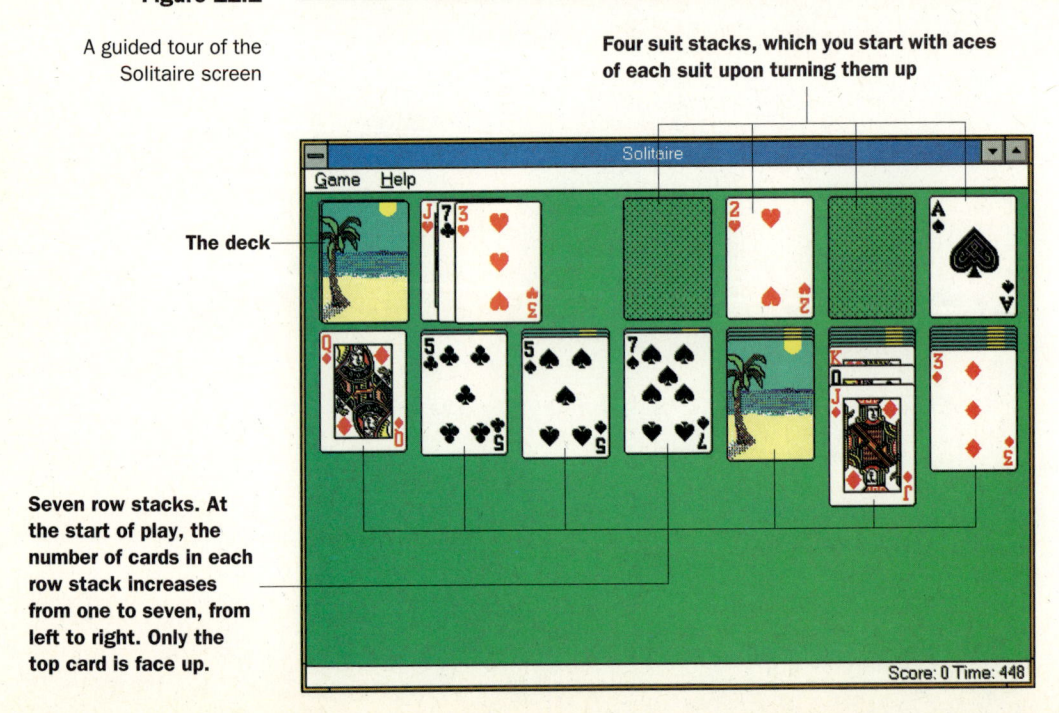

A guided tour of the Solitaire screen

Four suit stacks, which you start with aces of each suit upon turning them up

The deck

Seven row stacks. At the start of play, the number of cards in each row stack increases from one to seven, from left to right. Only the top card is face up.

The Object of the Game

The object of Solitaire is to use all the cards in the deck to build up the four suit stacks from ace to king. You have to turn up the aces yourself first, because only once in a blue moon do you begin with any cards dealt into the suit stacks.

Playing Solitaire involves turning up cards and throwing them into the appropriate pile (if you can manage it). If you can't lay a card you turn up from the deck directly into the suit stacks, use the row stacks as a holding ground. However, in the row stacks, you are limited to alternating red and black cards in descending order.

If you get to the end of the deck and haven't finished the game (and you never will), you turn over the deck (in a virtual kind of way) and continue to draw cards. All the time, the clock is ticking away, eroding whatever points you've gained, so playing fast, tactically, and accurately is essential.

Playing the Game

When you begin playing Solitaire, first check the cards you have turned up: Can you place any of them in descending order on a card of a different color suit? Are there any aces that could start a suit stack? If not, click on the deck to turn up a card, and ask yourself the same questions again.

By default, Solitaire deals three cards at a time. Of these three, you can only attempt to place the top one. If this proves too frustrating (the second one is usually the one you really want to place), select Game, Options, Draw One. This will start a new game.

When you click on the deck, Solitaire shows either the first or third card in the deck, depending on which Draw option you select from the Options dialog box.

If you don't hit paydirt dealing from the deck, remember you can move a card in a row stack to another row stack, and the top card of any row stack to a suit stack. If you manage to shift cards from a row stack and uncover a face-down card in a row stack, you can turn the card face up and bring it into play.

If you empty a row stack altogether, the only card you can use to begin another stack in its place is a king—the same principle is at work with empty suit stacks, but they can only be started with an ace.

When you make a move that plumbs new depths of stupidity (which will happen once or twice a game, if you're like me), don't kick yourself—just select Game, Undo to restore the cards. This technique works both on cards in the stacks and on those dealt from the deck.

During a Standard scoring game, you can turn over the deck once you've dealt your way to the bottom. Just click on the big zero to the left of the upturned deck to turn it over, and then continue playing.

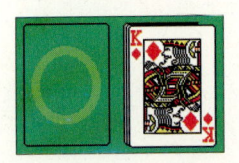

You win the game when you have used all the cards in the deck to build all four suit stacks from ace to king. You'll know when this is the case, because Windows puts on a 52-card gymnastic display to celebrate the fact. When this happens, have fun and enjoy the show—it won't happen too often.

To start a new game, select Game, Deal, or Game, Options, and select a different Scoring or Draw option.

Gratuitous Tip: Look, Ma, No Mouse

So good at Solitaire that you want to handicap your game? Or is your mouse hand getting tired? Try these keyboard shortcuts for rodent-free play.

Tab	Moves you from the deck to suit and row stacks
Left/Right Arrows	Moves you to the adjacent stack
Up/Down Arrows	Selects successive cards from a stack
Enter or spacebar	Picks up and releases a card or group of cards (or turns over a new card in the deck or a stack)

You can combine these keyboard actions to move several cards to another stack in one go: Press the Left or Right Arrow keys to move to the stack, and then use the Up Arrow key to select the highest-valued card in the series you want to move. Press Enter or the spacebar, and then shift the ministack using the Left or Right Arrow keys. Finally, press Enter or the spacebar to drop the cards at their destination.

If you are moving a card from the deck, press Tab to toss the card onto a suit or row stack.

Scoring

Just to confuse the issue, Solitaire has two scoring systems—Standard and Vegas—which you select from the Options dialog box. If you want to relax without being graded on your performance, turn scoring and timing off and truly recreate (not such a radical concept—try it sometime).

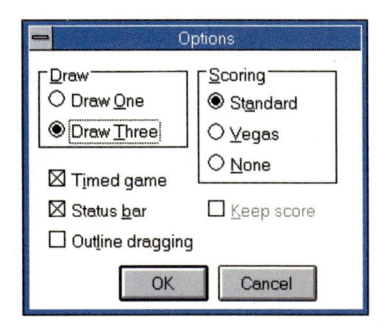

NOTE. *If you change the scoring option in the middle of a game, the game will end and you'll be dealt a set of stacks.*

Standard Scoring

In Standard scoring, correct moves earn you points, and the time you spend making them costs you points. You earn a bonus when you complete a timed game—the shorter the game, the larger the bonus.

Under Standard scoring, you win…

10 points per card moved to a suit stack

5 points per card moved from the deck to a row stack

And you lose…

15 points for each card you move from a suit stack to a row stack

20 points for each pass through the deck after the first three passes (with the Draw Three option selected)

100 points for each pass through the deck after the first pass (with the Draw One option selected)

Vegas Scoring

If your idea of fun is waving goodbye to quantities of money without seeing anything in return, try Vegas scoring. It's all the fun of America's neon playground without the smoke, noise, and free drinks to mar your concentration.

When you start out, you're already $52 down. The theory appears to be that decks of cards cost $52 in Las Vegas (they cost less than $2 in the rest of the country). Your goal is to get into the black and stay there. Unlike Standard scoring, the passage of time is immaterial in Vegas scoring, and you don't get bonuses (just like the real Las Vegas). You get a flat $5 for each card you move to a suit stack, and that's all.

NOTE. *Select Options, Keep Score to keep a running total from game to game.*

Losing badly after a couple of games? As I mentioned earlier, this is the Las Vegas experience. Unlike the real thing, however, you can recoup your original ante with a quick trick: Select Games, Options, and under Scoring, Select None or Standard. Then press Enter, reselect the Vegas option, and press Enter again.

Dealer! Fresh Deck, Please!

The first time you fire up Solitaire, it's programmed to provide a different design for the back of the cards every session. If one of them takes your fancy, select it from the Game, Deck, Select Card Back menu.

Each of the four deck designs shown in Figure 11.2 include little animated pictures. My theory is that they are intended to distract and give Windows the advantage in the game. Either way, they are fun to look at. The deck designs in question are the sunny beach with the palm tree—in which the sun plays tricks every minute or so. The hand holding three aces shows the fourth ace popping out from beneath the sleeve several times a minute. The robot's lights and dials never stop moving. And the spooky castle features flapping bats.

However, once you've picked a deck design, you're locked into that design until you manually select another. But you can return to the halcyon days when the deck design was random. Revert to unpredictable deck designs by firing up Notepad and editing SOL.INI—Solitaire's own setup file.

The job's pretty easy, because there's often only one line in SOL.INI: *BACK=* followed by a design name. Delete the design name, leaving a solitary word and equals sign, and save the changes to the file as you leave Notepad. You'll never know what to expect when you fire up Solitaire again.

Gain a Tactical Advantage

Now that you know how to play and how Windows grades your performance, here are a few hints about getting the better of the mean machine.

Figure 11.2

These four deck designs distract you with their little animations. While they are fun, don't be fooled into using these in a timed game—you'll lose big-time.

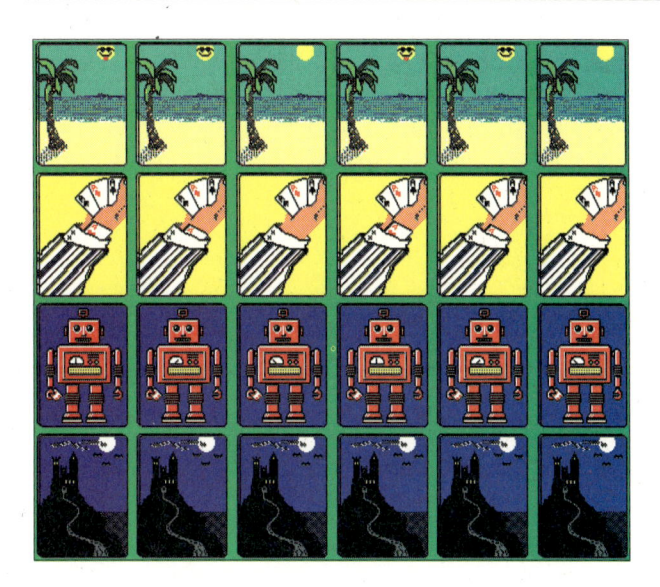

A Winning Strategy

We've already established that the Canfield/Klondike strain of Solitaire is based on the luck of the draw, but technique can help you get the better of the game. For example, whenever possible you should shift cards between row stacks—especially a run of cards from a large stack—rather than turning a new one from the deck. When you have a choice of fresh cards to turn up (either from the row or the deck), you are more likely to get lucky.

It's always a good idea to avoid dealing from the deck, because you incur a heavy point penalty whenever you reach the end of the deck.

Although there's also a penalty involved, you may sometimes want to play cards off the suit stack. It's not a desirable move, but if it can keep you from conceding a game, it's a worthwhile sacrifice.

Another technique to use when playing three cards off the deck is not to play all three (of the set of three you turn over) at a time—especially of the first set of three. This ensures that the second time through the pack by threes you'll hit different cards. Also, you might use the first pass through to scope out where the aces are and to figure out what to play on the second pass to get the aces to come up on the third pass.

Both these techniques may lose you points, but hey, who's counting?

Stop the Clock

Since passing time actually degrades your score under Standard scoring, stopping the clock can keep your score buoyant. It's easy enough to do: Click the

Minimize button or press Alt+Spacebar, followed by N, to minimize the window. Timing stops when the game's just an icon. Double-click on the minimized Solitaire icon, and the clock starts up again.

Of course, you don't get much of a chance to analyze your options this way, unless you get tricky first: Press Alt+PrintScreen a couple of times to capture the Solitaire window to the Clipboard. Then run the Clipboard Viewer to check the cards before you return to the game.

Don't Miss a Trick

Especially while you're learning the game, decrease your risk of missing a valuable opportunity by using the Outline Dragging feature. Select Game, Options, and choose Outline Dragging. This option provides a visual clue as to which stack you can legally place a card on.

With Outline Dragging switched on, drag each card you turn up over the stacks. If you pass over one on which you can drop the card, the stack will turn into an outline—about as big a visual hint as you'll need that this is where the card belongs.

Periodically, it's a good idea to drag whole stacks around over other ones to check whether an opportunity has arisen.

Let Your Windows Do the Stacking

Save time when stacking cards in the upper row. Don't drag the card, make Windows do it for you (after all, Windows—even on a 286—is much quicker than you are). If you turn over a card that belongs on one of your four stacks, just double-click on it. Windows takes it where it belongs right away.

Cheat!

You need one card, but—frustration of frustrations!—you're drawing three at a time, the one you want is the second of the three, and you can't drop the first anywhere. Don't fret—you *can* get to the second card. Select Undo to return the cards to the deck. Then hold down three keys—Ctrl+Alt+Shift—at the same time, and click on the deck again. Only one card will turn over. Keep holding down those three keys, and you'll cycle through the deck one card at a time.

■ Minesweeper

If Solitaire is all about gaining points (or money), Minesweeper appeals to a more primal instinct—survival. The premise is simple: You're marching through a minefield of at least 64 squares, and your task is to uncover all the safe zones in the field without being reduced to street pizza; when you step on one mine, all the mines in the field go off, and you've lost.

Minesweeper

Despite its gory punishment of losers, Minesweeper isn't a standard shoot 'em up war game. It's actually a game of logic and deductive reasoning. As you can see in Figure 11.3, you're given a count of mines adjacent to any safe square you select, and in many cases, that's enough information to skirt around most of the trouble zones. Of course, sometimes you don't have all the information you need, so there's a strong element of luck involved in winning the game.

Figure 11.3

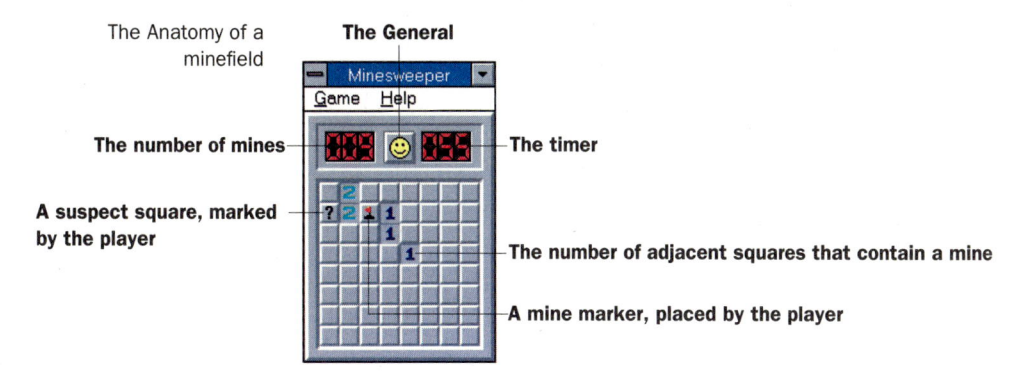

The Anatomy of a minefield

- The General
- The number of mines
- The timer
- A suspect square, marked by the player
- The number of adjacent squares that contain a mine
- A mine marker, placed by the player

The Object of the Game

Your mission: You are the commander of a scouting party, ahead of several platoons advancing into enemy territory. The General has charged you with uncovering all the safe squares in the minefield so that the platoons can navigate the field intact.

Your tools: You have three tools at your disposal for divining a course:

- A bargain-basement metal detector that can't pinpoint the exact location of a mine, but can tell you how many are in the immediate vicinity

- An unlimited supply of mine markers (activated by a single click on the right mouse button)

- An unlimited supply of suspect zone markers (activated by two clicks on the right mouse button)

Intelligence report: You know exactly how many mines have been planted in any given field—the information is up in the "LCD" readout to the left of the General. Apart from these fragments of information, you have only your wits to get you through the danger zone safely.

Your problem: Time is not on your side. To the right of the General, the clock ticks inexorably on. The quicker you get the job done, the better.

Playing the Game

Only one thing is certain in Minesweeper: The first step you take won't blow you up. After that, you're on your own. In the 64 squares of the beginner-level minefield, there are by default ten mines—meaning that approximately one square in six is wired to blow.

Taking the first step is easy (even if the consequences aren't); you just click once on a square—any square. The timer on the General's right begins counting and the expression on the General's face changes from a benevolant smile to a cartoon of Edvard Munch's screamer until you release the button. Ignore him... he's the most panic-stricken officer in the army. Release the button, and one of a few things will happen.

One or more squares will be marked off. If the single square you clicked contains a number, that's a count of the mines in the 8 squares that touch the square you clicked on—if the number's large, you're on shaky ground.

If you're lucky, you'll have hit a square with no adjacent mines, which precipitates a "sweep." A sweep uncovers each square it touches until it reaches the squares that live next to mines; a sweep looks like the first frame in Figure 11.4. Sweeps, therefore, consist mainly of blank, uncovered squares, fringed with numbered squares—and the more sweeps, the faster the game.

Figure 11.4

The anatomy of a losing game of Minesweeper: (a) the sweep, (b) the General worried by a new move, (c) you're hosed (you clicked on the wrong square)

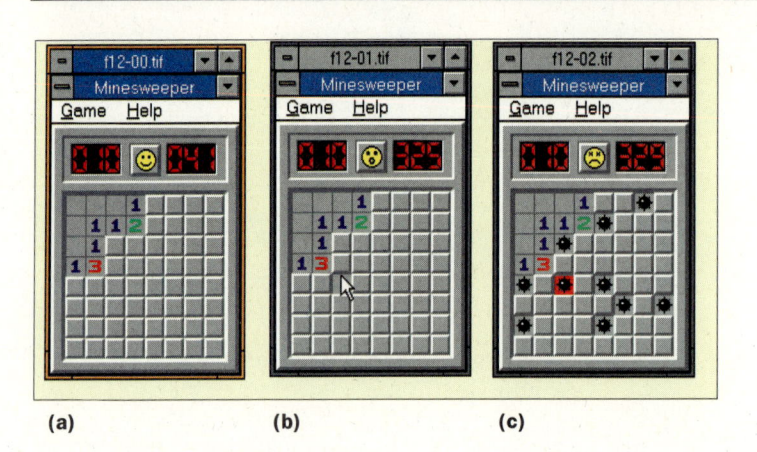

(a) (b) (c)

The trick now is determining which squares do cover mines, which may cover mines, and how to treat them. If you uncover all the safe squares without setting off a mine, you win. If you uncover a mine instead of marking it, you're hosed.

Unless you start out with a sweep, you have to make a couple of moves in the dark to glean enough information to intelligently deduce the best course of action. Determine the number of untouched squares next to an uncovered, numbered square. If the number of untouched squares is the same as the number on the uncovered square, they're all mines, and you should mark them as such.

If you know that a square is a mine, mark it with a single click of the *right* mouse button. When you do, the counter in the upper-left corner of the playing area reduces its number by one, even when you mark a perfectly safe square. If you click on a square by accident, just click on it twice to restore it to an unmarked square.

If you're pretty sure that a square's not safe, but you won't bet the farm on it (or risk buying the farm, for that matter), double-click on it with the *right* mouse button. If the Marks (?) option under the Game menu is checked (as it is by default), a question mark will appear over the square, and the mine counter won't deduct one from the score. It's easy enough to change a square marked with a question mark to a mine: Click on it twice with the right mouse button.

Knowing when to mark a square as a mine is the key to winning the game fast. Once you have marked at least one square as a mine, you might be able to uncover more squares quickly by *clearing around* them. (See "Clear around a Square," below.)

The likelihood is that you'll blow the field up more often than not, but that's war for you. What's worse, when the mines blow, Minesweeper tells you where you messed up. Everywhere you marked a mine on a square where there wasn't a mine, the game sticks a big red X over the mine symbols. The General changes his customary smile to a deep frown, too. The best response to this is to click on the General's face—which will start a new game. It's amazing how quickly the military brass cheers up.

Clear around a Square

Once you've marked off squares with the mine marker, you may be able to clear several more squares in one move. Move the cursor to a numbered square adjacent to the marked mine, and click both mouse buttons at the same time. All the untouched squares that lie next to the square will depress and spring back again if you're not next to a properly marked mine. But any adjacent squares whose mines *have* been marked, will be uncovered automatically.

This technique, while handy, comes with a few restrictions: You can't clear around a square if you haven't marked enough mines in the neighborhood. For example, if you try to clear around a square labeled 3, and you have marked only two squares with mines, nothing will happen. Or if you try to clear around an uncovered square, nothing will happen.

Oh, yes, and if you try to clear around a square with an unmarked mine next door, it blows and the game is over. So while this is a handy option when you're sure of what you're doing, it's fricassee time for the novice.

Scoring

Minesweeper scoring is simple. The counter to the right of the General indicates your playing time. The faster you find all the mines, the better your score.

If you complete a game faster than anybody else has managed to do, a dialog box pops up asking you to enter your name for the hall of fame. Go ahead, you've earned it.

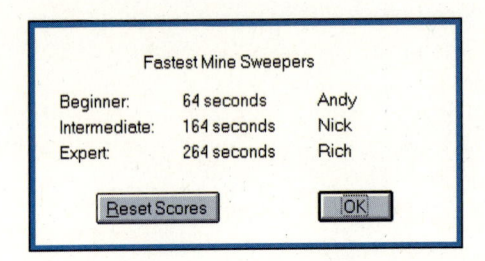

```
         Fastest Mine Sweepers

Beginner:       64 seconds    Andy
Intermediate:  164 seconds    Nick
Expert:        264 seconds    Rich

   [Reset Scores]         [OK]
```

To see a list of the fastest playing times, select the Game menu's Best Times option. If you see any game won in less than a couple of minutes, somebody cheated. Don't worry—you'll learn how to better your scores by smuggling in a better mine detector later in the chapter.

Gratuitous Cheating: Enter the Hall of Fame (through the Back Door)

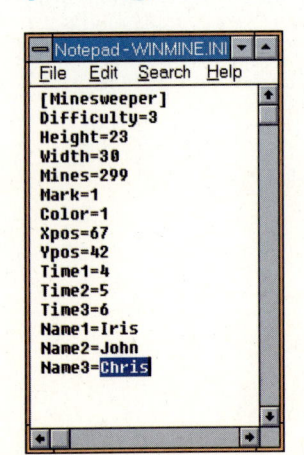

```
Notepad - WINMINE.INI
File  Edit  Search  Help
[Minesweeper]
Difficulty=3
Height=23
Width=30
Mines=299
Mark=1
Color=1
Xpos=67
Ypos=42
Time1=4
Time2=5
Time3=6
Name1=Iris
Name2=John
Name3=Chris
```

Were you ever irritated by the absurdly high scores some young punk earned at an arcade computer game? Did you ever long to be in the highest scorer league, but never came close? Sneak into the ranks of the miracle minesweepers by editing WINMINE.INI. Open the file in Notepad and scroll down to the *Time1=* through *Time3=* lines. Time1 is the beginner mode high score, Time2 is Intermediate, and Time3, Expert. *Name1=* through *Name3=* are the corresponding name lines. So pick a small number, and edit the default times of 999 with something low (but not too low, so as to give the game away). Then enter your handle in the Name lines. Well done!

The Minefield You Always Wanted

Played a few games as a beginner, and feel like moving up to something a little more advanced? Try out the different levels under the Game menu: Pick any size field shown in Figure 11.5 or make your own.

Figure 11.5

The art of playing dangerously. Minesweeper can be as simple or as perilous as you want it to be—but you'll always have to contend with ten or more mines.

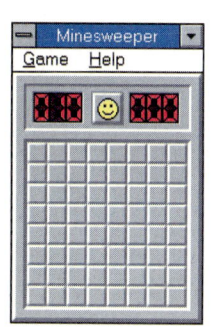

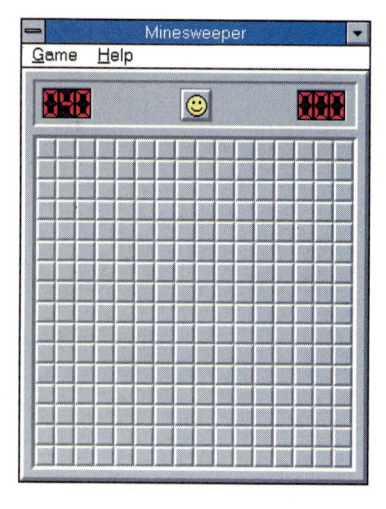

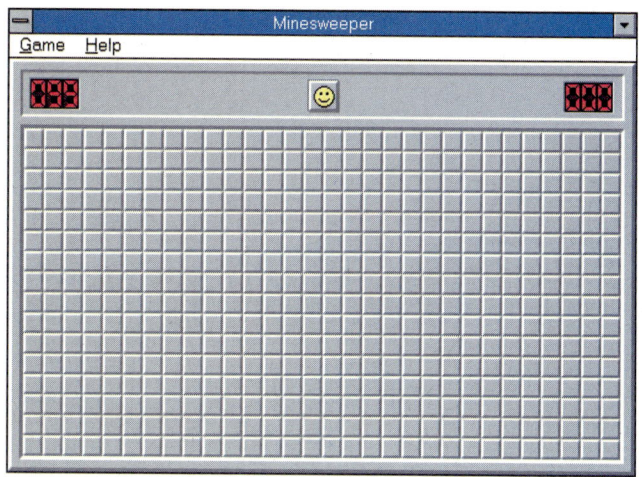

The beginner level, as you've already discovered, works on an 8-by-8-square grid laced with ten mines. The intermediate level is much bigger—16-by-16 squares and 40 mines—and the expert level is downright scary, sporting a 16-by-30-square grid with 99 mines.

But that's peanuts compared to what you can build using the Game menu's Custom option. Enter the dimensions for the layout, and the number of mines you want to avoid. The smallest field you can design is the beginner level—64 squares and ten mines. The biggest board is 24 squares high by 30 wide. The number of mines isn't so restricted, but it's best to reckon the number of mines with the Calculator so that there's one mine for every five or six squares.

Gain a Tactical Advantage

That about covers the basics. What you need now is to develop a technique for winning, and winning quickly. The best technique? Get help from every source you can. Even when the source could be categorized as an unfair advantage. Remember—Windows runs on machines capable of processing millions of instructions every second. You can handle more, but Windows doesn't get distracted. All's fair in games of war.

Feel Free to Be Uncertain

Play it safe: Mark the squares about which you're fairly uncertain with question marks. They won't lull you into a false sense of security like mine markers do, and they aren't dangerous either: If you clear a nearby uncovered square by pressing both mouse buttons, a suspect square that doesn't cover a mine can be uncovered automatically. Try the same trick with a safe square that's mistakenly marked as a mine, and the game's over.

Stop the Clock

Your score is based entirely on the time you take. To buy some time, press Alt+PrintScreen to copy the Minesweeper window to the Clipboard; then click on Minesweeper's Minimize button or press Alt+Spacebar followed by N to minimize the window. The clock stops and you can run the Clipboard Viewer to work out which squares are the most dangerous. When you've worked out the lay of the land, double-click on the minimized Minesweeper icon and continue.

Don't Mark—Win!

The point of Minesweeper isn't to mark every mine in the field—it's to uncover all the safe squares. Marking mines is convenient early on in the game, but once you're down to your last few squares, concentrate on uncovering the safe squares instead of wasting time (and thus eroding your score) marking the mines.

Cheat!

There's a beacon hidden in the Minesweeper code that, once activated, sends a signal when the cursor is over a mine. The problem is that the signal is a single pixel, almost concealed in the upper-left corner of the screen. The first step in sweeping mines with this virtual metal detector is removing your wallpaper—unless you have exceptionally plain wallpaper, the upper-left corner of your monitor won't show the one-pixel beacon clearly. First, click on the Control Panel, bring up the Desktop option, and select [None] under Wallpaper. Then make sure there's no pattern selected either. Click on OK, and select Minesweeper.

With Minesweeper in the foreground, hold down the Shift key with your right hand and type **XYZZY** with your left. Move the application up towards the upper-left corner of the screen (but don't let it obscure the corner itself). Now, hold down Ctrl and Alt, and move the mouse around the board. You will notice that the single pixel right on the corner of the the screen will change from black to white as you move the mouse. The pixel is black when the mouse is over a mine and white when it's over a safe square. The tactic: Click when the pixel's white!

■ What Was the Point of This Chapter?

In "Playing to Win," you learned how to play, score, configure, approach, and cheat at Solitaire and Minesweeper.

- *Windows Wasters*
- *Wasting Words*
- *The Chronicles of Wasted Spreadsheets*
- *A la recherche des screens perdus*
- *A Final Challenge*
- *What Was the Point of This Chapter?*

CHAPTER 12

Hunting for Easter Eggs

Uncovering evidence that Windows programmers waste more time than you ever dreamed possible.

They are hiding deep below the surface of your Windows applications. They are often very entertaining. They are fun routines that programmers encode when they are tired of being productive. And they are the epitome of wasted time.

In years to come, some enterprising historian of computer science will uncover the origins of the elusive animations that lie hidden in the code of Windows applications, but until then, their beginnings are shrouded in mystery. One thing is certain: They started as cast lists of the people who produced the software—a tribute to the hard work that went on behind the scenes. But the static gang screens soon evolved into the scrolling credits you see at the end of movies. Then the real fun began with all kinds of animation—many of which I'll uncover later in the chapter.

Many otherwise reputable software companies—from Microsoft to Borland to Lotus to Symantec—release programs laced with hidden routines. Your task, as a seasoned time-waster, is to find these routines in your software. Rumor has it that the difficulty of tracking them down is quite intentional; that way, they can pass undetected under the eagle eyes of project managers who frown upon such frivolities. The task of uncovering these hidden screens is referred to in programming circles as an "easter egg hunt," so the screens themselves are called "easter eggs."

■ Windows Wasters

Enough of the history. It's time to cut to the chase and uncover those eggs. To give you some idea of where to look for the screens, a crack team of *PC/Computing* editors has spent time (now totaling years) between assignments tracking them down. Even after such a concerted effort, we could find fewer than a dozen. It was a tough job, but somebody had to do it. Here are the fruits of our labors. Enjoy.

The Wallpaper That Built Windows 3.0

Although there are undoubtedly earlier examples of the static gang screen, the first major-league example was tucked into Windows 3.0. By contorting their fingers into a knuckle-cracking Digital Twister arrangement, early egg hunters uncovered perhaps the most boring wallpaper of all time. In those early days, it *was* a big thrill, although by today's standards, the results are rather feeble.

If you happen to have a spare copy of Windows 3.0 lying around on your hard disk, perhaps you'd like to surf this wave of nostalgia. Load the program, and while it's running, follow these steps:

1. Minimize all your applications, and then hold down F3.

2. Type **WIN3**, then release F3.

3. Press Backspace.

```
THE MAGICIANS:
aaronr amitc arthurc bobgu chipa chrisc chrisg clarkc craigc davidds davidw earleh fernandd
georgep glenns gunterz jaywant jimmat kens kensy lalithar marcw mikecole mikedr peterbe
philba ralphi richp rong sankar toddla tonyg
THE TESTERS:
bertm camp chrissh chriswil davidti dougr erich jeffst johnen johns korys lyndahl mattl randyg
richsa rong stephenb stuart terrib timg tycar
USER ED:
betsyt chrisbr chrisdo chrish danbr danda davee garyb joank jimgr jimro kathypf laurak laurap
lindah lindas loriw marcsm marionj michaelm niklas pauli peggy petrar robertaw rosem scottmc
sharot shelleym stevenwa tonye
PROGRAM MANAGEMENT:
davidcol ericst greglo jodys lisacr markwa melissmo timmcc
MARKETING:
celesteb danbo jonro richab sherryr tomja
SCENERY:
alig tandyt virginia susank
SPECIAL THANKS TO:
bobm chrisla donha kaikal lins neilk scottlu stevewo MSFT
MOMS:
chrisga julieg lorisi maryho sarahh
DADS:
billg russw steveb
```

The wallpaper turns into a list of the people involved in programming Windows, divided into groups. The Magicians, Testers, User Ed, Program Management, Marketing, Scenery, recipients of special thanks, and moms and dads involved in the project all get their strokes here. Each of them is listed by e-mail address, so if you felt like sending personal congratulations to one of the Windows 3.0 parents, say, billg (whoever that may be), all you'd need is Microsoft's InterNet ID—which for your information is microsoft.com.

When pioneering egg hunters tired of the information on their wallpaper (and let's face it, it doesn't take long), a quick click from the left mouse button was all it took to clear the display.

The Windows 3.1 Cartoon Carnival

Hidden in the bowels of Windows 3.1 is a cast list with a more 1990s set of production values. Waving flags, cartoon characters, and a full scrolling list of credits make this a veritable feature film—and when you see the various incarnations of the cartoon character, you'll appreciate that it's not only Hollywood that can morph one head into another.

Reaching the list is a three-step process that involves holding down the Ctrl and Shift keys while you open the Program Manager's Help About screen on three separate occasions—quite a chore, but here we go:

1. Hold down the Ctrl and Shift keys for steps 2 through 5.

2. In Program Manager, select Help, About Program Manager.

3. Double-click on the lefthand side of the Windows flag logo—where it disintegrates into small squares. Nothing will happen, so click on OK to close the box.

4. Again select Help, About Program Manager, and double-click on the main body of the flag. A tiny Windows flag blowing in the wind will appear next to a general dedication to the developers of Windows. This is peanuts compared to the real show. Click on OK to close the box.

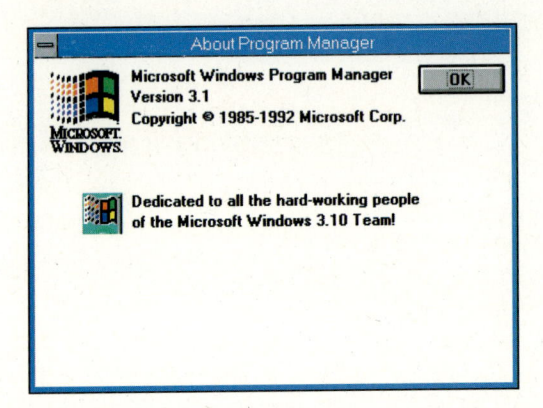

5. Once again, select Help, About Program Manager, and double-click on one of the panes on the right-hand portion of the flag, and watch the show.

A list of e-mail IDs will scroll by. The MC of the cartoon changes if you repeat the process and select a different pane on the Windows logo (in step 5). There are four heads in all (one for each pane)—including a ferret (or is it a teddy bear?) and Bill Gates.

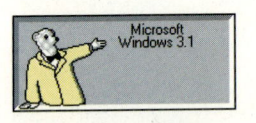

Norton Desktop for Windows Photographs and Philosophy

It's not pure Windows, but the Norton Desktop for Windows (NDW, versions 1.x and 2.0) is arguably the most popular third-party shell—a replacement for the Program Manager. If you use it, not only can you skip this book's chapter on program mismanagement, you can also catch a profound philosophical treatise, complete with monochrome headshots of the program's developers. To enjoy the show, follow these steps:

1. From the NDW shell, select Help, About.
2. With one hand, press and hold down three keys: N, D, and W (and brave the beeping this causes—it's for a good cause).
3. Click three times on the Norton Desktop icon.
4. Release the N, D, and W keys.
5. Wait.

After an eternity or two, while NDW is loading photographic images of the so-called Viper development team, a rogue's gallery will appear.

After the routine has had a chance to rest from its labors, it scrolls messages in the title bar to enlighten the masses with the sayings of such profound philosophers as Hilaire Belloc, Victor Hugo, Richard Nixon, Morrissey, and Anonymous.

■ Wasting Words

So much for Windows and its shell. Developers of all kinds of software like to leave their mark somewhere in their all-important projects. Take word processing programs, for example. There's no shortage of secret screens there. And what better way to overcome writer's block or writer's cramp than to take in a movie? And what better movie than one on your PC screen?

The Day the Word Stood Still

In Word for Windows 2.0's hidden monster movie, nineties technology meets fifties science fiction. Featuring six animated stick men and a large green monster, this time-waster can be played again and again. Its happy ending—

complete with cheers and fireworks—truly warms the heart (unless you like WordPerfect). Here's how to get to the show:

1. Start Word for Windows with any document open (even Document1).
2. Select Tools, Macro, and in the Macro Name box, type **spiff**. Press Enter or click on the Edit button.
3. In the macro box that appears, highlight and delete the lines *Sub MAIN* and *End Sub* as well as the blank lines between.
4. Close the macro document and save the changes.
5. Now choose Help, About, and click once on the Word for Windows icon.

Soon you'll see a few minutes worth of running men, a green monster that gets his comeuppance in the end, and the victors jumping up and down in triumph. Then there's a fireworks display with credits.

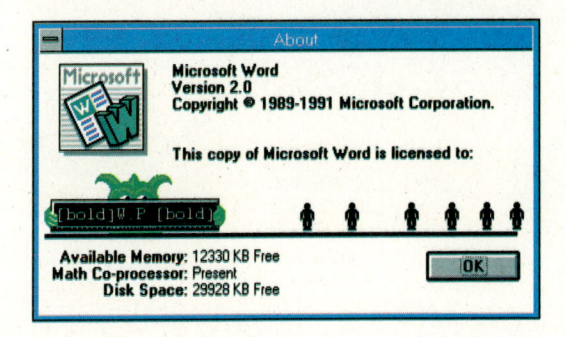

You can watch reruns any time during this Winword session by just repeating step 5—but be aware that this little routine tends to hog Windows resources. If you have a large print job or a BBS download going on in the background, this will bring it to a halt.

WARNING. *Don't save the global changes to the glossary when you quit Winword, because that affects your changes to the Spiff macro.*

Word for Windows 1's Fire in the Sky

Never upgraded to Word for Windows 2.0? Don't worry, there's still some fun to be had from the program's first incarnations. To bring up and watch a fireworks display, read on:

1. Open Word for Windows and in Document1, choose Format, Define Styles.
2. In the dialog box that pops up, press the Options button.

3. In the Based On box, type the word **Normal**. You'll get an error message—ignore it and click on OK to close the error box.

4. Click on Cancel to close the Define Style dialog box and return to the document.

5. Select Help, About.

6. Turn CapsLock on and press these four keys at once: O, P, U, and S. Then release the keys.

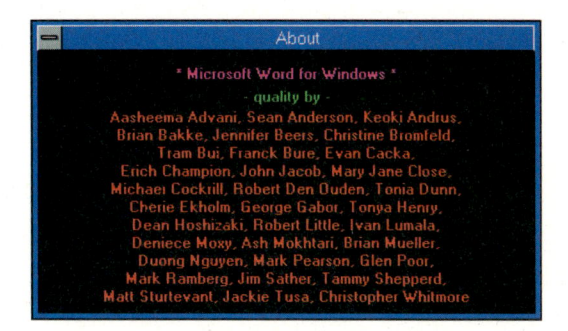

```
                        About
               * Microsoft Word for Windows *
                      - quality by -
           Aasheema Advani, Sean Anderson, Keoki Andrus,
             Brian Bakke, Jennifer Beers, Christine Bromfeld,
                  Tram Bui, Franck Bure, Evan Cacka,
              Erich Champion, John Jacob, Mary Jane Close,
              Michael Cockrill, Robert Den Ouden, Tonia Dunn,
                Cherie Ekholm, George Gabor, Tonya Henry,
                Dean Hoshizaki, Robert Little, Ivan Lumala,
                Deniece Moxy, Ash Mokhtari, Brian Mueller,
                 Duong Nguyen, Mark Pearson, Glen Poor,
                 Mark Ramberg, Jim Sather, Tammy Shepperd,
             Matt Sturtevant, Jackie Tusa, Christopher Whitmore
```

You'll catch a firework display with rolling credits—nothing too thrilling, but entertaining in a pinch.

Ami Pro 2.0's Video Tribute to Elvis

Lotus Development combined the teen obsessions of two decades—namely Elvis and video games—into a single masterly easter egg for version 2.0 of Ami Pro. The game is fun, but in the later stages, you'll probably wish, for the first and only time in your Windows experience, that you had a slower machine. (You might even miss Elvis the first couple of times you play.)

Here's how to begin the fun:

1. Choose Help, About Ami Pro.

2. Now hold down the Shift, Ctrl, and Alt keys as you follow steps 3 through 5.

3. Press F7.

4. Type the letters **S**, **P**, **A**, and **M**.

5. Note the amount of available memory (in kilobytes) listed in the lower-left corner of the Help About box. Enter the last digit in the available memory listing and then the third-to-last digit.

6. Release the Shift, Ctrl, and Alt keys.

210 Chapter 12: Hunting for Easter Eggs

What you'll see is a black screen with bouncing heads floating around on it. Beneath each head is a name, and you can guarantee each of them had a hand in developing the program. Click on a head, and it will disappear. As each head disappears, the remaining heads get faster and faster, until you're left with a few heads dodging around so quickly that you can barely keep up with them.

One of the heads (it seems to change every time) will turn into a remarkably familiar teen idol of the 1950s, bearing the name T. King. Try as you might, you can't get rid of this head with any amount of clicking. Reminiscent of supermarket tabloids, isn't it? Once you've had your fun and need to return to work, press Esc.

■ The Chronicles of Wasted Spreadsheets

The Windows spreadsheet wars of the early 1990s left no casualties, but the unusually unpleasant advertising campaigns from many of the major players made it clear that no love was lost between the warring factions.

The Chronicles of Wasted Spreadsheets   211

It's unsurprising, therefore, that the hidden screens in many of these programs exhibited a, shall we say, hearty partisanship in favor of the home development team.

Excel 4.0's Bug Buster

Want to know what the Excel programmers thought of their competition? Check out this little animation—with a cast of two icons and a lot of flying insects:

1. Open a blank document and select Options, Toolbars.
2. Click on the Customize button. In the Categories list box, select Custom.
3. From the top row of icons, select the Solitaire icon (don't pretend you don't know that one by now!) and drag it onto your regular toolbar.
4. Click on OK without assigning any command to the button, and click on Close to get rid of the Customize dialog box.
5. Maximize the worksheet by pressing the up-arrow in its upper-right corner.
6. Press Ctrl+Shift and click on the Solitaire icon.

A bouncing icon appears, breaks open to allow flies to buzz out, and is chased off by the Excel icon. In what is probably the first Windows-based reference to *Terminator 2: Judgment Day*, the words "No Problemo" appear. You can replay this animation any time in this or subsequent sessions by opening a new file and repeating steps 5 and 6.

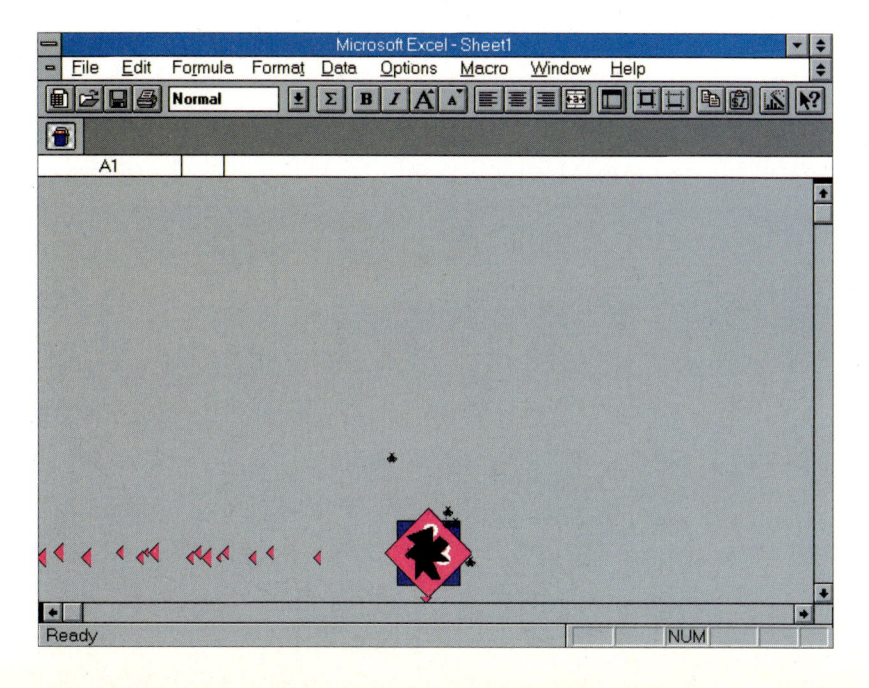

212 Chapter 12: Hunting for Easter Eggs

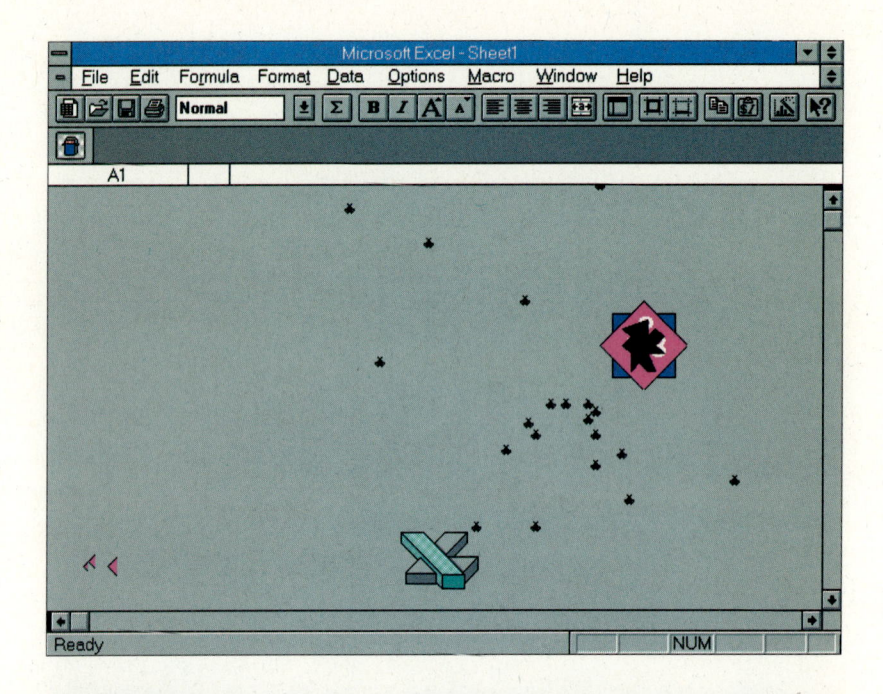

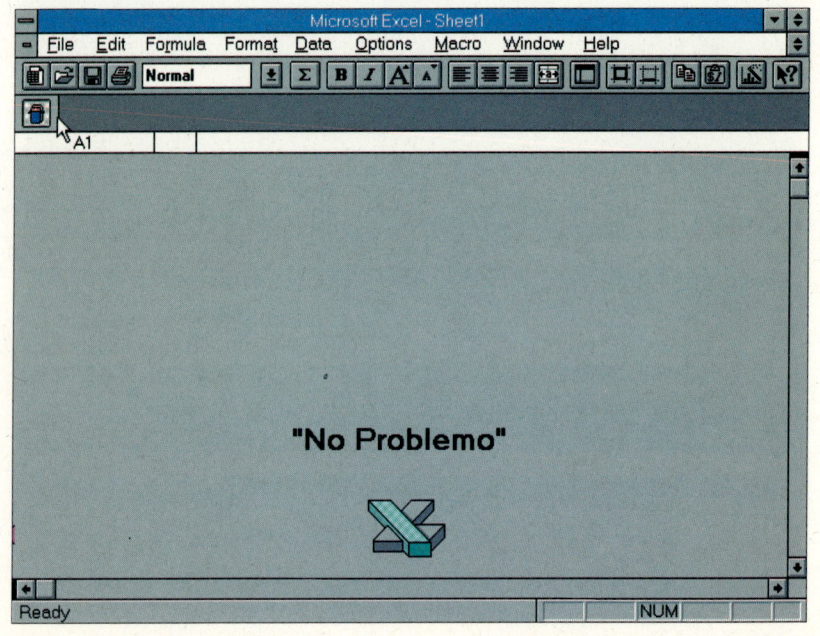

So Much for Pathos

Excel 3.0's animated screen reminds me of a recurring Monty Python joke. Michael Palin, dressed in a too-small, three-button suit plays mousy twit Arthur Pooty. In scene after scene, he suffers a catastrophic failure of nerve, and in a moment charged with high emotional content, he walks away from his past. He opens a door, walks out, and a 50-ton weight falls on him. The moral: So much for pathos.

Here's how to see the mighty Excel logo falling at top speed, followed by scrolling credits of the parties responsible for this sad moment:

1. In a blank worksheet, select Formula, Goto.

2. In the reference box type **IV16384** and click on OK. This brings you to the lower-right corner of the worksheet.

3. Click on the down and right scrollbar arrows until cell IV16384 is the only cell you can see.

4. Select Format, Row Height, and type **0**. Then click on OK.

5. Select Format, Column Width, and type **0**. Then click on OK.

6. Click on the button (it's the only thing left onscreen, so it's hard to miss!) and watch the action.

Who could follow that act?

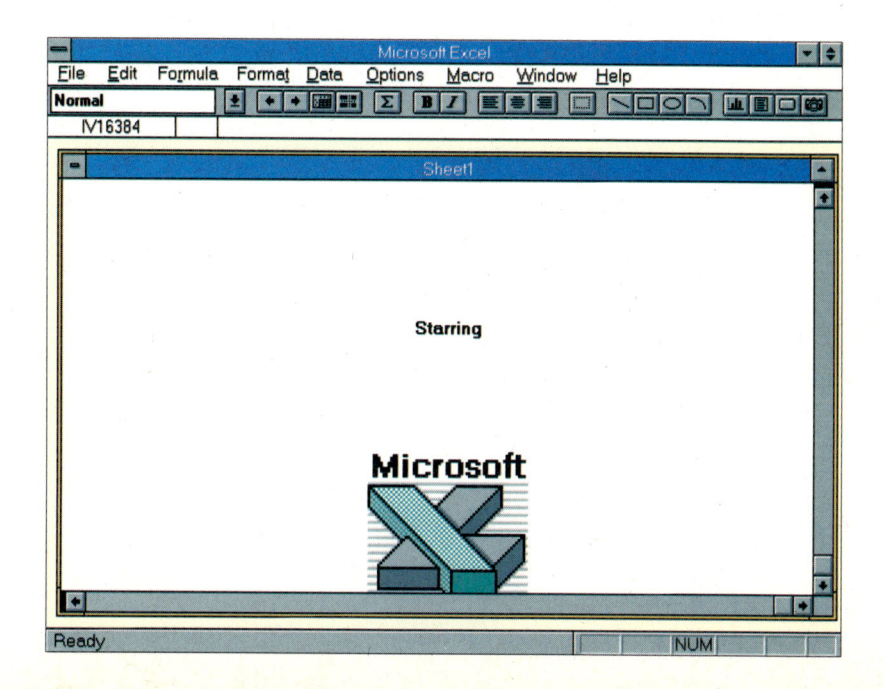

214 Chapter 12: Hunting for Easter Eggs

Terminator 1-2-3 1.1: Judgment Day

Not to be outdone by the Microsoft developers' tribute to Arnold Schwarzenegger's seminal celluloid work of 1991, the folks at Lotus Development added their own in 1-2-3 for Windows Release 1.1.

In a work that echoes themes from Excel's two earlier animations, the Lotus feature has all you could hope for in a rows-and-columns thriller. It comes with a play button in the lower-right corner of the spreadsheet. It sprinkles in falling icons. It offers a quotation from Schwarzenegger. And it's executed by a cast of dozens. Here's how to get started:

1. Open a new worksheet and maximize it.
2. Press the F5 (GOTO) key, specify cell address **IV8192**, and click on OK.
3. Drag the column width of the single cell that's showing to the leftmost point. When you release the mouse button, the column letters IU will appear above the cell.
4. Drag the bottom line of row 8192 up until its height is at its minimum value (namely, 1).

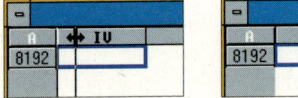

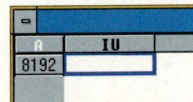

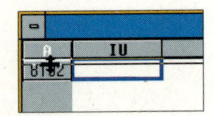

5. Click on the intersection of the row and column labels in the upper-left corner of the worksheets—it's labeled with the letter A.

In the fun that follows, two falling letters get vaporized by the starburst-laden 1-2-3 logo and a proverb in Spanish (mostly) appears at the head of the cast list. Truly an inspirational moment…

"Hasta la vista, baby!"

The Rockport Staff

Quattro Pro for Windows and the Elegant Meal

While Microsoft and Lotus play their games of retaliation, Borland goes for a more sedentary and sophisticated pace. Their hidden screen is static without being dull, taking the form of a swanky bistro's multifonted menu. Here's how to get past the *maître d'hôtel*:

1. Type in any text in any cell in a workbook, and press Enter.
2. Select Data, Parse from the menu.
3. Click on the Create Button.
4. Click on the Edit button.
5. Hold down the Shift key, and press the question mark key three times.

On the third stroke of the question mark, the menu for Cafe Borland will pop up. The chefs and tasters of the fare on the menu are mentioned by name, along with the recommended meal for the day from the French chef Philippe.

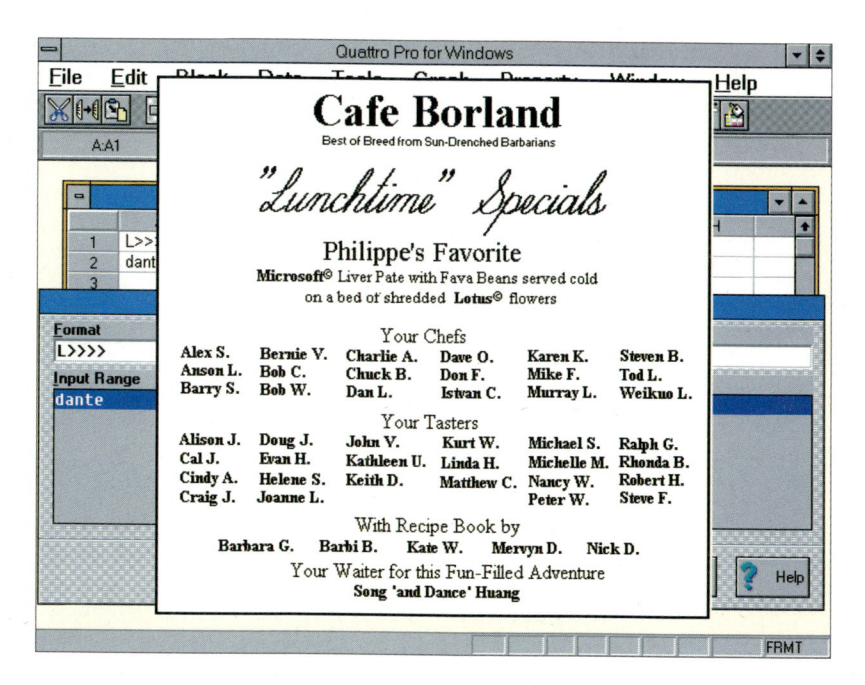

■ A la recherche des screens perdus

Many of the hidden screens you find (eventually), aren't based on fierce competition that exists (at least in the minds of developers) with similar applications. Some are just there to celebrate an application well programmed. Two such applications, CorelDRAW and Paradox for Windows, are cases in point.

CorelDRAW and the Hot Air Mouse

Anyone who's used CorelDRAW knows that its signature design is the hot air balloon. Examples of these balloons crop up everywhere from the packaging to icons to startup screens and copyright screens. One example features prominently in a hidden screen, too. Here's how to uncover it in CorelDRAW versions 3.0 and 4.0:

1. Select Help, About CorelDRAW!

2. In the About CorelDRAW! screen, locate the hot air balloon icon in the upper left corner. In version 3.0 of the program, hold down Ctrl and Shift and double-click on the icon. In version 4.0, just double click on the icon.

3. An elongated About box will appear with a balloon at the base. Hold down the left mouse button to make the balloon rise up. Release the button, and the rising balloon will slow down and begin to descend. Hold it down again, the balloon will slowly rise up.

4. In version 4.0, there's an additional treat. Click a couple of times on the right mouse button, and impersonators of a certain celebrity will parachute out of the sky.

There you have it. The perfect melding of an established trade mark with an easter egg screen, coupled with a rudimentary flight simulator. The subtle acceleration and deceleration of the balloon when you depress and release the mouse button is strikingly like the effect of the burner in a hot air balloon. What more could you ask for (except possibly a little wind drift factor for realism)?

Paradox for Windows Plays Pdox and the Wolf

We've already established from Quattro Pro for Windows that Borland's secret screens have a touch of class. Paradox for Windows goes one better with a cast list with music: a little refrain from Prokofiev's magnum opus for children, *Peter and the Wolf*. For this cultural extravaganza, follow these steps:

1. In Paradox for Windows, select Help, About...

2. When the About dialog box appears, press Shift+Alt+C at the same time.

A new dialog appears, a virtual lake filled with fake waves and a number of duck couples (which of course is a reference to the product name, Pair o' ducks). A rather lame dialog takes place in speech bubbles between a few duck groups, with a couple of zingy lines, and a lot of names.

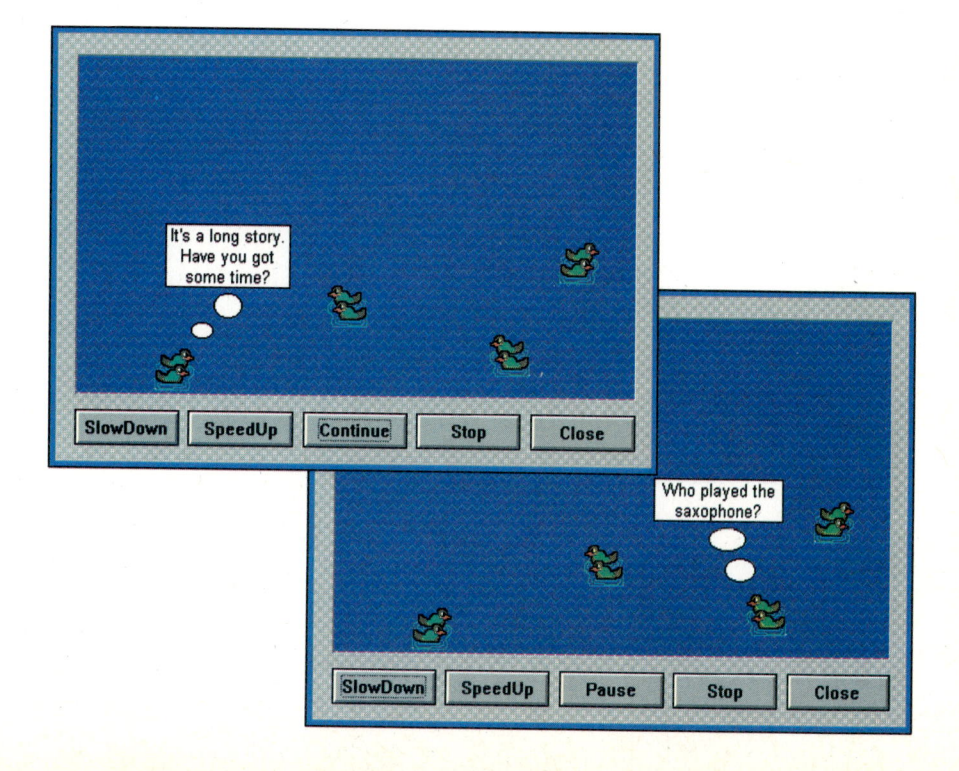

You have the option of speeding up the dialog, pausing it, or shutting it down, but you'll want to wait until the end, where the name of a sax-toting Frenchman appears to Peter's chorus (assuming your sound card or sound driver is enabled).

■ A Final Challenge

Those are all the Easter eggs that a dedicated team of crack time-wasters could uncover. True, other applications do produce cast lists, but nothing as dramatic or well-hidden as the real eggs. Lotus Notes, for example, will scroll names through the title bar when you select Help, About, and click on the words Lotus or Iris from the third paragraph—it's like an Easter egg, but it's too easy to find. Most hDC Microapps, including Express and Power Launcher, will throw up a static cast list if you select Help, About, and press Ctrl+Shift as you double-click on the spot where the starburst appears on the hDC logo. And PC Tools for Windows has a little fireworks show and cast list: From the Desktop application, select Help, About Desktop, then hold down Ctrl+Shift and on the Desktop icon, double click with *both* mouse buttons (this takes a little practice, but it can be done). A few niceties spice up the display. A single click anywhere in the window with the left mouse button will shift the center of the fireworks to wherever you clicked. And a single click with the right mouse button will make the fireworks burst at random from anywhere on the screen. But these routines are small potatoes.

Your challenge is to uncover more of these routines in the applications you use daily. As new versions of programs are released, the old directions given here will no longer lead to buried treasures. Your task, then, is to take all you've learned in this book about wasting time in Windows, and use it to uncover these routines. The road is hard, the frustrations many, and the rewards…well, they outweigh the pain.

So why are you waiting? Put this book away, fire up that PC, and don't just sit there—waste some time!

■ What Was the Point of This Chapter?

"Hunting for Easter Eggs" had no point. It merely proved that you're not the only one who wastes time in Windows. The developers of Windows applications hide fun little routines in their programs that are well-nigh impossible to find. However, if you look hard enough, you can find them in:

- Windows 3.0 and 3.1
- Norton Desktop for Windows

What Was the Point of This Chapter? 219

- Word for Windows 1.1 and 2.0
- Ami Pro (the best game I never paid for)
- Excel 3.0 and 4.0
- 1-2-3 for Windows 1.1
- Quattro Pro for Windows
- CorelDRAW 3.0 and 4.0
- Paradox for Windows
- Sundry hDC applications, Lotus Notes, and PC Tools for Windows
- Probably many more (though I couldn't find them)

■ Appendix: Programs on the Disk

The disk in the back of this book is loaded with as many time-wasting utilities as possible. Some of these are disguised as productivity tools—programs you'll work with, but *enjoy* working with. The rest are unadulterated fun. But like any Windows application, they need to be installed and understood before you can start using them.

So, gentle reader, here are the programs you'll find on the disk....

■ Programs You'll Work With

Before and After Batch Files

File name: BEFAFTER.EXE

Copyright: 1993, Dylan Tweney

Status: Freeware

Why You Need Them

These DOS batch files help you track the changes other programs make to your hard disk when you install them. BEFORE.BAT takes a "snapshot" of your current system configuration, and after you've installed an application, AFTER.BAT logs all the changes.

How to Install Them

To use the Before and After batch files properly, you should install them right away. Follow these steps:

1. Select your Windows directory in the File Manager and choose File, Create Directory to create a new subdirectory under it. Type **INSTALL** to name the new subdirectory, and click on OK. (Note: You can name the INSTALL directory whatever you want, but it must be a subdirectory of the Windows directory for the batch files to work properly.)

2. Copy BEFAFTER.EXE from the companion disk into the new INSTALL directory.

3. Double-click on BEFAFTER.EXE in the File Manager. It's a self-extracting archive, so you'll briefly see a DOS screen as the files are extracted, and then you'll be returned to Windows.

4. Back in the File Manager, press F5 to refresh the File Manager screen. You'll see six new files: BEFORE.BAT, AFTER.BAT, BEFORE.PIF, AFTER.PIF, BEFORE.ICO, and AFTER.ICO.

5. Use the PIF Editor to open BEFORE.PIF and AFTER.PIF, and make sure the path names listed for the command line and working directory are correct. (If your Windows directory is anything other than C:\WINDOWS, you'll need to change that part of each path in the .PIF files.) Save the changes to the .PIF files and return to Windows.

6. Finally, create Program Manager items for BEFORE.PIF and AFTER.PIF, using the included .ICO files for their icons. That's all there is to it!

How You Use Them

Before you install any application—for DOS or for Windows—double-click on the BEFORE icon in the Program Manager. You'll see a DOS window appear as BEFORE.BAT begins recording your system information. BEFORE.BAT will keep you informed of its progress; when it's done, you'll be returned to Windows.

Install your application. After its installation is complete, double-click on the AFTER icon in the Program Manager. When you see the Parameters prompt, type the name of the application you just installed —you can use any name up to eight characters in length. Then press Enter or click on OK—AFTER.BAT will compile a list of all the changes and additions to your system.

WinZip 4.0

File name: WINZIP4.EXE

Copyright: 1991–1993, Nico Mak

Status: Shareware, $29

Register: Nico Mak, P.O. Box 919, Bristol, CT 06011–0919

Benefits of registration: Receive disk with latest version; no "*nag screen*" (request for registration during the program's startup).

Why You Need It

You need WinZip to extract the files on the disk that have the .ZIP extension. WinZip increases your disk space by compressing files you don't use all the time into archive files. This program uses the file-compression program PKZIP (if you have it) or LHA (on the disk).

How to Install It

If you already have PKZIP or LHA installed, make a note of the directories where those files are located. You'll need to know their paths when you configure

WinZip, the first time you run it. Use File Manager to find the files PKZIP.EXE, PKUNZIP.EXE, ZIP2EXE.EXE, and LHA.EXE, and write down their full paths. Now you're ready to install WINZIP4.EXE:

1. If you've already installed BEFORE and AFTER, run BEFORE.BAT now to take a snapshot of your system, so you can identify all the changes WinZip's installation makes.

2. Create a directory on your hard disk to hold the WinZip files. In the File Manager, choose File, Create Directory, and type a name for the WinZip directory (for example, **WINZIP**). Then click on OK.

3. Copy WINZIP4.EXE from the companion disk into the new WinZip directory.

4. Double-click on WINZIP4.EXE in the Program Manager to extract all of WinZip's files from this self-extracting archive file. You'll briefly see a DOS screen as WinZip's files are extracted.

5. When you are returned to the File Manager, double-click on WINZIP.EXE to run WinZip. When WinZip is activated for the first time, the Welcome and Configuration dialog boxes appear. WinZip will also offer to add its icon to your Program Manager Accessories group. (Agree to the offer and move the icon later, if you'd prefer the icon elsewhere.)

6. When you're done configuring WinZip, installation is complete. If you ran BEFORE.BAT before installing WinZip, run AFTER.BAT now. When you see the dialog box that prompts you for "Parameters," type **WINZIP**. AFTER.BAT will record all changes to your system in the file WINZIP.TXT in your INSTALL subdirectory.

How You Use It

When you see a file with a .ZIP or .LZH extension in the File Manager, just double-click on it to launch WinZip and open the archive file. WinZip shows you a list of the files compressed within the archive file. To extract files, just select the files you want and click on the Extract button. WinZip will ask you to specify the directory where you want to put the extracted files, and then it will decompress them to that directory.

LHA Version 2.13

File name: LHA213.EXE

Copyright: 1991, Haruyasu Yoshizaki

Status: Freeware

224 Appendix: Programs on the Disk

Why You Need It

LHA version 2.13 is a file-compression program, or "archiver," which you can use to compress files, decompress them, or make self-extracting archive files. It's free, and all you need is one executable file to do everything. It works just fine with WinZip, too.

How to Install It

To install LHA version 2.13, follow these steps:

1. First use the File Manager to create a new directory on your hard drive to hold the LHA files. Choose File, Create Directory, type a directory name, and click on OK.

2. Copy the self-extracting archive file LHA213.EXE from the companion disk to this new directory.

3. Once you've copied LHA213.EXE onto your hard drive, double-click on it in the File Manager. You'll see a DOS screen with a brief description of LHA. Press Y on the keyboard to extract LHA's files. When the program is done extracting, it returns you to the File Manager.

4. In the File Manager, press F5 to refresh the screen, and check the files that were extracted. There should be four: LHA.EXE, the actual program you use for extracting and archiving files; LHA.HLP, a text file (*not* a Windows Help file) giving a brief overview of LHA's commands; LHA.DOC, a text file providing more extensive documentation; and HISTORY.ENG, a short history of LHA's various versions.

5. Once you've verified that these four files are present on your hard drive, you may delete LHA213.EXE from your hard drive. LHA is ready to use.

How You Use It

Use LHA with WinZip to archive files you want to compress. If you're feeling intrepid, LHA.HLP provides an introduction to using LHA from the DOS command line.

Plug-In for Program Manager Version 1.30

File name: PLUG-IN.ZIP

Copyright: 1992, Plannet Crafters, Inc., all rights reserved

Status: Shareware, $20

Register: Plannet Crafters, Inc., 2580 Runic Way, Alpharetta, GA 30202

Benefits of registration: No nag screen; receive disk with latest version; access to technical support; more custom cursors.

Why You Need It

The Program Manager alone doesn't look good enough or do a good enough job. Plug-In adds custom cursors, special icons for groups, an enhanced File Run dialog box with a command history, and more.

How to Install It

To install Plug-In, follow these steps:

1. Plug-In's installation routine adds files to your Windows directory and modifies Windows system files, so run BEFORE.BAT before beginning to install Plug-In.

2. Use the File Manager to create a directory for Plug-In on your hard disk.

3. Switch to a drive window that shows the contents of the companion disk, and double-click on the file PLUG-IN.ZIP to open it in WinZip.

4. Click on the Extract button in WinZip.

5. Specify the directory you created for Plug-In on your hard disk, and click on OK to extract the files from the archive.

6. Close WinZip when it's done extracting files, and return to the File Manager.

7. In the File Manager, double-click on the file PLUGIN.EXE to start Plug-In. Follow the prompts to complete the installation.

8. After Plug-In's installation is complete, run AFTER.BAT to log the changes it made to your system.

How You Use It

Plug-In makes a host of improvements to the Program Manager and your desktop. The best way to learn how to use it is just to start playing with it. To configure Plug-In's settings, choose Options, Configure Plug-In. Help for Plug-In is available on the Program Manager's Help menu; rely on it to get your bearings.

■ Programs You'll Play With

Fish! 3.0

File name: FISH3.ZIP

Copyright: 1990–1993, Tom and Ed's Bogus Software

Status: Shareware, $24.95

Register: Tom and Ed's Bogus Software, Shareware Upgrade, 15600 N.E. 8th St., Suite A3334, Bellevue, WA 98008

Benefits of registration: Receive disk with latest version; can save creations from the Fish Editor; includes over 60 unique fish.

Why You Need It

Fish! 3.0 turns your desktop into an aquarium filled with dozens of brightly colored fish. It's a screen saver, too. Not only that, you can use its Fish Editor to create your own animated fish and control the way they move across the screen.

How to Install It

To install Fish! 3.0, follow these steps:

1. Fish! 3.0's installation procedure puts files in your Windows directory and modifies WIN.INI, so run BEFORE.BAT before you start to install the program.

2. Put the companion disk into the floppy drive. Use the File Manager to open a drive window for your floppy drive. Double-click on FISH3.ZIP to open the file in WinZip.

3. Click on the CheckOut button. Click on OK when WinZip displays the dialog box asking you to confirm the CheckOut directory. WinZip will extract the files to the temporary directory, and it will create a temporary Program Manager group with icons for each of the files.

4. When WinZip returns you to the Program Manager, double-click on the SETUP.EXE icon in the CheckOut group.

5. If you want Fish! 3.0 to run whenever you start Windows, leave the X in the box labeled "Run fish when Windows starts." Otherwise, click on the box to remove the X.

6. Click on Install.

7. Close WinZip, and click on Yes when it asks if you want to delete all the files in the temporary directory.

8. Run AFTER.BAT to record the changes made to your system. When you see the Parameters prompt, type **FISH** and click on OK. A list of the additions to your system will be compiled in the file FISH.TXT in your INSTALL subdirectory.

How You Use It

Fish! 3.0 automatically starts when the installation is complete, and it will also start up every time you run Windows if you chose that option. If it isn't already running, choose File, Run from Program Manager, type **FISH** and press Enter. Once Fish! 3.0 is running, click anywhere on the desktop to call up the Fish menu.

Assorted TrueType Fonts

File name: FONTS.ZIP

Status: Public domain

Why You Need Them

You don't have enough fonts on your system.

How to Install Them

To gain access to more TrueType fonts, follow these steps:

1. In the File Manager, double-click on the file FONTS.ZIP on the companion disk to open the file in WinZip.

2. Click on the CheckOut button. Make a note of the pathname of the CheckOut directory when WinZip asks you to verify it. Once you've written it down, click on OK. WinZip will extract the files to a temporary directory and will create a temporary Program Manager group with an icon for each of the files.

3. When WinZip returns you to the Program Manager, open the Control Panel. Double-click on the Fonts tool.

4. Click on the Add button. Use the directory window to switch to the CheckOut directory where WinZip put the extracted files. The fonts' names appear in the Fonts window.

5. Select the fonts you want, or click on Select All to select the entire group.

6. Make sure there's an X in the check box labeled Copy Fonts to Windows Directory.

7. Click on OK. Once all the fonts are installed, exit the Fonts tool and close the Control Panel.

8. Close WinZip, and answer Yes when it asks you if it should delete the CheckOut directory and group.

How You Use Them

The fonts are ready for use in any application that handles TrueType fonts. There are five character fonts—Basque Light, Black Chancery, Chopin, Garamond, and Saint Francis. The other two fonts, Inter and Mapmaker Thin are made up of symbols, like the Windows Symbol and Wingdings fonts.

AZ Icon Edit Version 1.7

File name: AZICONED.ZIP

Copyright: 1991, AZ Computer Innovations

Status: Shareware, $20

Register: AZ Computer Innovations, P.O. Box 10514, Glendale, AZ 85318

Benefits of registration: No nag screen; notification of future upgrades; discount on future versions.

Why You Need It
With AZ Icon Edit, you can create, modify, and save icons that you can use for program items in the Program Manager.

How to Install It
To enter the wild world of custom icons, follow these steps:

1. Use the File Manager to create a directory on your hard disk for AZ Icon Edit.
2. In the File Manager, double-click on the file AZICONED.ZIP on the companion disk to open this archive file in WinZip.
3. Click on Extract. Select All Files, and browse to the AZ Icon Edit directory you just created. Click on Extract.
4. Close WinZip.
5. To run AZ Icon Edit, choose File, Run from the Program Manager, click on Browse, and change to the AZ Icon Edit directory. Select AZICONED.EXE. Click on OK, and then click on OK again to run the program. Alternatively, create a program item for AZICONED.EXE in the Program Manager.

How You Use It
Once you've started AZ Icon Edit, just start drawing the icon you want in the icon editing space. Select a color and use the mouse to paint that color into the editing screen. AZ Icon Edit features tools for manipulating, rotating, and flipping the image. There's even a "capture" button that lets you take a snapshot of any icon-sized square on your screen, and then edit that.

Assorted Icons

File name: ICONS.ZIP

Copyright: 1993, Matthew Lake

Status: Freeware

Why You Need Them

These are good "rough sketches" that you can use when you want to create personalized versions using AZ Icon Edit.

How to Install Them

To install this assortment of icons, follow these steps:

1. In the File Manager, double-click on the file ICONS.ZIP on the companion disk. WinZip will start, and the files archived in ICONS.ZIP will be listed.

2. Click on Extract.

3. Ensure that you've selected the All Files radio button. Specify your Windows directory, your AZ Icon Edit directory, or any other directory where you want to keep your .ICO files.

4. Click on Extract. After WinZip extracts the files, close WinZip. The icons are ready to be used.

How You Use Them

To assign icons to any Program Manager program item, select that item's Properties dialog box (hold down the Alt key as you double-click the item). Click on Change Icon, and then click on Browse. Switch to the directory where your .ICO files are located. Select an icon file, and then click on OK. Click on OK again to return to the Properties dialog box. Click on OK once more to return to the Program Manager. The new icon will appear on the item.

To edit one of these icons, open AZ Icon Edit. Choose File, Open, and specify the icon file you want to edit. Click on OK to open it and begin editing.

Meta-Mouse Version 1.4

File name: METAMS.ZIP

Copyright: 1992, 1993, Farpoint Software

Status: Shareware, $12

Register: Farpoint Software, 2501 Afton Court, League City, TX 77573-3438

Benefits of registration: Receive disk with most recent version.

Why You Need It

Meta-Mouse makes your mouse cursor easier to see and more attractive as well. You can choose from a wide variety of mouse cursors.

How to Install It

To install Meta-Mouse, follow these steps:

1. Put the companion disk in your floppy drive, and open a drive window for that floppy in the File Manager.
2. Double-click on the file METAMS.ZIP to open it in WinZip.
3. Click on Extract.
4. Switch to your Windows directory. Then click on Extract to decompress the two files—METAMOUS.EXE and METAMOUS.DOC—in your Windows directory. The Meta-Mouse installation is complete!

How You Use It

Run Meta-Mouse from the File Manager by choosing File, Run, typing **META-MOUS**, and clicking on OK. (Or create a Program Manager icon for it—and put it in your Startup group to make Meta-Mouse run every time you start Windows.) Once Meta-Mouse is running, click once on its minimized icon, and select Setup from its menu. Pick the options you want, and click on OK when you're done.

Hot Spot!

File name: HOTSPOT.ZIP

Copyright: 1993, David Veith, LMDC

Status: Shareware, $4

Register: LMDC, 1438 169th Place NE, Bellevue, WA 98008

Benefits of registration: Good karma (that's what LMDC says!)

Why You Need It

Hot Spot! enables you to start a screen saver on demand or to prevent your screen saver from engaging even when the time limit has elapsed.

How to Install It

To install Hot Spot!, follow these steps:

1. Open a drive window in the File Manager that shows the contents of the companion disk. Double-click on the archive file HOTSPOT.ZIP to open it in WinZip.
2. In WinZip, click on the Extract button.

3. Ensure that you've selected the All Files button, and then specify the directory where you want to put the Hot Spot! files. There are only three files—HOTSPOT.EXE, HOTSPOT.HLP, and README.TXT.

4. Click on Extract. When it's done extracting the files, close WinZip.

5. If you haven't picked a Windows screen saver, open the Control Panel now. Double-click on the desktop icon, and specify the screen saver you want. Then click on OK, and close the Control Panel.

6. Run Hot Spot! by double-clicking on HOTSPOT.EXE in File Manager or by creating a program item to run HOTSPOT.EXE.

How You Use It

Once you've opened Hot Spot!, you can start your screen saver in two ways: double-click on the minimized Hot Spot! icon on your desktop or move the mouse cursor to the "hot spot" corner of your desktop. To configure Hot Spot!, click once on its minimized icon, and select Hot Spot Setup from the menu. If you need help, click on the Hot Spot icon and select Help from its menu.

Paint Shop Pro

File name: PAINTSP.ZIP

Copyright: 1990-1992, JASC Inc., all rights reserved

Status: Shareware, $49

Register: JASC, Inc., 17743 Evener Way, Eden Prairie, MN 55346

Benefits of registration: No nag screen.

Why You Need It

Paint Shop Pro lets you view and manipulate images in a wide variety of file formats; further, it lets you convert images from one file format into another. Unlike Paintbrush, it reads and writes RLE files, which are similar to .BMP wallpaper files, but usually much smaller in file size.

How to Install It

To install Paint Shop Pro, follow these steps:

1. Put the companion disk in your floppy disk drive, and open a File Manager window for it. In the File Manager, double-click on the file PAINTSP.ZIP. WinZip will open the file.

2. Click on the CheckOut button. Click on OK to make WinZip extract the archived files to a temporary directory, and create a temporary Program Manager group to hold icons for the files.

3. Once WinZip is finished extracting the files, you'll be returned to the Program Manager with the CheckOut group visible. Double-click on the Setup icon to install Paint Shop Pro.

4. Paint Shop Pro's setup dialog box appears. Ensure that the "Source Drive & Directory" correspond to the temporary directory you're using. If you want to install Paint Shop Pro to a different directory, type it in the Destination Drive & Directory box. Then click on OK.

5. Once Paint Shop Pro's installation is complete, close WinZip. Click on Yes when WinZip asks you if it should delete the CheckOut group and directory.

How You Use It

Run Paint Shop Pro by double-clicking on its icon in the Program Manager. To view a graphic file image, choose File, Open, specify the file type, and browse to the directory it's in. Once you've found the file, double-click on it to open it. Use Paint Shop Pro to manipulate the image all you like. When you're done, save it in its own format or choose File, Save As to save in a different file format.

Assorted Windows Wallpaper Files

File name: PAPER.ZIP

Status: Freeware

Why You Need Them

You need more Windows wallpaper in your collection. Also, there's a bonus .PCX file you can use to trick friends and co-workers.

How to Install Them

To install the wallpaper files, follow these steps:

1. In the File Manager, view the contents of the floppy disk. Double-click on PAPER.ZIP to open the file in WinZip.

2. In WinZip, click on Extract.

3. Specify your Windows directory as the directory where you want the extracted files placed.

4. Click on OK. When all the files are extracted, close WinZip.

How You Use Them

Open the Control Panel and double-click on the Desktop tool. In the Wallpaper box, pick any of the new .BMP files to make it your wallpaper. Or use Paintbrush to view the images, including BOX_MINE.PCX, which contains a variety of scary Windows error messages.

Screen Saver Collection #1

File name: SAVERS.EXE

Copyright: 1991, Gordon Harris

Status: Shareware, $5

Register: Gordon Harris, Data Arts, 3349 Humboldt Ave. S, Minneapolis, MN 55408

Benefits of registration: That warm fuzzy feeling you get knowing you're supporting the shareware concept.

Why You Need It

Because you're tired of the paltry five screen savers that ship with Windows 3.1. This collection adds five more screen savers that are completely compatible with Windows and much better looking than Flying Windows.

How to Install It

To install the screen savers, follow these steps:

1. In the File Manager, select File, Create and make a new directory called Savers on your hard disk.
2. Copy SAVERS.EXE in the File Manager to the Savers directory.
3. Click on the name SAVERS.EXE in the hard disk subdirectory.
4. When the files are done decompressing, delete SAVERS.EXE from the hard disk.

How You Use It

Run the Control Panel and double-click on the Desktop icon to select a new screen saver. The Screen Saver Collection's screen savers will appear along with the standard Windows ones in the drop-down list. Pick the one you want, click on Test to see what it looks like, and click on Setup to configure the saver. Pick CYCLE.SCR to make your screen saver cycle through all available screen savers. Also included is a file, SAVERS.WRI, which has information on the screen savers and how to register the program.

.WAV Files and PC Speaker Sound Driver

File name: SOUNDS.ZIP

Copyright (driver): Microsoft, 1992

Copyright (sounds): Public domain

Why You Need Them

Everyone needs more .WAV files, right? And if you don't have a sound card, the sound driver plays .WAV files over your lowly PC's speaker!

How to Install Them

To install the .WAV files (and the sound driver if you need it), follow these steps:

1. In the File Manager, open a window for the companion disk. Double-click on the file SOUNDS.ZIP to open it in WinZip.

2. If you already have a sound card, you don't need the speaker driver. Select all the files in SOUNDS.ZIP by pressing Ctrl+/ (Control-forward slash); then hold down Ctrl and click on SPEAKER.ZIP to deselect it. Click on Extract. If you don't have a sound card and want to install the speaker driver, just click on Extract to decompress all the files.

3. Select a destination directory for the files. If you have a .WAV file directory, put the files there—otherwise copy them into your Windows directory.

4. Click on Extract. If you're not installing the PC Speaker Driver, you're all done—close WinZip and go play with your .WAV files.

5. To install the PC Speaker Driver, you first need to decompress SPEAKER.ZIP, which is included in SOUNDS.ZIP. In WinZip, choose File, Open, browse to the directory where you extracted the files from SOUNDS.ZIP, and select SPEAKER.ZIP. Click on OK to open the archive.

6. Use the View button to read the text files AUDIO.TXT, LICENSE.TXT, and SPEAKER.TXT.

7. Select the last three files in the archive: OEMSETUP.INF, SPEAKER.DRV, and SPEAKER.TXT. Select all three by clicking on OEMSETUP.INF and then holding down Shift and clicking on SPEAKER.TXT.

8. Click on Extract. Specify the same directory where you put your .WAV files, and click on Extract.

9. Close WinZip.

10. Run the Control Panel, and double-click on the Drivers icon.

Appendix: Programs on the Disk **235**

11. Click on the Add button. Select "Unlisted or Updated Driver" from the list, and click on OK.

12. When the Control Panel prompts you to insert the disk with the driver, click on Browse. Switch to the directory where you extracted the files from SPEAKER.ZIP, and click on OK. Click on OK again.

13. The Control Panel displays "Sound Driver for PC-Speaker." Click on OK to install it. Your PC speaker will briefly make some noises as the driver is installed.

14. When the PC Speaker Setup dialog box appears, configure the speaker's volume and playback speed to suit your taste. Click on Test to hear what the settings sound like. When it sounds right, click on OK.

15. Click on the Restart Now button to restart Windows immediately. After Windows fires up, the sound driver is ready to use.

How You Use Them

Use the Windows Sound Recorder accessory to test the .WAV files and your speaker driver, if you installed it. Start the Sound Recorder, and choose File, Open to open one of your new .WAV files. Click on the Play button to hear the sound.

Toilet

File name: TOILET.ZIP

Copyright: 1993, R. E. Frazier

Status: Shareware, $5

Register: Robert E. Frazier, 7414 Mesa College Dr. #32, San Diego, CA 92111

Benefits of registration: Support shareware software development.

Why You Need It

Deleting files with the File Manager is rather dull, and it's tough to undo a mistake. Not only is Toilet more entertaining, but when you mistakenly drop a file into it, you can retrieve it. Alternatively, you "flush" the toilet to get rid of those files for good.

How to Install It

To install Toilet, follow these steps:

1. In the File Manager, open a window on the companion disk, and double-click on the file TOILET.ZIP to open it in WinZip.

2. In WinZip, click on Extract. Select any directory where you want to put TOILET.ZIP, and click on Extract to put it there.

3. Close WinZip. Toilet is now ready to use.

How You Use It

In the Program Manager, choose File, Run, browse to the directory where you put TOILET.ZIP, select the file, and then click on OK. If you like, create a Program Manager program item to launch Toilet from your desktop. Once you've started Toilet, it appears minimized on your desktop. To delete files, drag them from the File Manager onto the Toilet icon. If you want to get them back, click once on Toilet and select Undelete File from the menu that pops up. To get rid of the files, click on Toilet and choose Flush Toilet to delete them permanently.

Index

Numbers in bold indicate figures

A

After batch file, 142–144, 221–222
Ami Pro, hidden developer credits, 209–210
applications. *See* programs
archived files, 160–162, 222–224
Arrange Icons, 73–75
arrow. *See* cursor control
ascenders, 109
ASCII characters, 113, 115–116
Auto Arrange option, 73, 74
automatic save, disabling, 129
AZ Icon Edit, 78–84, 228

B

baseline, 109
batch files, installing programs with, 142–144, 221–222
beep. *See* sound control
Before batch file, 142, 144
bitmap (.BMP) files, customizing wallpaper with, 23, 29
blink rate, 61
booting. *See* startup
button bars, 140–141

C

Calculator, creating icon for, 81–83
capital letters, overuse of, 114
cascading windows, 135, **136**
characters
    elements of, 109–110
    special, 113, 115–116
    uppercase and italic, 114
Cistern Configuration Editor, 162–163, 253–236
Clock Saver (screen saver), 50
color
    in cursor control, 60, 64–65, 67
    in icons, 76, 77, 79–80
    in wallpaper customization, 35–36, **37**
command line histories, adding to File Run dialog box, 137
compressed files, 160–162, 222–224
Control Panel, directly accessing options, 23. *See also* particular option
CorelDRAW, hidden developer credits, 216–217
.CUR files, 69
cursor control
    basic shapes, 59
    blinking cursor, 65–66
    color of, 60, 64–65, 67
    double-click speed, 63–64
    files for, 69
    I-beam blink rate, 61
    mouse tracking speed, 62–63
    mouse trails, 60–61
    multiple pointers, 67–68
    non-Microsoft mice and, 68
    overview, 59–60
    shape, 66–68

D

dash, em, 115
deleting files
    disabling, reminder for, 148
    saving disk space by, 160, 162–163
    with Toilet, 162–163, 235–236
descenders, 109
directories, managing. *See* File Manager
disks, hard. *See* hard disks
DOS PATH, 4
double-click speed, 63–64

E

"Easter eggs." *See* hidden routines and screens
echo, adding to sound, 98
em dash, 115
end, the, 241
endless loop. *See* loop, endless
error messages, as wallpaper, 31–33
events
    lists of, in macros, 177
    sounds for, 92–95
Excel, hidden routines and screens, 211–213
exiting
    disabling automatic save during, 129

Index

F

macros for, 174–177
extended character set, 113, 115–116

File Manager
    adding shortcuts with macros, 170–174
    archiving files, 160–162
    arranging file windows, 156–157
    associating files with programs, 158–160
    changing file detail and order, 149–151
    changing fonts in, 149, **150**
    changing views in, 151–155
    deleting files, 160, 162–163, 235–236
    disk labels, 153–154
    icons for components, 151
    modifying reminders, 148
    rearranging directories, 157–158
    rearranging files, 157–158
    saving disk space, 160–163, 235–236
    spacing elements in, 157
    tiling windows in, 152–153
files. *See also particular file type*
    loading during startup, 6
    managing. *See* File Manager
    provided with book. *See* programs
Fish (screen saver), 54–56, 57, 225–227
Fishes (screen saver), 50
Flying Windows (screen saver), 43
.FON files, 119, 121
fonts
    adding, 111–113
    building comparison list, 116
    components and terminology, 108–109
    editing, 119–122
    evolution, 107–108
    in File Manager windows, 149, **150**
    judicious use of, 113–115, 116
    provided with book, 227
    removing, 111
    special characters, 115–116
    storing in folders, 116–119
    TrueType. *See* TrueType fonts
    typefaces vs., 108
    Windows's standard, 110–111
.FOT files, 117, 118

G

games
    Minesweeper. *See* Minesweeper
    Solitaire. *See* Solitaire
graffiti, as wallpaper, 30–31

group icons, changing, 76–78

H

hard disks
    labels for, 153–154
    saving space on, 160–163
hDc Microapps, hidden developer credits, 218
here, you are, 238
hidden routines and screens
    Ami Pro developer credits, 209–210
    CorelDRAW developer credits, 216–217
    discovering, 218
    Excel bug buster animation, 211–212
    Excel developer credits, 213
    hDc Microapps developer credits, 218
    Lotus Notes developer credits, 218
    Lotus 1-2-3's Schwarzenegger tribute, 214
    Norton Desktop developer credits, 206–207
    overview, 203–204
    Paradox developer credits, 217–218
    PC Tools developer credits, 218
    Quattro Pro developer credits, 215
    Windows developer credits, 204–206
    Word fireworks, 208–209
    Word monster movie, 207–208
Hot Spot, 49, 230–231
hourglass. *See* cursor control
hyphens, overuse of, 114

I

I-beam. *See* cursor control
icon control
    altering existing icons, 80–81, 84
    arranging, 73–76
    assigning program to, 86–87
    changing font in label, 122
    changing group icons, 76–78
    creating icons, 81–83, 84
    grouping and displaying, 84–87
    icon editors for, 78, **79**
    overview, 72
    retouching, 86
    setting colors and shapes, 79–80
    standard icon choices, 72–73
icons
    assigning to a button bar, 140–141
    assigning macros to, 171
    creating. *See* icon control
    managing. *See* icon control
    overview, 71–72

provided with book, 228–229
setting up screen savers as, 46–48
for sound files, 101–102
initialization (.INI) files, editing, 14–18
installing programs
    with batch files, 142–144
    with Plug-In, 140
italics, 114

K

keyboard, playing Solitaire from, 190

L

leading, 110, 114
letters. *See* characters
LHA, 160, 223–224
line-spacing, 110, 114
Load, Run vs., 17
logo, Windows. *See* startup, logo
loop, endless. *See* endless loop
Lotus, hidden routines and screens
    Notes, 218
    1-2-3, 214

M

macros
    adding shortcuts to applications with, 170–174
    assigning to icons, 171
    capturing screens with, 178–180
    changing default settings for, 173
    checklist for using, 180–182
    examples, 166–170
    importance of planning in, 174, 180
    linking, 170
    lists of events in, 177
    merging from one file to another, 174
    overview, 165–166
    playback speed, 168
    quitting all applications with, 176–177
    quitting Recorder with, 174–176
    running from command line, 171
    testing, 173–174, 182
Mallory, George Leigh, 129
Marquee (screen saver), 44–45
Meta-Mouse, 64–67, 229–230
Minesweeper
    cheating, 198, 201
    customizing minefield, 199–200
    object of game, 195
    overview, 194–195

playing, 196–197
scoring, 198
strategies and tricks, 197, 198, 200–201
MORICONS file, 72, 78
mouse
    modifying control of. *See* cursor control
    playing Solitaire without, 190
Mouse Action option, 148
Mystify (screen saver), 43–44

N

Newpaper utility, 27
Norton Desktop, hidden developer credits, 206–207

O

object linking and embedding (OLE), 99–103
Object Packager, creating sound library with, 101–103
Outline Dragging, use in Solitaire strategy, 194

P

Paintbrush
    changing startup icon with, 11–14
    customizing wallpaper with, 27–34
    sizing images in, 29
PaintShop Pro, 25–26, 231–232
Paradox, hidden developer credits, 217–218
passwords, screen savers and, 46, 47, 51, 56
patterns, in wallpaper creation, 36–37
PC speaker driver, 90–92, 234–235
PC Tools, hidden developer credits, 218
.PCX files, customizing wallpaper with, 29
PIF Editor, relocating, 157–158
Plug-In
    cursor control with, 67–68
    icon control with, 76–78
    installation and basic use, 224–225
    Program Manager control with, 137–140
pointer. *See* cursor control
point size, 109, 114
printing, file association and, 159
Print Screen
    customizing wallpaper with, 27, **28**, 33–34
    in macros, 178–180
PROGMAN.EXE file, 72–73, 76–78
PROGMAN.INI file, 14, 16–18, 128, 129
program groups. *See* Program Manager

240 Index

Program Manager
    adding command line histories, 137
    button bars, 140–141
    changing Startup group, 138–139
    copying groups, 138
    disabling automatic save, 129
    disabling groups, 139
    minimizing groups to icons, 138
    program installation. *See* installing programs
    program launch shortcut, 132
    QuickRun menu. 137–138
    rearranging applications, 130–132, 138
    renaming, 18
    reordering group list, 141
    sizing, 130, 131
    standard arrangement, 128–129
    switching between applications, 133–136
programs. *See also particular program*
    accessing directly, 4
    adding shortcuts to, 170–174
    associating files with, 158–160
    AZ Icon Edit, 78–84, 228
    Before and After batch files, 142–144, 221–222
    Fish, 54–56, 57, 225–227
    Hot Spot, 49, 230–231
    installing. *See* installing programs
    LHA, 160, 223–224
    loading multiple from single icon, 171–172
    managing. *See* Program Manager
    Meta-Mouse, 64–67, 229–230
    PaintShop Pro, 25–26, 231–232
    Plug-In. *See* Plug-In
    quitting with macros, 174–177
    screen savers, 54–56, 57, 233
    speaker driver, 90–92, 234–235
    Toilet, 162–163, 235–236
    wallpaper files, 232–233
    .WAV files, 234–235
    WinZip, 160, 222–223

Q

Quattro Pro, hidden developer credits, 215
QuickRun menu, 137–138
Quilt Saver (screen saver), 50
quitting. *See* exiting
quotation marks, typographer's, 114

R

Recorder. *See* macros
Recursive. *See* Recursive
reminders, modifying, 148
Run, Load vs., 17

S

sans serif vs. serif, 109
Save Changes on Exit, disabling, 129
SAVERS.EXE, 50
scalable fonts, 108
screens
    capturing with macro, 178–180
    changing backgrounds. *See* wallpaper, customizing
    printing. *See* Print Screen
screen savers
    accessing via icons, 46–48
    basic control of, 42–43
    Clock Saver, 50
    Fish, 54–56, 57
    Fishes, 50
    Flying Windows, 43
    Marquee, 44–45
    Mystify, 43–44
    passwords and, 46, 47, 51, 56
    provided with book, 54–56, 57, 233
    Quilt Saver, 50
    rotating, 52–54
    Starfield Simulation, 43
    starting on demand, 49, 230–231
    Various Stuff, 51
serif vs. sans serif, 109
shortcut keys
    launching applications with, 132–133
    in macros, 181–182. *See also* macros
    switching between applications with, 134
"smart" quotes, 114
Solitaire
    changing deck designs, 192, **193**
    keyboard-based play, 190
    object of game, 189
    overview, 188
    playing, 189–190
    scoring, 191–192
    strategies and tricks, 192–194
sound control
    adjusting volume and duration, 91
    changing event sounds, 92–95
    combining sound files, 97–98
    descriptions for sounds, 95
    echo, 98

Index **241**

organizing sounds into scrapbook, 99–103
overview, 89–90
playing backwards, 98
removing special effects from, 99
replaying sounds, 95–99
sound speed, 98
speaker driver, 90–92
viewing sound waveform patterns, 96–97
Sound Recorder, 95–99
speaker driver, 90–92, 234–235
special characters, 113, 115–116
special effects (sound), 96–99
Starfield Simulation (screen saver), 43
startup
    accessing applications directly, 4
    bypassing startup items, 19
    customizing startup group, 17–18, 138–139
    editing .INI files, 14–18
    files loaded during, 6
    Load vs. Run, 17
    modifying WIN.COM program, 4–5
    operation explained, 6
    sound, 92
startup logo
    creating, 10–14
    customizing, 8–10
    removing, 6–8
SYSTEM.INI file, 14–16, 121
system fonts, 119–122

T

Task List, disabling, 34
text
    macros for, 169–170
    visual considerations, 114
tiling windows, 135, 136, 152–153
time stamps, 151
time, well spent, 1–236
Toilet, 162–163, 235–236
toolkits, arranging Program Manager by, 132
tracking speed, 62–63
TrueType fonts. *See also* fonts
    described, 108
    making into system fonts, 122
    provided with book, 227
    Windows's standard, 116–117
.TTF files. *See* TrueType fonts
typefaces, fonts vs., 108. *See also* fonts
type size, judicious use of, 114
typography, basic elements of, 109–110

U

underlining, 114
uppercase, overuse of, 114
useless tip, completely, 177

V

Various Stuff (screen saver), 51
Vegas scoring (Solitaire), 191
volume control, 91

W

wallpaper, customizing
    basic procedure, 22–23
    with .BMP files, 23, 29
    color and pattern in, 35–37
    without Control Panel, 27
    with error message, 31–33
    files provided with book, 232–233
    with graffiti, 30–31
    with Paintbrush, 27–34
    positioning, 23–24
    with Print Screen, 27, 33–34
    rotating automatically, 27
    saving memory in, 25–26
.WAV files, 92, 96–98, 234–235
WIN.COM program, 4–5
windows
    File Manager, arranging, 151–153
    sizing, 130, 131
    switching between, 133–136
    tiled vs. cascaded, 135, 136
WIN.INI file
    fonts and, 117, 121–122
    icons spacing via, 75–76
    mouse settings, 63
    overview, 14
    Run and Load lines in, 16, 17
    sound and, 93
WINMINE.INI file, 198
WinZip, 160, 222–223
Word, hidden routines and screens, 207–209
word processors, use in .INI file editing, 14, 15
Write, associating files with, 159–160

X

x-height, 109

Imagination.
Innovation. Insight.

The How It Works Series from Ziff-Davis Press

". . . a magnificently seamless integration of text and graphics . . ."
Larry Blasko, The Associated Press, reviewing *PC/Computing How Computers Work*

No other books bring computer technology to life like the *How It Works* series from Ziff-Davis Press. Lavish, full-color illustrations and lucid text from some of the world's top computer commentators make *How It Works* books an exciting way to explore the inner workings of PC technology.

ISBN: 094-7 Price: $22.95

ISBN: 129-3 Price: $24.95

PC/Computing How Computers Work

A worldwide blockbuster that hit the general trade bestseller lists! *PC/Computing* magazine executive editor Ron White dismantles the PC and reveals what really makes it tick.

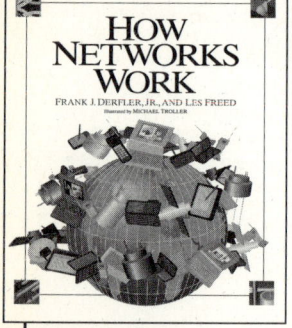

ISBN: 133-1 Price: $24.95
Available: October

How Macs Work

A fun and fascinating voyage to the heart of the Macintosh! Two noted *MacUser* contributors cover the spectrum of Macintosh operations from startup to shutdown.

How Software Works

ISBN: 146-3 Price: $24.95

This dazzlingly illustrated volume from Ron White peeks inside the PC to show in full-color detail how software breathes life into the PC. Covers all major software categories.

How to Use Your Computer

Conquer computerphobia and see how this intricate machine truly makes life easier. Dozens of full-color graphics showcase the components of the PC and explain how to interact with them.

All About Computers

This one-of-a-kind visual guide for kids features numerous full-color illustrations and photos on every page, combined with dozens of interactive projects that reinforce computer basics, making this an exciting way to learn all about the world of computers.

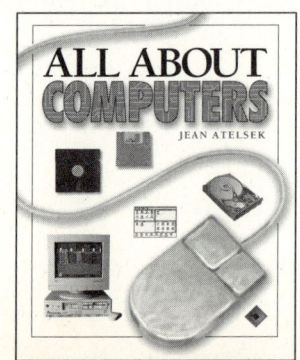

ISBN: 155-2 Price: $19.95

How Networks Work

Two of the most respected names in connectivity showcase the PC network, illustrating and explaining how each component does its magic and how they all fit together.

ISBN: 166-8 Price: $15.95 Available: October

**Available at all fine bookstores or by calling
1-800-688-0448, ext. 100.**

ZD PRESS
ZIFF-DAVIS

Arrrgh!

Don't you just hate it when software doesn't work the way you expect? When simple problems block your progress for hours? When your resident techie isn't around, the technical support hotline is constantly busy, on-line help is no help at all, the manual is hopeless, and the book you have tells you everything except what you really need to know?

Don't you just hate it?

We do too. That's why we developed *HELP!*, a groundbreaking series of books from ZD Press.

HELP! books mean fast access to straight answers. If you're a beginner, you'll appreciate the practical examples and skill-building exercises that will help you work confidently in no time. If you're already an experienced user, you'll love the comprehensive coverage, highly detailed indexes, and margin notes and sidebars that highlight especially helpful information.

ISBN: 1-56276-014-9
Retail Price: $27.95

We're launching the *HELP!* series with these all-new books:

HELP! WordPerfect 6.0—WordPerfect insider Stephen G. Dyson has created the most complete single source of techniques, examples, and advice that will help you clear the hurdles of WordPerfect 6.0 quickly and easily.

HELP! Microsoft Access—Best-selling author Miriam Liskin gives you fast access to the complete feature set of Microsoft's leading-edge Windows database program. Sample databases included on disk!

ISBN: 1-56276-099-8
Retail Price: $29.95

HELP! Paradox for Windows—Popular database and spreadsheet authority Lisa Biow provides one-stop solutions to the challenges of Borland's high-powered new database manager.

More *HELP!* is on the way soon for WordPerfect for Windows, Lotus Notes 3.0, DOS 6.0 and Windows NT 3.1. So if you hate struggling with software as much as we do, visit your favorite bookstore and just say *HELP!*

ISBN: 1-56276-039-4
Retail Price: $27.95

Available at all fine bookstores or by calling 1-800-688-0448, ext. 101.

ZIFF-DAVIS ZD PRESS

MAXIMIZE YOUR PRODUCTIVITY WITH THE TECHNIQUES & UTILITIES SERIES

Borland C++ Techniques & Utilities

Master programmer Kaare Christian leads this performance-oriented exploration of Borland C++, version 3.1. Focusing on object-oriented programming using the Borland class libraries, he shows you how to increase productivity while writing lean, fast, and appealing programs.

ISBN: 054-8
Price: $39.95

PC Magazine DOS 6 Techniques & Utilities

Based on his national bestseller *PC Magazine DOS 5 Techniques and Utilities*, Jeff Prosise puts essential tools and techniques into your hands with this power-user's guide to DOS 6. The two disks are packed with 60 powerful utilities created specifically for this book.

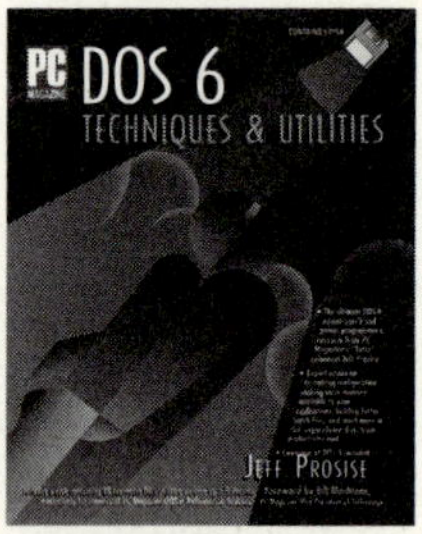

ISBN: 095-5
Price: $39.95

Techniques & Utilities Series book/disk resources from Ziff-Davis Press are designed for the productivity-conscious programmer or power user. Expert authors reveal insider techniques and have written on-disk utilities and support files so you can apply new skills instantly. If you're a serious programmer or user who wants to get things done quickly and work more effectively, then these are the ideal guides for you.

Look for more performance-oriented titles in the months ahead.

ISBN: 035-1
Price: $39.95

ISBN: 010-6
Price: $39.95

ISBN: 008-4
Price: $29.95

PC Magazine Turbo Pascal for Windows Techniques & Utilities

Neil J. Rubenking guides programmers through the power and intricacy of programming in Turbo Pascal for Windows. Included are two disks that contain all the source code examples from the text.

PC Magazine Turbo Pascal 6.0 Techniques & Utilities

This is the ideal guide for serious users who want to get things done. Neil J. Rubenking reveals tips and techniques that will enable you to unleash the full power of Turbo Pascal 6.0.

PC Magazine BASIC Techniques & Utilities

This guide presents an unprecedented level of coverage of BASIC's internal operation for the QuickBASIC and BASIC 7 programmer. Ethan Winer reveals insider techniques that will allow you to dramatically increase your productivity with BASIC.

ZIFF-DAVIS ZD PRESS

Available at all fine bookstores, or by calling 1-800-688-0448, ext. 102.

Insider Networking Secrets Revealed by Renowned Experts Frank J. Derfler, Jr., and Les Freed

Frank J. Derfler, Jr., and Les Freed have pooled their knowledge to create the most extensive guides to networking and communications. Active in the PC industry since its birth, Freed is the founder of DCA's Crosstalk division, and Derfler is senior networking editor of *PC Magazine* and the writer of the magazine's "Connectivity" column. You can be assured you are learning from highly respected experts in the computer industry with the most up-to-date information available.

With the wisdom of Derfler and Freed, you will boost your network system performance and productivity in no time.

PC Magazine Guide to Windows for Workgroups
ISBN: 120-X
Price: $22.95

Both users and administrators will get up and running fast and enjoy an instant boost in workgroup productivity with the help of this concise, easy-to-read guide.

PC Magazine Guide to NetWare
ISBN: 022-X
Price: $39.95

Les Freed and Frank J. Derfler, Jr. present tips, tricks, and techniques that make this best-selling book/disk package the essential survival guide to NetWare.

PC Magazine Guide to LANtastic
ISBN: 058-0
Price: $19.95

Best-selling authors and networking experts Frank J. Derfler, Jr., and Les Freed show you how to master the full power of LANtastic.

PC Magazine Guide to Connectivity, Second Edition
ISBN: 047-5
Price: $39.95

This supercharged second edition of the connectivity bible from Frank J. Derfler, Jr., includes *PC Magazine*'s most up-to-date product information, plus a special section on modem communication. You'll receive two disks that contain a full-featured e-mail program, performance-testing utilities, and many other application and utility programs.

PC Magazine Guide to Modem Communications
ISBN: 037-8
Price: $29.95

Acclaimed experts Les Freed and Frank J. Derfler, Jr., cover the fundamentals of modem communications, and provide scores of tips and insights on purchasing the right equipment and using bulletin board systems and modems for business applications. A valuable companion disk includes scripts for accessing on-line services, a file compression/decompression utility, and many more time-saving programs.

PC Magazine Guide to Linking LANs
ISBN: 031-9
Price: $39.95

Network authority, Frank J. Derfler, Jr., shows you the most effective ways to share network resources with the LAN down the hall or around the globe. This essential guide gives practical advice on quality, cost, and compatibility for dozens of popular products.

ZIFF-DAVIS ZD PRESS

Available at all fine bookstores, or by calling 1-800-688-0448, ext. 104.

The Quick and Easy Way to Learn.

Teaches DOS 6
ISBN: 1-56276-100-5
Price: $22.95

Teaches WordPerfect 6.0
ISBN: 1-56276-105-6
Price: $22.95

Teaches Word for Windows 2.0
ISBN: 1-56276-065-3
Price: $22.95

We know that PC Learning Labs books are the fastest and easiest way to learn because years have been spent perfecting them. Beginners will find practice sessions that are easy to follow and reference information that is easy to find. Even the most computer-shy readers can gain confidence faster than they ever thought possible.

The time we spent designing this series translates into time saved for you. You can feel confident that the information is accurate and presented in a way that allows you to learn quickly and effectively.

Teaches Microsoft Access
ISBN: 1-56276-122-6
Price: $22.95

Teaches DOS 5
ISBN: 1-56276-042-4
Price: $22.95

Teaches OS/2 2.1
ISBN: 1-56276-148-X
Price: $22.95

Teaches cc:Mail
ISBN: 1-56276-135-8
Price: $22.95

Teaches WordPerfect 5.1
ISBN: 1-56276-032-7
Price: $22.95

Teaches Ami Pro 3.0
ISBN: 1-56276-134-X
Price: $22.95

Teaches Microsoft Project 3.0 for Windows
ISBN: 1-56276-124-2
Price: $22.95

Teaches Excel 4.0 for Windows
ISBN: 1-56276-074-2
Price: $22.95

Teaches 1-2-3 Release 2.3
ISBN: 1-56276-033-5
Price: $22.95

Teaches Windows 3.1
ISBN: 1-56276-051-3
Price: $22.95

ZIFF-DAVIS ZD PRESS

Available at all fine bookstores, or by calling 1-800-688-0448, ext. 103.

Ziff-Davis Press Survey of Readers

Please help us in our effort to produce the best books on personal computing. For your assistance, we would be pleased to send you a FREE catalog featuring the complete line of Ziff-Davis Press books.

1. How did you first learn about this book?

Recommended by a friend . . . . ☐ -1 (5)
Recommended by store personnel . . . . ☐ -2
Saw in Ziff-Davis Press catalog . . . . ☐ -3
Received advertisement in the mail . . . . ☐ -4
Saw the book on bookshelf at store . . . . ☐ -5
Read book review in: _____ ☐ -6
Saw an advertisement in: _____ ☐ -7
Other (Please specify): _____ ☐ -8

2. Which THREE of the following factors most influenced your decision to purchase this book? (Please check up to THREE.)

Front or back cover information on book . . . ☐ -1 (6)
Logo of magazine affiliated with book . . . . . . ☐ -2
Special approach to the content . . . . ☐ -3
Completeness of content . . . . ☐ -4
Author's reputation . . . . ☐ -5
Publisher's reputation . . . . ☐ -6
Book cover design or layout . . . . ☐ -7
Index or table of contents of book . . . . ☐ -8
Price of book . . . . ☐ -9
Special effects, graphics, illustrations . . . . ☐ -0
Other (Please specify): _____ ☐ -x

3. How many computer books have you purchased in the last six months? _____ (7-10)

4. On a scale of 1 to 5, where 5 is excellent, 4 is above average, 3 is average, 2 is below average, and 1 is poor, please rate each of the following aspects of this book below. (Please circle your answer.)

Depth/completeness of coverage   5 4 3 2 1 (11)
Organization of material   5 4 3 2 1 (12)
Ease of finding topic   5 4 3 2 1 (13)
Special features/time saving tips 5 4 3 2 1 (14)
Appropriate level of writing   5 4 3 2 1 (15)
Usefulness of table of contents   5 4 3 2 1 (16)
Usefulness of index   5 4 3 2 1 (17)
Usefulness of accompanying disk   5 4 3 2 1 (18)
Usefulness of illustrations/graphics 5 4 3 2 1 (19)
Cover design and attractiveness   5 4 3 2 1 (20)
Overall design and layout of book 5 4 3 2 1 (21)
Overall satisfaction with book   5 4 3 2 1 (22)

5. Which of the following computer publications do you read regularly; that is, 3 out of 4 issues?

Byte . . . . ☐ -1 (23)
Computer Shopper . . . . ☐ -2
Corporate Computing . . . . ☐ -3
Dr. Dobb's Journal . . . . ☐ -4
LAN Magazine . . . . ☐ -5
MacWEEK . . . . ☐ -6
MacUser . . . . ☐ -7
PC Computing . . . . ☐ -8
PC Magazine . . . . ☐ -9
PC WEEK . . . . ☐ -0
Windows Sources . . . . ☐ -x
Other (Please specify): _____ ☐ -y

Please turn page.

6. What is your level of experience with personal computers? With the subject of this book?

	With PCs	With subject of book
Beginner...............	☐ -1 (24)	☐ -1 (25)
Intermediate............	☐ -2	☐ -2
Advanced..............	☐ -3	☐ -3

7. Which of the following best describes your job title?

Officer (CEO/President/VP/owner)........ ☐ -1 (26)
Director/head......................... ☐ -2
Manager/supervisor.................... ☐ -3
Administration/staff................... ☐ -4
Teacher/educator/trainer............... ☐ -5
Lawyer/doctor/medical professional...... ☐ -6
Engineer/technician.................... ☐ -7
Consultant............................ ☐ -8
Not employed/student/retired............ ☐ -9
Other (Please specify): _____ ☐ -0

8. What is your age?

Under 20............................. ☐ -1 (27)
21-29................................ ☐ -2
30-39................................ ☐ -3
40-49................................ ☐ -4
50-59................................ ☐ -5
60 or over........................... ☐ -6

9. Are you:

Male................................. ☐ -1 (28)
Female............................... ☐ -2

Thank you for your assistance with this important information! Please write your address below to receive our free catalog.

Name: _____
Address: _____
City/State/Zip: _____

Fold here to mail.

1447-08-03

BUSINESS REPLY MAIL
FIRST CLASS MAIL   PERMIT NO. 1612   OAKLAND, CA

POSTAGE WILL BE PAID BY ADDRESSEE

Ziff-Davis Press
5903 Christie Avenue
Emeryville, CA 94608-1925
Attn: Marketing

NO POSTAGE
NECESSARY
IF MAILED IN
THE UNITED
STATES

■ TO RECEIVE 5¼-INCH DISK(S)

The Ziff-Davis Press software contained on the 3½-inch disk included with this book is also available in 5¼-inch format. If you would like to receive the software in the 5¼-inch format, please return the 3½-inch disk with your name and address to:

Disk Exchange
Ziff-Davis Press
5903 Christie Avenue
Emeryville, CA 94608

■ **END-USER LICENSE AGREEMENT**

READ THIS AGREEMENT CAREFULLY BEFORE BUYING THIS BOOK. BY BUYING THE BOOK AND USING THE PROGRAM LISTINGS, DISKS, AND PROGRAMS REFERRED TO BELOW, YOU ACCEPT THE TERMS OF THIS AGREEMENT.

The program listings included in this book and the programs included on the diskette(s) contained in the package on the opposite page ("Disks") are proprietary products of Ziff-Davis Press and/or third party suppliers ("Suppliers"). The program listings and programs are hereinafter collectively referred to as the "Programs." Ziff-Davis Press and the Suppliers retain ownership of the Disks and copyright to the Programs, as their respective interests may appear. The Programs and the copy of the Disks provided are licensed (not sold) to you under the conditions set forth herein.

License. You may use the Disks on any compatible computer, provided that the Disks are used on only one computer and by one user at a time.

Restrictions. You may not commercially distribute the Disks or the Programs or otherwise reproduce, publish, or distribute or otherwise use the Disks or the Programs in any manner that may infringe any copyright or other proprietary right of Ziff-Davis Press, the Suppliers, or any other party or assign, sublicense, or otherwise transfer the Disks or this agreement to any other party unless such party agrees to accept the terms and conditions of this agreement. This license and your right to use the Disks and the Programs automatically terminates if you fail to comply with any provision of this agreement.

U.S. GOVERNMENT RESTRICTED RIGHTS. The disks and the programs are provided with **RESTRICTED RIGHTS**. Use, duplication, or disclosure by the Government is subject to restrictions as set forth in subparagraph (c)(1)(ii) of the Rights in Technical Data and Computer Software Clause at DFARS (48 CFR 252.277-7013). The Proprietor of the compilation of the Programs and the Disks is Ziff-Davis Press, 5903 Christie Avenue, Emeryville, CA 94608.

Limited Warranty. Ziff-Davis Press warrants the physical Disks to be free of defects in materials and workmanship under normal use for a period of 30 days from the purchase date. If Ziff-Davis Press receives written notification within the warranty period of defects in materials or workmanship in the physical Disks, and such notification is determined by Ziff-Davis Press to be correct, Ziff-Davis Press will, at its option, replace the defective Disks or refund a prorata portion of the purchase price of the book. **THESE ARE YOUR SOLE REMEDIES FOR ANY BREACH OF WARRANTY.**

EXCEPT AS SPECIFICALLY PROVIDED ABOVE, THE DISKS AND THE PROGRAMS ARE PROVIDED "AS IS" WITHOUT ANY WARRANTY OF ANY KIND. NEITHER ZIFF-DAVIS PRESS NOR THE SUPPLIERS MAKE ANY WARRANTY OF ANY KIND AS TO THE ACCURACY OR COMPLETENESS OF THE DISKS OR THE PROGRAMS OR THE RESULTS TO BE OBTAINED FROM USING THE DISKS OR THE PROGRAMS AND NEITHER ZIFF-DAVIS PRESS NOR THE SUPPLIERS SHALL BE RESPONSIBLE FOR ANY CLAIMS ATTRIBUTABLE TO ERRORS, OMISSIONS, OR OTHER INACCURACIES IN THE DISKS OR THE PROGRAMS. THE ENTIRE RISK AS TO THE RESULTS AND PERFORMANCE OF THE DISKS AND THE PROGRAMS IS ASSUMED BY THE USER. FURTHER, NEITHER ZIFF-DAVIS PRESS NOR THE SUPPLIERS MAKE ANY REPRESENTATIONS OR WARRANTIES, EITHER EXPRESS OR IMPLIED, WITH RESPECT TO THE DISKS OR THE PROGRAMS, INCLUDING BUT NOT LIMITED TO, THE QUALITY, PERFORMANCE, MERCHANTABILITY, OR FITNESS FOR A PARTICULAR PURPOSE OF THE DISKS OR THE PROGRAMS. IN NO EVENT SHALL ZIFF-DAVIS PRESS OR THE SUPPLIERS BE LIABLE FOR DIRECT, INDIRECT, SPECIAL, INCIDENTAL, OR CONSEQUENTIAL DAMAGES ARISING OUT THE USE OF OR INABILITY TO USE THE DISKS OR THE PROGRAMS OR FOR ANY LOSS OR DAMAGE OF ANY NATURE CAUSED TO ANY PERSON OR PROPERTY AS A RESULT OF THE USE OF THE DISKS OR THE PROGRAMS, EVEN IF ZIFF-DAVIS PRESS OR THE SUPPLIERS HAVE BEEN SPECIFICALLY ADVISED OF THE POSSIBILITY OF SUCH DAMAGES. NEITHER ZIFF-DAVIS PRESS NOR THE SUPPLIERS ARE RESPONSIBLE FOR ANY COSTS INCLUDING, BUT NOT LIMITED TO, THOSE INCURRED AS A RESULT OF LOST PROFITS OR REVENUE, LOSS OF USE OF THE DISKS OR THE PROGRAMS, LOSS OF DATA, THE COSTS OF RECOVERING SOFTWARE OR DATA, OR THIRD-PARTY CLAIMS. IN NO EVENT WILL ZIFF-DAVIS PRESS' OR THE SUPPLIERS' LIABILITY FOR ANY DAMAGES TO YOU OR ANY OTHER PARTY EVER EXCEED THE PRICE OF THIS BOOK. NO SALES PERSON OR OTHER REPRESENTATIVE OF ANY PARTY INVOLVED IN THE DISTRIBUTION OF THE DISKS IS AUTHORIZED TO MAKE ANY MODIFICATIONS OR ADDITIONS TO THIS LIMITED WARRANTY.

Some states do not allow the exclusion or limitation of implied warranties or limitation of liability for incidental or consequential damages, so the above limitation or exclusion may not apply to you.

General. Ziff-Davis Press and the Suppliers retain all rights not expressly granted. Nothing in this license constitutes a waiver of the rights of Ziff-Davis Press or the Suppliers under the U.S. Copyright Act or any other Federal or State Law, international treaty, or foreign law.